THE ASSESSMENT OF PERFORMANCE AND COMPETENCE

L. Walklin

Stanley Thornes (Publishers) Ltd

First printed in 1991 by:
Stanley Thornes (Publishers) Ltd
Ellenborough House
Wellington Street
CHELTENHAM
GL50 1YW
United Kingdom

98 99 01 02 03 / 10 9 8 7 6 5

A catalogue record for this book is available from the British Library

ISBN 0–7487–1115–5

371.2/

Typeset by Techset, Gateshead, Tyne & Wear
Printed and bound in Great Britain by Redwood Books, Trowbridge, Wiltshire

CONTENTS

FOREWORD

The competence-based curriculum is now well established and competence is achieved through a range of opportunities that may be presented to the learner within the workplace, training workshop and college. Perhaps the most exciting result of the 'Competence Curriculum' is the integration of educational, training and experiential elements of learner activity. These have sometimes been viewed as separate elements of the learner's development, reinforcing the notion of a *dichotomy* between education and training.

The introduction of Youth and Employment Training initiatives as work-based schemes gave early recognition of the importance and benefits of work experience as a key aspect of competence. These schemes further promoted the benefits of relating this 'on-the-job' experience to the vocational education and training provided 'off-the-job'.

Qualifications are being developed to standards and levels acceptable to the National Council for Vocational Qualifications (NCVQ) and Scottish Vocational Education Council (SCOTVEC). These qualifications identify competences to be achieved and demonstrated to the required standard by the learner. This approach suggests new responsibilities for both the learner and the teacher if competence is to be developed, practised and assessed through relevant learner-centred activities. The assessment of competence is a key activity both to identify achievement and as the basis for accreditation. The range of activities within which assessment takes place requires those involved with the learner to be familiar with, and capable of, undertaking appropriate assessment responsibilities.

The Assessment of Performance and Competence clearly presents and considers the sequence of curricular planning, teaching and assessment activities necessary to ensure that learner competence can be developed and the level of performance monitored. The author outlines a logical approach to competence assessment which is relevant to the learner, whether in a workplace, college or training environment.

The author's readable style and choice of topic areas will allow those involved in the assessment of competence to find both explanation and direction. He draws on substantial experience in industry, vocational education, training and staff development to present the subject in a usable form for the practitioner. The book is a welcome complement to others by the author and appears at a time when there is increasing emphasis on the assessment of competence and limited guidance and support for those engaged in the process.

Ray Chave
Vice Principal
Bournemouth and Poole College
of Further Education
1991

ACKNOWLEDGEMENTS

The author and publishers are grateful to the following for permission to reproduce copyright material:

The City and Guilds of London Institute for permission to reproduce specimens of current certification documentation and instruments relating to the C & G 9293 Direct Trainers and Assessors Award.

The Employment Department Group – Training, Enterprise and Education Directorate (TEED), formerly the Training Agency, for numerous references to content of its publications.

The Engineering Industry Training Board for permission to reproduce a specimen entry taken from an EITB Training Log Book.

The Further Education Unit (FEU) for numerous references to content of its publications.

The Health and Safety Executive and HMSO for references to publications concerning the monitoring of safety, health and hygiene, guidance on Electricity at Work Regulations 1989 and information about COSHH Assessments.

The Hotel & Catering Training Company for permission to reproduce documentation relating to the CaterBase qualification scheme.

The Joint Unit for Certificate of Pre-Vocational Education (CPVE) & Foundation Programmes for permission to reproduce documentation relating to the DES/ Joint Board CPVE Framework and Award. Thanks are also due to its representatives: Sue Fifer, Head of The Joint Unit; Elizabeth Selwood, Regional Co-ordinator; Helen Aylett, CPVE Senior Development Officer; Lois Wolffe, Marketing Officer and Helen Rodgers, Moderator; for advice concerning current policy and procedures.

The London Chamber of Commerce and Industry Examinations Board for permission to reproduce the Competence Transcript, Unit Certificate and full Certificate for the Business Administration National Vocational Qualification Level 1. Thanks are also due to Aileen Thompson, Head of NVQ Unit (LCCI) and Business Administration lecturers Eve Bowyer and Janette Derham for their help and advice concerning London Chamber of Commerce and Industry Examinations Board NVQ awards.

The National Council for Vocational Qualifications for permission to reproduce the NVQ Assessment Model and documentation relating to joint certification and the NROVA.

The Principal, The Bournemouth and Poole College of Further Education for permission to reproduce trainer training and other documentation designed by the author and drafted by Brian Snape, College Media and Information Co-ordinator.

The Road Transport Industry Training Board and the National Joint Council for permission to reproduce documentation relating to the RTITB Modular Training scheme and the National Craft Certificate. Thanks are also due to John Old, Training Officer, RTITB for advice concerning skills testing.

William Collins, Sons and Co. Ltd for a reference to the philosophy of Immanuel Kant.

Roger Scott-Simons, Head of Training Programmes, Dorset Skills Training for information relating to Government Sponsored Training.

Every attempt has been made to contact copyright holders, but we apologise if any have been overlooked.

Disclaimer

The persons named in this book have no existence outside the imagination of the author and have no relation whatsoever with any company or person bearing the same name or names. They are not even distantly inspired by any individual known or unknown to the author, and all incidents are pure invention.

HOW TO USE THIS BOOK

The Assessment of Performance and Competence may be read from cover to cover or used for spot reference. A list of topics is given at the front of each chapter and this is intended to help readers form an overview of the extent of coverage.

Performance criteria relating to the role of trainer, trainee or assessor are embedded in the text. They are inset in heavy type as are suggestions for meeting the high standards now demanded when planning, preparing, delivering, monitoring and evaluating training provision and learning opportunities.

Relevant complementary or underpinning knowledge is outlined in the text and methods of dealing with training functions ranging from initial assessment to accreditation of competence are discussed.

INTRODUCTION

Quality education, training and staff development is the key to survival in business and the wider community today and a spur to future development and growth. Commitment to a quality approach in the design and implementation of training is now demanded in order to meet the high expectations of everyone seeking to update their knowledge and skills. Trainers, training consultants and human resource managers will therefore need to achieve self-imposed high quality standards for the provision of tutoring and learner support so as to match outcomes with learner entitlement.

A systematic audit of all training operations will need to be carried out. Every aspect of recruitment and training provision beginning with initial assessment and ranging across: induction, safe working, planning and delivering training, assessing performance at work and accrediting achievement of competence will need to be carefully monitored and evaluated. Full implementation of National Vocational Qualifications (NVQs) and Scottish Vocational Qualifications (SVQs) will call for considerable change in training philosophy and the measurement of performance at work in every occupational area.

Performance-related and competence-based trainer's, assessor's, verifier's, APL adviser's and workplace monitoring officer's awards are being progressively developed and continuously updated. These awards and associated underlying training and developmental work provide standards that will help staff meet the challenge presented by the needs, performance criteria and targets of training functions.

Increasing emphasis is now being placed on giving candidates credit for prior achievement and this has led to a demand for an enlarged army of competent advisers. Their role will be to help others to identify existing competence and to assist them to present themselves for assessment. This new force will comprise supervisors and managers within a business, college tutors, careers officers and people working in personnel and training whose role embraces guiding and advising others towards vocational qualifications or GNVQs.

With this in mind an appendix has been added which is intended to supplement information about assessing prior learning and achievement given elsewhere in the text.

It is hoped that by relating what is described in this handbook to their work, readers will be better able to meet rigorous quality standards that now apply to each and every training initiative. What is more, detailed guidance is provided for trainers who need to provide tangible evidence of their competence in the form of currently accepted practice or approved qualifications based on Training & Development Lead Body standards.

Les Walklin
1993

Note
Since this book was typeset the Training Agency has become the Employment Department Group – Training, Enterprise and Education Directorate (TEED). Hence all references to the Training Agency should be taken to refer to TEED.

CHAPTER ONE

DEVELOPING STANDARDS

Chapter coverage

Standards-based systems
Analysing work content – functional analysis
Process used for analysis
Defining performance criteria
Competence
Assessment specifications
Writing objectives
Validity and reliability
Quality assurance in accreditation

Standards-based systems

There are a number of basic requirements for the successful introduction of a **standards-based system** of assessment. Understanding the concept of assessing competence against performance criteria is not as easy as some would like to suggest. Anyone who is liable to act hastily without considering what assessment is all about should think twice before getting involved.

Commitment and support from the top is a prerequisite for success in any new initiative and workplace assessment is no different in this respect. If the accreditation of achievement is seen to be important to senior managers this message will be filtered down to all other levels. Any programme of accrediting competence will be doomed to failure without the visible enthusiastic support of workplace trainers, assessors and supervisors who know what is involved in the process.

The concept of **developing standards** includes features such as: analysing work content within an occupation; defining the key purposes of jobs involved; identifying related units and elements of competence; defining performance criteria and assessment specifications based on objectives; validity and reliability of training outcomes and quality assurance in assessment. These features are discussed overleaf.

Analysing work content – functional analysis

The process of examining in detail the work activities that go on in an occupation in order to discover its essential features has been described as **functional analysis**.[1]

A **function** is part of the normal activity of a person performing a specific role. When a worker is able to consistently carry out these functions to specified standards that person is said to be competent.

An **analysis** is carried out in order to separate the whole occupational area into its constituent parts and to examine each function of the job holder's role in terms of units and elements of competence.

A group of specialists set up by the Training Agency suggested that a functional analysis to develop standards should proceed as follows:

- Describe the key purpose of the occupational area.
- Ask: 'What needs to happen for this to be achieved?'
- Repeat the process until the functions being identified are at **unit level**.
- Repeat the process for each unit until the functions are at **element level**.[2]

The group give examples of functional analysis, one of which is reproduced in Figure 1.1. In this case the analysis relates to the occupational area: '**commercial horticulture**'. The key purpose selected is: 'to **provide ornamental beds and borders**' and this is broken down into functions identified at **unit level**.

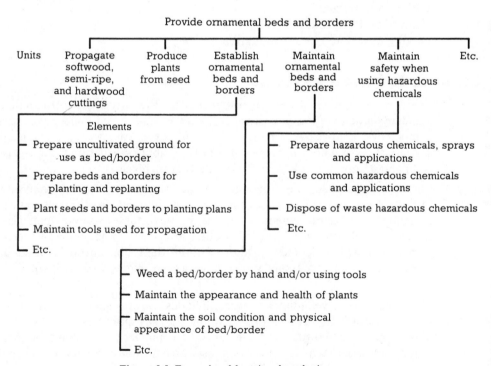

Figure 1.1 Example of functional analysis

Source: Guidance Note 2 – Training Agency p. 12[3]

Then, following the procedure suggested, the question: **'What needs to happen for this to be achieved?'** is asked for each unit. This yields a comprehensive list of **elemental functions** that enable the **key purpose** to be fulfilled.

Standards with **performance criteria** can then be written for the list of elements. This neat package can provide opportunities for practical work performed to be assessed while horticulturists are demonstrating 'can do' activities.

Process used for analysis

The four stages involved in producing the functional analysis are shown in Figure 1.2. As can be seen the starting point is identifying and describing the key purpose of the job to be studied. Functions that describe the activities of the job holders are then specified for those involved at all levels within the organisation. Once a clear picture of what goes on to fulfil the key purpose is obtained the person making the analysis is able to 'home-in' on the individual roles of those carrying out the work in particular units.

The final stage requires the analyst to shape and list units of competences that are crucial to the worker's achievement of results of the right quality and standard.

While thinking specifically about unit content the analyst will also be considering several essential elements of skilled performance encountered daily wherever work is carried out:

– working together skills
– task skills
– planning skills
– contingency management skills.

Working together skills

Working together skills comprise all those aspects of personal effectiveness and getting on with others that are essential to good relations in the workplace. Attitudes and related feelings may exert a considerable influence on a person's approach to the working environment. **Environmental skills** embrace the ability to work within conditions of service and contract of employment and to achieve results that will help move the organisation forward or at least maintain its position in the market place. They might be described as skills that are not specifically task oriented but without which a worker might find it difficult to demonstrate a consistent level of performance at work.

Team work
Peer group learning and support is valued by those who are able to get together to talk about their work. This is particularly true of people who lack the confidence to go it alone or who do not have sufficient study skills or work experience to properly understand principles underlying modules or units of competence to be assessed.

Task skills

A **task** is a specific piece of work required to be done in connection with a key purpose. A **skill** is the ability, either innate or acquired by training and practice, that enables a person to perform a task expertly. **Manual proficiency** is often a prominent

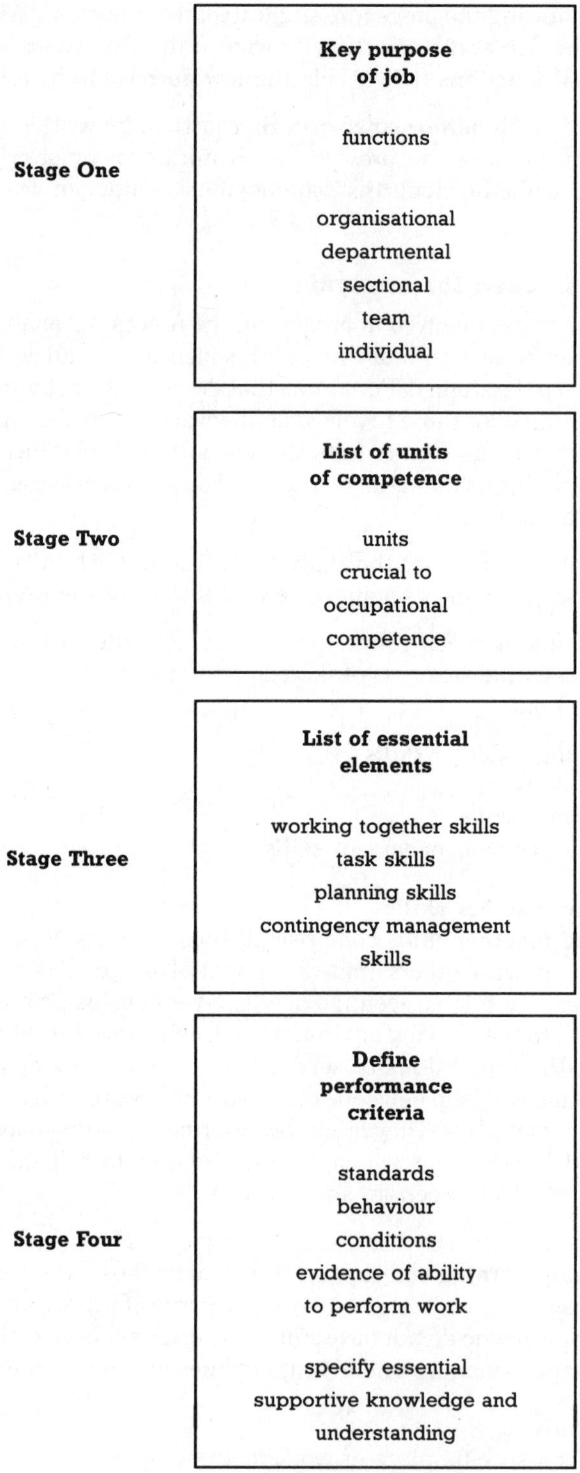

Stage One

> **Key purpose
> of job**
>
> functions
>
> organisational
> departmental
> sectional
> team
> individual

Stage Two

> **List of units
> of competence**
>
> units
> crucial to
> occupational
> competence

Stage Three

> **List of essential
> elements**
>
> working together skills
> task skills
> planning skills
> contingency management
> skills

Stage Four

> **Define
> performance
> criteria**
>
> standards
> behaviour
> conditions
> evidence of ability
> to perform work
>
> specify essential
> supportive knowledge and
> understanding

Figure 1.2 Producing a functional analysis

Based on: 'A process to develop standards'[4]

feature of a skilled person's performance at work but knowledge and understanding is implicit in the performance of work at any level. **Task skill** is the combination of knowledge, experience, attitude and performance skill needed to carry out specified tasks.

Planning skills

A **plan** is a detailed scheme or method for attaining an objective. This is fine when plenty of time is available to work out every detail, to dot the i's and cross the t's. There is no doubt that people who plan every move carefully do not often make silly mistakes. They seldom, if ever, find themselves short of this or that, but not every work situation calls for this level of attention to detail. It can be wasteful of time that could be more productively spent doing other things. What is certain though is that in many cases: 'failing to plan is planning to fail'.

A skilled person spends a little time thinking about what is to be done and how best to set about completing the task on time and at the right quality without wasting a lot of effort. This is where the expert will adopt a **planning-led approach** when the task calls for it. This method of working often leads to better results than flying by the seat of one's pants and reacting to one mini-disaster or shortage after another.

> When assessing competence it is easy to recognise a candidate who has planned the method of tackling a task and has neatly assembled all resources needed to perform competently.

Contingency management skills

Contingencies are things that may or may not happen. Accidental things that happen by chance or without obvious or known causes come under this heading. In the workplace they may be known as 'snags' – that hinder or impede progress or 'cock-ups' – that indicate work has been done badly and may need rectification. Making a 'botch' of something is a way of saying that work is sub-standard or spoiled.

In each of the instances given, something has gone badly wrong and somehow or other things have got to be put right. It is the way that the rectification or alternative course of action is handled that needs to be managed.

Management is the technique or practice of managing or controlling the use of physical and human resources. A **manager** is a person who directs or manages processes, materials and other people.

In the past it was commonly believed that managers had to be members of the executive or administration of an organisation and that responsibility for running the show was delegated only to top, middle or line managers. Rank and file had little say in the way things were done. This is not true today. Good leadership is replacing the old 'carrot and stick' approach. Everyone in organisations are now being encouraged to take part in some way in the management of their employing organisation. Members of the workforce are becoming quality conscious and realise that they must take a fair degree of responsibility for what they do.

> The ability to manage tasks and to organise working method should be encouraged at all levels. This facility often forms the foundation of the whole system of working within an organisation.

Defining performance criteria

The definition of competences and the writing of associated performance criteria enables evidence of the ability to perform work to be assessed. In addition to a demonstration of practical skills the achievement of competence criteria will embrace the ownership of essential supportive knowledge and understanding.

**Define
performance
criteria**

standards

behaviour

conditions

evidence of ability

to perform work

specify essential

supportive

knowledge and

understanding

Figure 1.3 Defining performance criteria

Competence

A well-known definition of **competence** is: 'the demonstration of knowledge, skills and attitudes required to perform a given task or act', but in a particular occupational area such as a salon an alternative might be: 'the ability to perform occupational or work-related activities and to demonstrate underpinning knowledge, skills, understanding and personal effectiveness to standards required and demanded by employers and customers in actual working conditions'. The word '**standards**' keeps cropping up. It has to, for without standards who could say what competent performance at work means?

> The assessor will need to be satisfied that the candidate is not only able to demonstrate correctly those physical skills involved in carrying out a range of tasks but is also able to handle contingencies and to cope when something goes wrong.

Standards defined

A '**standard**' may be defined as a specification by which the qualities required of something may be tested or compared. Standards specify distinct performance goals. When assessing competence, standards will be written into any specification of behaviour that will test a person's ability to demonstrate appropriate skills.

A competent person will be able to perform consistently and reliably and will regularly maintain at the standard specified an effective and efficient output. Standards form the bedrock upon which the framework of National Vocational Qualifications (NVQs) has been built. Without standards it would be difficult if not impossible to say whether or not a person is performing competently, since standards are a measure of competence. It therefore follows that the skills, knowledge and understanding needed to perform at the right standard will define the vocational and educational training back-up that should be available to candidates from training providers and their trainers.

The assessor will check that occupational standards are being met by candidates and that they are working correctly, efficiently and safely.

CaterBase criteria

The CaterBase 'Front of House' List of Performance Criteria[5] reproduced in Figure 1.4 is a good example of well-conceived criteria, many of which could be applied to other occupational areas. The essential elements of skilled performance described above are well represented in the list.

Competence in the Performance Criteria given must be displayed throughout the period of assessment for every CaterBase Module.

Assessment specifications

The performance standards to which candidates need to be trained may be defined in a document called an **assessment specification**. This document is often used by companies who write their own 'in-house' criteria additional to those of any awarding body concerned.

Some trainers and assessors like to produce specifications to meet local needs that are additional to those identified nationally. Others prefer to have fairly precise guidelines against which to assess candidates. Rather than rely entirely on their own opinion as to just how well candidates are performing against the criteria established by external authorities, they compare performance against the specification.

Behavioural objectives that specify: 'what the candidate is expected to be able to do in order to demonstrate competence' provide the performance criteria. For example, a candidate may be required to be able to: 'weigh-up to an accuracy of plus or minus five grammes and pack four 200 gramme sachets of ground coffee within one minute'. Here, performance criteria are precisely stated and competence can readily be assessed. There can be no doubt about the outcome; either the candidates can do it or they can not.

Assessors will refer to the assessment specification or assessment guide in order to confirm: what are the performance criteria to be met; what will count as evidence of competence; how much will need to be assembled or seen and the methods by which such evidence must be collected.

The assessment is mainly objective. There can be little variation in assessors' opinions about decisions made.

The following Performance Criteria relate to work methods in the Front of House area. Competence in these Performance Criteria must be displayed throughout the period of assessment for each module. Individual modules will not be deemed to be complete until the work method section has been signed by the assessor.

Performance Criteria

1 Presents smart appearance and maintains personal hygiene.
- Keeps body clean and fresh.
- Keeps face clean.
- Keeps teeth clean and breath fresh.
- Keeps hands/fingernails clean and manicured.
- Keeps hair clean, neat and appropriately styled.
- Maintains clean shaven face or clean, trimmed beard/moustache.
- Does not wear jewellery, make-up and perfume to excess.
- Does not display unpleasant personal habits e.g. chewing gum, touching nose.
- Wears correct, clean, pressed, well-maintained, and well-fitting clothing/uniform.
- Wears correct, clean, well-maintained and well-fitting footwear.

2 Adheres to safe working practices.
- Does not create hazardous situations.
- Eliminates and/or reports all hazards.
- Eliminates and/or reports all equipment defects.
- Follows instructions when operating equipment.
- Leaves equipment safe after use.
- Complies with fire prevention, extinction and evacuation procedures.

3 Adheres to hygienic working practices.
- Eliminates and/or reports all hygiene hazards.
- Reports all medical conditions which affect hygiene.
- Washes hands when appropriate.
- Covers minor cuts, abrasions, burns and other minor skin disorders with clean dressing.

4 Employs efficient methods of work.
- Uses correct equipment and materials.
- Uses equipment and materials correctly.
- Has equipment and materials correctly arranged and to hand.
- Maintains equipment and materials in good order.
- Does not waste materials.
- Follows energy conservation procedures for electricity.
- Performs tasks in specified/logical order.
- Paces work correctly.
- Is punctual for work.
- Takes pride in presentation of work.
- Works conscientiously.
- Works with honesty.
- Works without unnecessary noise.
- Copes with pressure.
- Uses initiative where appropriate.
- Keeps work area tidy.

Figure 1.4 (cont.)

5	Uses effective interpersonal skills.	– Uses clear, precise and natural speech. – Acknowledges/greets customers politely and with a smile. – Listens carefully to customers. – Has positive manner. – Is alert and attentive to customers. – Displays ability to work as a member of a team. – Adopts correct posture. – Listens carefully to work instructions. – Accepts correction. – Written communication is clear, accurate and correctly presented.

Figure 1.4 CaterBase 'Front of House' list of performance criteria

Writing objectives

An objective may contain up to three parts:

- A description of what is to be demonstrated as evidence that the candidate is competent to undertake the task.
- A statement describing the important conditions (if any) under which the behaviour is expected to occur.
- The acceptable performance level specifying how well or to what standard the candidate must perform to be considered competent.

The chief advantages of using objectives are that they:

- Help in planning and delivering training.
- Let all concerned know what is expected of them.
- Emphasise what it is that must be learned and demonstrated.
- Help candidates judge their own progress.
- Provide a basis for the assessor's accreditation of performance.

Examples
The following examples contain some or all of the three component parts that may comprise the objective.

The candidate will be able to:

- Prepare, cook and present for service a four-egg plain omelette.
- Fit correctly a 13 amp plug to an electric fire.
- Using a Colchester Lathe produce within 45 minutes from a metal blank supplied, a Shaft Part No 4920, correct to drawing specification and tolerances.
- Without referring to any books or notes write in legible handwriting with not more than four spelling mistakes a 200-word description of the role of beauty therapy salon receptionist.

Validity and reliability

Validity defined

When planning training and assessment in the workplace or elsewhere, we must ensure that the content and process is **valid**. The assessment method must fit what is to be assessed. This means that the accreditation of competence covers what is required to be achieved in terms of performance criteria.

> It is of the utmost importance to ensure that candidates will be able to perform anywhere, competently, in their occupational roles.

In order to be properly validated: 'Competence must be demonstrated and assessed under conditions as close as possible to those under which it would normally be practised'.[6]

> Before carrying out an assessment a clear picture of what is critical, important and relevant to successful achievement leading to an award should be in the assessor's mind.

> Assessors also need to be aware of the tendency to 'home-in' on aspects of the candidate's performance that particularly interest them. Value judgements and bias on their part can affect objectivity of the assessment.

Reliability defined

Assessments should be **reliable**. The extent to which an assessment of competence is consistently dependable and reliable when carried out by different assessors or by a single assessor with different candidates, or at different times of day and in different places, is a measure of the **reliability** of the accreditation.

Performance criteria usually provide a description of conditions and standards against which competence may be judged. Competence is then confirmed by completing all the criteria for success on a 'can-do' basis. This limits to a considerable extent subjectivity and variation in assessors' opinions.

> The reliability of an assessment may be influenced adversely by the workplace accreditor's workload and ability to manage time and stress. When assessing achievement is regarded as being a 'bolt-on' activity, the consistency of results may well vary considerably.

General factors that may affect reliability include: the form and content of the assessment and the environment in which it takes place. Assessor-related factors include: spoken or written language used for instructions, cultural bias and style of supervision. Candidate-related factors include: mental, physical and emotional state, degree of motivation and relationship with the assessor.

> 'Awarding bodies should develop systems for monitoring assessment practices to ensure they are sound and enable standards of delivery to be maintained.'[7]

Quality assurance in accreditation

In order to ensure continuing credibility of NVQ awards and the process of workplace accreditation it is necessary to employ assessment methods that will limit variance in quality of accreditation.

Each and every element of competence must be assessed to standards indicated by the performance criteria.

The **National Council for Vocational Qualifications (NCVQ)** will be interested in making certain that the method adopted captures valid evidence of competence although it does not specify particular types of assessment to be used.

> 'Assessments should be carried out according to procedures specified by the awarding body for the particular NVQ.'[8]

This is not new. For many years, BTEC Moderators and CGLI Assessors have been monitoring standards across Britain. Proposals for offering programmes and provision for implementation and accreditation to required standards must be validated by the awarding body before the 'go ahead' is given to centres. Verification of implementation by the centre to agreed standards required during delivery of the programme is part of the normal monitoring processes, as is a review of outcomes.

> Validation of competence of workplace assessors in terms of their ownership of occupational area knowledge and skills and their ability to review, assess and accredit candidates to agreed standards, is essential to the maintenance of quality of assessment. Assessor competence is a key criterion to participation in assessing achievement.

Notes

1 *Developing Standards by Reference to Functions – Guidance Note 2*, Employment Department Group Training Agency, Moorfoot 1989, p. 8.
2 Ibid p. 8.
3 Ibid p. 12.
4 Ibid pp. 8–11.
5 *Front of House Performance Criteria WM05*, CaterBase, Hotel & Catering Training Company (formerly Hotel & Catering Training Board), London. Crown Copyright 1986.
6 *The NVQ Criteria and Related Guidance*, NCVQ, London, January 1988, para 2.3.3.
7 *The NVQ Criteria and Related Guidance*, NCVQ, London, January 1988, para 4.11.
8 *The NVQ Criteria and Related Guidance*, NCVQ, London, January 1988, para 4.11.

CHAPTER TWO

INITIAL ASSESSMENT AND INDUCTION

Chapter coverage

Identification and initial assessment
Initial assessment and review
Access and initial assessment
Role of student services in colleges
Role of client support services – access and initial assessment
Student services – induction and assessment role
Analysis of individual training needs
Meeting training needs
Database operation
Skills audit
Organisational needs
Bridging the training gap
Purpose of initial assessment
Subsequent assessments
Criterion-referenced testing and norm-referenced testing
Assessing induction
The employing organisation
Induction programme for new starters
Personnel matters
Training agreement factors
Health and Safety at Work Act, 1974
Training plans and programmes
Learning opportunities and methods
Session training plans
Checklists

Identification and initial assessment

It is important to assess all people seeking access to vocational education and training opportunities. There is also a need to continuously review and assess the training needs of industrial and commercial workers, new starters and trainees, the purpose being to help in the planning of training and to promote occupational competence.

The object of **identification and initial assessment** is to help trainers and learners sort out what it is that they wish to achieve. Action plans can be produced and relevant training arranged to meet needs as far as is possible bearing in mind available resources and the ability of individuals to attain their occupational aims. Some of the purposes of initial assessment and review are set out in Figure 2.1.

Initial assessment and review

Purpose:

- To help candidates to clarify learning needs and to create an action plan.
- To help candidates see how the opportunity to accredit existing skills and to plan for the learning of new skills can help them to move forward or to enhance career opportunities.
- To prioritise importance of action plan content and to derive a sequence of learning, bearing in mind costs and benefits of decisions made.
- To monitor and record progress against earlier action plans. To clarify confusion or lack of understanding. To adjust current action plan accordingly.
- To write sets of aims and objectives designed to enable sought-after skills to be defined and understood.
- To identify tasks and workplace activities that will enable new skills to be learned and practised and existing skills to be accredited.
- To agree the settings and context in which the achievement of competence may be demonstrated and accredited.
- To analyse and reflect upon the relevance of candidate's experiences in the workplace to the achievement of competence.
- To review supporting evidence of competence and to allow for guidance, counselling and monitoring of the learning process and outcomes of assessment.
- To carry out accreditation processes for prior learning and to discuss how best to integrate new competences when learned into daily workplace activities.

Figure 2.1 Initial assessment and review

In progressive companies and elsewhere, such as in Government Sponsored Training like Employment Training and Youth Training, the identification of training needs and related assessments are designed to meet the needs of individuals, while at the same time relating to operational plans of the employing organisation or occupational area. Individual training programmes may be based on outcomes of the analysis of training need.

Access and initial assessment

Matching individual needs and expectations with related education and training provision is the key to success in the attainment of competence in an occupation or subject.

Access to suitable learning opportunities has in the past not always been easy and at best a compromise between what the client was seeking and whatever course or training was already 'on the shelf'. Today there exists demand for a wider range of training provision. This is needed to fulfil the expectations of employers seeking to provide quality products and services backed by a well-trained and competent workforce.

In order to meet this challenge, providers will need to set up or improve access and initial assessment. A more responsive vocational education and training service is called for. For example, a central admissions unit could be located within Student Services.

Role of student services in colleges

Student Services is the name given to the college department that deals with matters affecting the student as a client. In some cases this work is undertaken by a **Student Counsellor** working alone but with access to all college departments and support services or external referral agencies. Not all colleges provide these services, although it is now becoming a necessity rather than a luxury as competition for students hots up. With the introduction of NVQs, higher priority is being given to providing the kind of facilities that are needed to back-up assessment and accreditation of prior learning. Clients seeking information on accreditation and curriculum entitlement (their share of the education and training cake) now expect a better deal than that on offer in the 1980s and before. They need to gain access to the right person to help them without first being needlessly directed from one place to another. They deserve to be interviewed in a quiet, comfortable and private room. They require to be treated in a sensitive way by supportive and honest people who know what they are talking about. They are, after all, customers without whom the college would fail.

Another key role would be to facilitate access to learning and to make it easy for clients to get out of the system what they need rather than what happens to be on offer. A model that might suit schools and colleges but which is transferable to other training providers and employers is shown in Figure 2.2.

Working on a **systems approach,** clients would be directed to the **central admissions unit** which would act as a filter. Competent staff would offer a user-friendly counselling and guidance service to people looking for learning opportunities.

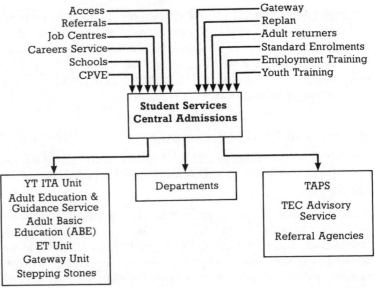

Figure 2.2 Role of Client Support Services – access and initial assessment

For many clients, mainstream education and training provision would be geared to satisfying their needs. Such people would be directed to the department where adequately trained academic staff would be able to give detailed information on subjects and routes to progression. They would be set on the right track – that leading to the achievement of their goals.

Clients with learning difficulties or problems that cannot readily be resolved and those needing help with career choice would be referred to qualified staff based in support units.

The layout of a typical services unit is shown in Figure 2.3. Departmental assessors experienced in initial assessment procedures and the accreditation of prior learning link with Student Services. They are in contact with subject specialists who are able to offer 'in-depth' study guidance to clients. At peak periods such as during annual enrolment (if this mode of enrolment survives) these key staff would be seconded to the central admissions unit within Student Services in order to cope with the normally heavy demand. At other times close liaison would be maintained and assessors would be on call to give advice.

Terminals provided would enable clients to access national and local databases (see also Chapter 8).

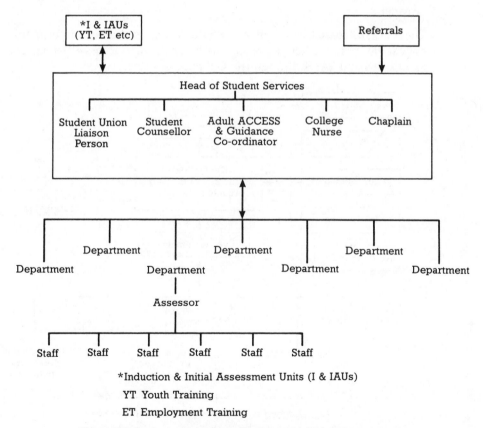

*Induction & Initial Assessment Units (I & IAUs)

YT Youth Training

ET Employment Training

Figure 2.3 Student services – induction and initial assessment role

Analysis of individual training needs

It is likely that anyone who is working or preparing to work will have some learning need. The way things are going today calls for rapid responses from the workforce. The rate at which technology is changing, how we need to do things and what we need to do at work, together with more demanding customer expectations, means that we have to do something about keeping up-to-date. We need to constantly adjust to these demands made of us and learn new things that will help us to move on. We need to be competent and this applies whether our status is that of trainee, skilled worker, supervisor, trainer or assessor.

Meeting training needs

Once needs have been identified, information on the availability of education and training opportunities should be readily available to all clients wishing to gain access to the provision. This is where suitable databases can be helpful to providers seeking to meet individual training needs.

Database operation

The database operation shown in Figure 2.4 would be very useful when attempting to match **demand-led** needs with **supply-led** provision. The model uses a typical college as the main provider although the concept is transferable to any other major provider.

The **NVQ Database** (see Chapter 8) would be a main source of information for the college database and **key persons** would be available to access other databases such as ECCTIS and TAPS through the facility.

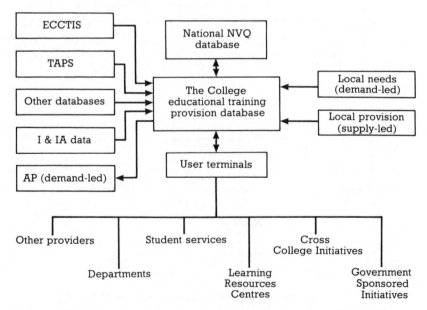

I & IA = Induction & Initial Assessment (needs based data)

AP = Action Plans (meeting clients' competence based needs)

Figure 2.4 Database operation

Qualifications and training opportunities on offer would be accessed using the college educational training provision database or that of Student Services. User terminals operated by staff from many sources, such as those shown in Figure 2.4, would input and access data needed to maintain the service at the right standard. The input/output model would serve to match as far as possible supply and demand.

The college database
The database shown in Figure 2.5 could be operated by Student Services. It would provide detail of 'What's on offer' to clients who arrive seeking information and guidance as to how their needs might be met. Once again qualified staff from departments and those with special responsibility for cross-college initiatives would be on hand to supplement detail provided by the database. Outcomes of training in the form of NVQ-related achievement and other qualifications are fed back into the database and this data is useful when monitoring and evaluating the training provision.

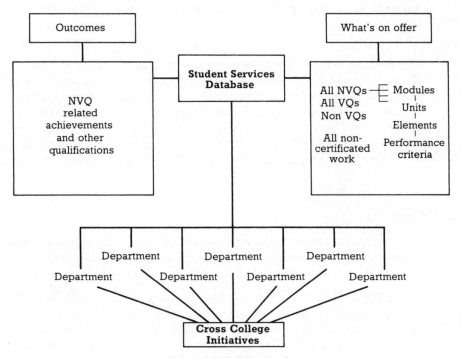

Figure 2.5 College database

Other databases
Connecting with the college Student Services database would be others as shown in Figure 2.6. Youth Training and other Government Sponsored Training databases would contain such records as are permitted together with information on training provision and needs.

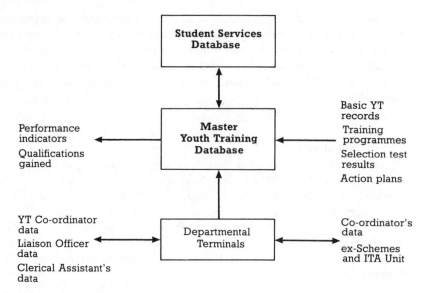

Figure 2.6 Government sponsored training databases: example of 'other database' input to SSU database

The training manager's requirements and trainee choices would be input to the database, together with initial assessment needs-based data, selection test results and action plan content. A 'best match' would result and this, together with data relating to NVQs and other qualifications, could be used to formulate performance criteria to be used as a basis for negotiating the training programme. Trainee achievement would also be input to generate performance indicators as a measure of outcomes of training, qualifications gained and other scheme-specific statistics.

Skills audit

Whether an assessment and review of learning needs is carried out together with an experienced trainer/counsellor or alone by **self-analysis** may not be too important. What is important is for people to be able to identify what skills they already have.

Those involved in the analysis should be encouraged to talk about their needs during induction or when the training group first assembles. Some will be surprised to find themselves in a situation where their personal views are sought. For many this will be the first time. Others may be confused because they may feel that they are not yet in a position to tell someone else what it is that they wish to learn. If people are asked to write a list of things they need to know, without any kind of help, prompting or support, they are likely to come out with the old adage: 'How shall I know what it is that I do not know and yet need to know?'

A suitable starting point could be to ask the group to discuss among themselves or with the trainer, their **aptitudes, abilities** and extent of their **prior experience.** They might then be invited to ask themselves: 'What skills do I own?' and to write a list of their achievements.

In this way a non-threatening climate for needs identification may be established. By building on what they can already do, any negative views of themselves in terms of feelings of inadequacy can be swept away. Strengths will be identified and a **positive self-image** built. It is not helpful to focus too heavily on weaknesses.

Taking into account their background knowledge, standard of basic education, special learning difficulties and what they hope to achieve during subsequent training, it may be possible at this stage to agree realistic expectations and outcomes that will go some way to balance individual and organisational needs.

Alternatively, comparison could be made of what they can do against a **checklist of competences** relating to their occupational area. The resulting skills audit can then be compared with a list of competences that will be needed to work at the right standard. Personal development needs that do not directly relate to work skills may also be identified during the process.

The difference between what they are competent to do now and what they will need to be able to do in the future is known as the **training gap.** Once the gap has been agreed the next stage will be to establish a priority for learning. Those concerned could ask themselves: 'What are my priorities? What skills do I need to develop now?' and 'What skills will I need to develop in the future? and 'How will my learning needs be met?' The object of carrying out the identification of training needs during induction is to help trainers and trainees clarify learning needs and to create an **action plan.**

The assessor will expect to see evidence that a procedure for the analysis of training needs is being implemented in the workplace.

Systems for recording, categorising and prioritising individual and organisational needs should be operating.

Candidates should be able to demonstrate that positive action has been taken to ensure that both sexes are treated fairly in terms of equal opportunity and avoidance of sex discrimination.

The assessor will need to check that action plan content and sequence of learning has been prioritised so as to give the best match between trainee's and employer's needs.

The assessor could usefully discuss with candidates their ideas about training programme content and method. Candidates could be asked to identify tasks and workplace activities that will enable trainees to learn most effectively.

The assessor may need to question the candidate about the employer's needs and expectations as far as the trainee is concerned and take this into consideration when verifying evidence of the candidate's identification of the learner's needs.

Organisational needs

Trainer/assessors will be wearing at least two hats during **initial assessment** and identification of training needs sessions. They will be seeking to help fulfil the purposes listed in Figure 2.1 in order to meet learners' expectations, while at the same time bearing in mind the employer's needs.

Staff developers and trainers should be looking for a good match between **organisational needs** and needs of the individual. The proposed training provision should address both sets of needs.

Bridging the training gap

The new knowledge, skills and attitudes that form the competences to be gained may be achieved during a combination of 'on-the-job' and 'off-the-job' learning experiences. The amount of **'memorising'**, **'understanding'** and **'doing'** activity through which learning will be achieved will depend on the nature of the **element of competence** to be mastered and the related **performance criteria**.

No one learning method will suit everyone. It may therefore be beneficial for learners to try self-managed learning or networking with others. Open and distance learning with trainee access to flexible learning facilities available in Accredited Centres and Further Education Colleges are gaining popularity.

> The candidate being assessed will need to demonstrate that the trainees supported in one way or another by the trainer and employer have shared responsibility for gaining the competences identified as the 'training gap'.
>
> The assessor may wish to discuss with the candidate and trainees the range of learning opportunities provided and methods available to the learners.

Purpose of initial assessment

Initial assessment is intended to influence decisions concerning a trainee's placement and progress. It is no use trying to fit a square peg into a round hole. While in many cases school leavers and others may not have had the opportunity to develop all of their potential aptitudes there will always be some occupations for which they would probably be unsuited. Some form of selection may be necessary. **Trainability testing** is often first used to get an idea of a trainee's suitability for training in given competences.

Trainability tests may be applied to trainees before or during **induction.** The tests are practical and involve the person in performing a specific job-related task for which they have been given prior instruction. The number of errors made is noted and a **performance rating** is allocated. The tests measure **job aptitude** and **training potential.**

After the test the trainer and trainee together discuss performance and make a mutual decision as to whether the applicant is likely to benefit from training in the skills needed to perform the job. This could well be the first negotiating experience for some trainees, so great care should be exercised to make it a pleasant one.

In the book *People and Work*[1] the following advantages of using trainability testing are given:
'Trainability testing can help to:

- Save wasting expensive training on unsuitable applicants.
- Reduce average training time.
- Involve instructors in selection.
- Check claims of previous experience.
- Channel applicants into work appropriate to their skills.
- Highlight potential weak spots.
- Indicate probable length of training required and likely overall level of competence.'

Trainability test results can help trainees to assess their own potential. The tests enable them to:

- Demonstrate practical skills.
- Build up confidence.
- Get a taste of the job.
- Meet the trainers and assessors.
- Avoid unnecessary stress caused by failing to meet performance targets during training.

The trainer's role in the initial assessment procedure is to make the trainees feel at home, to conduct the assessment fairly and efficiently and to encourage them to reflect upon their experiences. Negotiation then follows, during which the trainee's competences and strengths are identified, assessed and recorded.

Subsequent assessments

Throughout the training programme formal assessments can be made. Informal assessments may also be made and these involve negotiating with trainees or carrying out **trainee-centred reviewing.**

Criterion-referenced testing, in which a trainee is assessed relative to certain pre-determined standards, specified in performance criteria, may be used in preference to **norm-referenced testing** that compares the trainee's performance with other trainees or to an average for a group of trainees. With criterion-referenced tests the trainee will 'pass' if performance against standards meets the standard. This system of assessment depends to some extent on the trainer adopting a modular approach to training where successful completion of one learning step leads on to the next.

Norm-referenced testing has in the past often been applied to nationally-set examinations for a large number of candidates. With this type of testing, individual scores are compared with the scores of all other candidates. Norm-referencing is not ideal for vocational training assessment. If results are taken on face value, it would appear that those who score high marks have learned more than lower scorers. This is not always true because unless all aspects of performance are included in the terminal tests, the scores will bear little relationship with total achievement.

Trainers and assessors must be able to:

- Explain the purpose of initial assessment in a programme of negotiation and be clear as to their own role in the process.
- Explain the criteria on which performance standards are set.
- Identify an appropriate range of assessment methods.
- Use suitable assessments to measure trainees' performance or help them to carry out self-appraisal against each learning objective or performance criterion.
- Operate a recording and reviewing system founded on the use of initial and ongoing formative assessment.

Making initial assessments

The methods used for making assessments will normally be chosen to suit the person to be assessed. If self-assessment is not possible then assessment may be made with the trainer and trainee working together using methods such as:

- Checklist or series of structured questions.
- Guided individual discussion.
- Group discussion.
- Setting trainees a task or problem.
- Observing trainees in the workplace during the course of their normal work.
- Observing trainees undertaking set tasks specified by the employer, Lead Body, CGLI, workplace trainer, assessor or other agent.

In the case of the assessment of **functional literacy and numeracy,** the Training Agency define **functional reading** as: 'the ability to read things that are relevant for work'. The Training Agency say that: 'the highest priorities should be given to things that matter most in the job'. They define **functional writing** as: 'The ability to communicate in writing where it is important in work'.[2]

The Training Agency suggest that: 'A set of structured questions can uncover a lot of information about the person's skills and attitudes; combined with an informal invitation to carry out a number of simple tasks, quite an accurate initial assessment can be made'.[3]

Self-assessment questions devised by the Careers and Occupational Information Centre are reproduced in Figures 2.7 and 2.8. The questions may be used to help trainees think about reading and mathematical skills that will be essential to future performance in their chosen employment.

The assessor when observing the candidate's achievement of competence in the area of planning and delivering induction will have much to monitor and the process could well take several hours. A guided discussion with trainees as well as the candidate will need to be highly interactive and based on key elements given in suitable checklists.

Evidence in support of the candidate's claims of achievement will be selected by the assessor in accordance with the performance criteria relating to the element of competence being assessed. Such evidence will need to cover all criteria concerning the element.

How's your maths?	would like help	can do with pen and paper	can do with calculator	can do in head	no need
addition					
subtraction					
multiplication					
division					
fractions					
decimals					
percentages					
ratios					
weights and measures					
time: using 12 hour clock					
using 24 hour clock					
analogue digital					
using a calculator					
others					
(list)					

The main areas I would like to work on are:

_____

_____

_____

_____

I would like to start on:

_____

_____

_____

_____

Figure 2.7 'How's Your Maths?'

Source: 'Working with unemployed people.' Careers and Occupational Information Centre, 1987 (see *Literacy and Numeracy*, Training Agency, Sheffield, 1989 p. 7)[4]

How's your reading?	confident	not so confident	need help	no need
reading a newspaper or magazine				
job adverts				
timetables				
maps				
instructions				
letters				
forms and leaflets				
catalogues				
labels				
diagrams				
dictionaries				
phone directories				
reference books				
predicting (getting meaning from the context)				
reading between the lines				
skimming and scanning				

Figure 2.8 'How's Your Reading?'

Source: 'Working on Reading', Careers and Occupational Information Centre, 1988 (see *Literacy and Numeracy*, Training Agency, Sheffield, 1989 p. 6)[5]

Assessing induction

Induction

To **induct** a person is to formally install them in a company or training scheme or to initiate knowledge of what the particular **organisational area** or **workplace** is all about. Induction is the act of accepting new starters or trainees into an organisation soon after their appointment. The process allows a **training agreement** to be negotiated. The effectiveness and completeness of the staff development officer's or trainer's planning and delivering of induction to newcomers will be reflected in what the newcomers learn, understand and agree and the attitudes they form toward the company. Their subsequent performance may depend to a considerable degree on the kind of deal they get during induction.

The employing organisation

During primary induction the presentation should include a description of the employing organisation and an explanation of its **mission**. The fact that any organisation is in business to provide goods and services that people need and to do so at a profit should be stressed. Survival, an important aspect of the business, might usefully be mentioned.

Organisations can be structured in many ways but whether the operation is that of a **sole trader, partnership** or **PLC** all have one thing in common – they all have to operate within a **legal framework.** Obviously, some reference needs to be made to the employing organisation's framework and possibly to the differences between **private** and **public companies.** The role of **shareholders, directors** and **employees** could also be covered but only insofar as is necessary to meet the trainees' needs. Too much detail may serve to confuse and baffle.

The core of many organisations comprise: **management, staff, product development, production, marketing** and **finance** although there may be other elements. Trainees will need to get a clear picture of how each part of their organisation fits with other parts and in particular how the work of their section or department fits into the whole scheme of things. Whether the firm be large or small, motivation and commitment to high quality performance will be enhanced if they can see how their personal occupational skills will contribute to the success of the enterprise.

> The assessor will check that the candidate together with trainees have examined the purpose and operation of the employing organisation and that the trainees have a clear picture of its structure.

> The assessor will check that the workplace trainer has explained to trainees how their job skills and occupational area role is matched with opportunities within the employing organisation and that they understand what has been said.

Induction programme for new starters

First impressions are important. How we feel about someone when meeting them for the first time will influence our attitude toward them on subsequent meetings. The same goes for staff joining a company. They will appreciate a proper induction. A better attitude will result from a little time taken welcoming newcomers, making them feel at home and settling them into their new surroundings. The likelihood of their leaving due to anxiety or confusion will be reduced if they are properly integrated into the company and with the people who work there.

Induction is the time to give information about the organisation that will affect the new starters and to introduce them to their supervisors, the job and the training opportunities available to them.

Typical outline programmes listing some factors that will be of benefit to new staff are given in Figures 2.9, 2.10 and 2.11. As can be seen, the programmes cover some of the aspects of policy and procedures that are important to new starters and to the success of the company.

Content of the induction will vary according to the needs of individuals concerned and those of the company or employing department. Its duration and phasing will depend upon company size and induction policy. In some cases a general induction covering the programme suggested in Figure 2.9 may be delivered, followed by mini-inductions spread over a defined period.

The organisation
mission
history and development
structure and management
products and marketing
finance
growth and development plans

Personnel matters
reception process
policies, rules and procedures
conditions of employment
education and training
disciplinary and grievance procedures
services to staff
health, safety, first aid, hygiene, housekeeping and protective clothing
race relations and equal opportunities
personal needs allowances
welfare and employee benefits

Facilities
washrooms and toilets
first aid room, cloakroom, lockers
rest room and canteen
parking
telephone

Workplace and job
tour of premises
hours, wages and incentives
work arrangements
work standard and quality assurance (BS5750)
tools, equipment and methods
performance appraisals

Staff
supervision
trainers
other workers
union representative

Monitoring
help available
follow-up meetings
counselling

Figure 2.9 Induction programme

INDUCTION PROGRAMME

	MONDAY	TUESDAY	WEDNESDAY	THURSDAY	FRIDAY
9.30–11.00	Job Link Video Ice Breakers	Telephone Techniques	First Aid	Environ-mental Health	Self Defence
11.00–11.30	Coffee	Coffee	Coffee	Coffee	Coffee
	Induction Test	Telephone Techniques	Health & Safety	Environ-mental Health	Self Defence
12.30–1.30	Lunch	Lunch	Lunch	Lunch	Lunch
	Police Sheet + Video	Telephone Techniques	PAYE	Bank Talk	NROVA
2.30–3.00	Coffee	Coffee	Coffee	Coffee	Coffee
	Police Talk	Telephone Techniques	Communica-tions	Bank Talk	Test Paper + Residential Video
4.00	Finish	Finish	Finish	Finish	Finish

Figure 2.10 Induction programme

Care should be taken to provide a good reception and make the new-comer feel welcome on the first day.

Key information should be shared first. Information overload should be avoided by extending the induction period over the shortest practicable period.

The **induction** outlined in Figure 2.10 contains a mix of activities that might suit trainees in clerical and secretarial or sales occupations (SOC Major Groups 4 or 7). In addition to a fairly standard programme designed to meet the needs of young people, a day of activity is included for a talk followed by practice concerning telephone techniques. The self-defence session would be mainly practical, while PAYE would probably take the form of a lecture supported by a question and answer session.

A typical **workplace induction** programme is given in Figure 2.11. Trainees will already have received a general induction and the building craft skills induction programme would be delivered on joining the Construction Department. All newcomers to practical work need some induction and this is especially true in labour intensive occupations and where power tools, lifting, scaffolding and heavy plant are involved.

Due to the nature of construction work and the people working in craft and related occupations too much passive listening and paper-based activity may not be welcomed. As it is necessary to make an impact when delivering the induction a good deal of 'hands-on' activity could usefully be provided. This is allowed for in the

Day	9	10	11	12	1	2	3	4	5
Mon 9/7	Assemble, welcome by head and tour of department Meet staff		Outline of scheme and induction programme			Health & Safety at Work Act (1974) First aid films Accidents & fire precautions Electricity at Work Regs (1989) COSHH			
Tues 10/7	Training log books Recording procedures Administration		Banking and finance matters			Site safety Introduction to working platforms			
Wed 11/7	Union representative UCATT		Scaffolding			Erecting scaffolding			
Thurs 12/7	Portable power tools		Hand tools			Lifting and transporting and stacking materials			
Fri 13/7	Starting, stopping and maintaining mixers and compressors					Mixing concrete and mortars			

Figure 2.11 Induction programme – building craft skills

programme of suggested activity that emphasises site safety and safe-working practices. The induction timetable prepares trainees for dealing with hazards that may be encountered when working on-site. It may be the only time that trainees will gain prior insight into potentially dangerous aspects of construction work.

> Programme content enables trainees to experience a systematic concentrated induction into the use of tools and equipment connected with their future work role. This hopefully will promote safe working practices and reduce the risk of injury while at work.

Personnel matters

Policies are plans of action adopted by a company. **Procedures** define courses of action to be followed by employees in order to achieve the desired policy outcomes. The workforce will need to become fully conversant with company policy and procedures. In the case of service industries and jobs such as checkout operator the induction of new starters and trainees may well embrace policy matters such as those given in Figure 2.12.

Trainer responsibilities

A **trainer** is a person employed to plan and deliver practice and instruction that will provide opportunities for trainees to reach an agreed standard of proficiency or to enable them to meet **performance criteria** specified in a given training programme or unit of competence.

Resources in the form of people and materials that will be used throughout the training and learning programme should be selected and evaluated so that trainees derive maximum achievement from the learning experience in terms of time, resources and energy invested.

Training plans covering content, resources to be employed, timing and mode of delivery should be prepared during the planning stage prior to delivery. Any plans produced should be reviewed and updated in the light of experience gained during their use.

> The assessor will check with trainees that candidates seeking accreditation have explained their responsibilities as trainers and facilitators of learning. The assessor will need to be reassured that trainees have been encouraged to ask questions and given ample opportunities to make their views known, and to show that they have all understood.
>
> The assessor will require the candidate to justify the use of method and resources used throughout the induction programme. Validity against performance criteria specified will be tested.
>
> Training plans covering the induction programme will be checked to ensure that training methods applied are suitable. The effectiveness of those adopted in terms of trainee learning outcomes will be evaluated and the value to trainees of related feedback challenged.

Hours of work
    weekly work schedules
    meals and rest periods
    length, timing and frequency of breaks

Staff dress
    regulation uniforms
    name badges
    shoes
    stockings to be worn
    cleanliness

Personal appearance
    hair condition/length
    cosmetics
    jewellery
    hands and fingernails

Gratuities
    extend courteous service
    accept no gratuities
    accept no gifts

Mass media
    no statements to press
    no interviews or recordings
    channel all such approaches to manager

Legal requirements
    written statement of main terms and conditions of employment
    variations in terms and conditions for casual staff
    parties to contract
    job title
    remuneration
    holidays and holiday pay
    pension entitlement
    sick entitlement
    disciplinary rules
    grievance procedures
    length of notice
    Health and Safety at Work Act 1974
    Intoxicating Substances (supply) Act 1985
    sale of solvent-based products – 'sniffing'

Staff sales
    payments for
    till receipts
    security checks

Figure 2.12 Company policy and procedure

Trainees' rights and responsibilities

A **right** is that which is due to a person. Rights are legitimate entitlements and may include specified privileges or allowances resulting from employment in a particular organisation.

Being **responsible** is being accountable for one's decisions and actions and for the outcomes. It involves the need to take rational decisions without supervision and taking the consequences for mistakes as well as credit for good results. A person who has control and authority over what he or she does must take, or at least share, the responsibility for outcomes.

The assessor will need to monitor the candidate's explanation of the trainees' rights and responsibilities as well as their own as trainer and be satisfied that the trainees have understood these in respect of the training to be undertaken and support that may be expected.

Administration

The process of managing the affairs of an organisation or training programme is called **administration**. There are certain administrative procedures that trainees must be familiar with. It is a requirement that during induction sessions workplace trainers provide trainees with sufficient information on the administration and other procedures that they will come across during their training within the work placement or employing company.

During induction, routine policies and procedures will need to be explained, related documentation issued and samples completed. Where possible procedures should be learned by **doing** or **carrying out** activities where and when they naturally occur rather than as exercises. Examples covered might include some of those given in Figures 2.13, 2.14 and 2.15.

```
- offer of employment
- training agreement
- training programmes
- training plans
- performance criteria and units of competence
- assessments and reviews
- individual action plans
- planned work experience
- off-the-job training
- records of achievement
- identification and initial assessment/preparation
- guidance and counselling provision
- health and safety policies
- travel claims
- sickness and absence reporting
```

Figure 2.13 Policies and procedures

The assessor will question trainees in order to confirm whether or not the candidate, acting as a trainer, has successfully communicated accurate information on administrative and other workplace or training provider procedures.

Examples of correctly completed documents submitted by trainees to the scheme manager or employer may be called for to support the candidate's claim for accreditation of competence in this area.

Form of agreement	
Expectations	
Trainer	**Trainee**

Trainee will:
– participate willingly
– attend training sessions
– read and follow all workplace and
  college rules and conditions
– comply with the law (Health & Safety
  at Work Act 1974, Electricity at
  Work Regulations 1989, etc.)
– maintain contact with trainers and
  supervisors
– report absences, hazards and
  accidents
– keep a diary and logbook
	To receive:
	– induction and initial assessment
	– action plan
	– training plan
	– planned work experience
	– off-the-job training
	– liaison support
	– guidance and review
	– assessments
	– record of achievements
	– insurance cover
	– safe working environment

Other factors	
Outcomes	**Administration**

– identification of:
   strengths
   interests
   aptitudes
   abilities
– training potential
– work skills and competence
– experience
– suitable employment
– National Vocational Qualifications or
  other awards
	– equal opportunities
	– status of trainee
	– attendance pattern
	– hours of work
	– holiday entitlement
	– sickness reporting
	– grievance procedures
	– disciplinary procedures
	– safety and hygiene
	– first aid and accidents
	– counselling
	– company rules and regulations

Figure 2.14 Training agreement factors

Training Agreement

Trainee's name ....

Address ....

....

....

I have read and I understand the agreement that we have negotiated and declare that I will follow the rules and regulations set out in the Agreement.

Signed .... Trainee

Signed .... Employer

Date ....

Figure 2.15 Training agreement declaration

Health and Safety at Work Act, 1974

Consideration of the implications for trainers and trainees of the **Health and Safety at Work Act, 1974** is given in Chapter 3. It is however essential that trainers can demonstrate that, during induction, they have explained the employer's and the trainees' responsibility under the Act.

> The assessor will check with the candidate and trainees that they are able to monitor the safety of their working environments and that they can implement fire, accident and emergency procedures, can maintain appropriate records and ensure a safe working environment.

Training plans and programmes

Documents detailing personal training programmes will need to be produced jointly by trainer and trainee during or before the formal induction session.

Some plans detail methods, resources and opportunities by which **negotiated objectives** or **performance criteria** may be attained or they may take the form of either of those given in Chapter 3. But sometimes the programme is less detailed as in Figure 2.16.

The example gives key information about the trainee's planned achievement targets and how and when training will take place. Targeted review interview dates are agreed together with estimated dates for completion of training.

The format of an alternative training programme is shown in Figure 2.17. This type of form allows for short-term plans to be written and for reviews to be made on an ongoing basis.

The documents serve as evidence of a series of formative reviews and assessments and sheets can be filed in the trainee's portfolio of records and used to support claims of achievement.

> Personal programmes will be examined by the assessor to ensure that proposed training is based on units and elements of training relating to the trainee's occupational area.
>
> In order to assess the effectiveness of the trainer/trainee negotiations the trainees will be required to state and justify the performance standard agreed for the job skills within their chosen occupational area. Statements made will be checked against selected elements of competence comprised of lists of performance criteria that together make up the element.
>
> The assessment will normally be made at the workplace and discussion with the candidate and trainees will probably be centred around the personal training programmes produced as evidence. Trainees may be asked to confirm that their training programmes were negotiated and agreed by them in cooperation with the candidate, and if appropriate, with other workplace trainers.

The Training Agency

YT

PERSONAL TRAINING PROGRAMME

This is your personal training Programme. It sets out what you are aiming to achieve in YT and how your training will take place. It also shows the dates for review interviews with your Managing Agent. The estimated date for completion for training is a rough guide to how much time you will need to achieve what is set down. However, at the end of this time you may wish to go further and add more training to achieve your programme.
Your Managing Agent will advise you.

Name _____ PANIANG TAMPRATEEP _____

Managing Agent _____ CHARLTON MARSHALL COLLEGE _____

Period from _JANUARY 1991_ to _DECEMBER 1991_ (estimated date of completion of training within YT)

SECTION 1 - VOCATIONAL QUALIFICATION TO BE ACHIEVED

Title THE RETAIL CERTIFICATE

NCVQ Level (England and Wales) _____ I _____

Awarding Body / Bodies _____ NRTC / CITY & GUILDS OF LONDON INSTITUTE _____

List here the separate component parts of the qualification (City & Guilds, Certificate, Skills tests, Knowledge tests, etc.)	Expected date of achievement
FOUNDATION UNITS (×6) PLUS OPTION UNITS : Product presentation Stock handling Price change Mail handling	28 June 1991
Any additional units to be achieved	
RSA WORD PROCESSING	After the foundation units have been achieved.

SECTION 2 - THE TRAINING

Off the job Training Location(s)	Dates
	from to
Charlton Marshall College	March 1991 – Sep 1991

On the job Training Location(s)	Dates
	from to
Henley Superstores PLC	1 Jan 1991 – 1 June 1991
Chez Mercien Fashions	2 June 1991 – 31 Dec 1991

Dates of formal review of progress achievements

weeks commencing:
4 March 1991
3 June 1991
2 Sep 1991
2 Dec 1991

Comments (including achievements before YT.).

Worked for one-year as part-time sales assistant in Alastairs Newsagents.
Member of school business enterprise project group
Gained relevant work experience during school
CPVE year
Awaiting GCSE results confirmation

RECEIVED BY TRAINEE

Signature _____ Date 4 January 1991

Figure 2.16 Personal training programme

SHEET NUMBER ☐

NAME:	PROJECT/PLACEMENT:
AIMS & OBJECTIVES:	
PRIOR LEARNING: (Units of Competence)	
TRAINING TO BE UNDERTAKEN: (Units and elements)	
HOW:	
WHERE:	
BY WHOM:	
DATES:	
ASSESSED: (By whom)	
LAST REVIEW DATE:	**SIGNATURE OF TRAINEE:**

Figure 2.17 Training programme

Learning opportunities and methods

Trainees should be given time to discuss with the trainer and with one another what **learning opportunities** and **methods** are or will be made available to them during their training programmes. The way people prefer to learn and the pace of learning varies from one person to another and there is no set pattern of learning that suits everyone. For these reasons it is essential that method and content is negotiated and agreed as far as is possible during the induction period. Work methods available should be chosen to suit the trainees' occupational area.

> The assessor will expect to see evidence that trainers have allowed trainees to agree or disagree with their training plans and methods of learning and as far as possible to have modified methods and plans to suit their individual needs, capabilities, aspirations and motivations.

The trainer has an obligation to check that trainees understand his or her instructions and to give them sufficient opportunities and encouragement to ask questions and challenge training provision.

> During discussions with trainees it will become obvious to the assessor either that trainees have been given opportunities to ask questions about their training programmes and to give opinions on their proposed training or that their programmes have been imposed without adequate negotiation.

Session training plans

Trainers need to put a good deal of thought into preparing suitable training session plans and providing suitable learning opportunities that will help trainees to learn efficiently, confidently and enjoyably. Session planning is discussed more fully in Chapter 3.

> The assessor will confirm with trainees that the candidate has told them about a range of learning opportunities available to them and also of the different methods of learning that they might use to achieve their learning objectives.
>
> The candidate will need to show that as far as is reasonably feasible, trainees have been given the opportunity to negotiate their individually preferred learning method.

Checklists

Assessment checklists designed by CGLI in connection with their 929 series of Trainers and Assessors Awards are reproduced in Figures 2.18, 2.19 and 2.20. The checklists and their usefulness for self-assessment and as preparation prior to formal assessment is discussed in this and other chapters. Each of the checklist items is self-explanatory.

The Trainee Checklist

A **trainee** is a person being trained for an occupation. The **Trainee Checklist** given in Figure 2.18 lists those elements of a workplace trainer's role that are essential to successful and acceptable performance in the planning and delivery of induction at the training location.

> The Trainee Checklist suggests questions that an assessor might need to ask trainees to confirm that the candidate for assessment has delivered a satisfactory induction.
>
> Where possible any teaching and learning should be participative and trainee-centred.

The Coaching Checklist

The coaching checklist given in Figure 2.19 relates to those elements of a trainer's role that are essential to all trainee training activities and especially to the induction sessions where trainers need to exercise great care.

TRAINEE CHECKLIST

DID THE TRAINER:		COMMENTS:
Explain how your occupational area fits in to the organisation		
Explain his/her responsibilities as your trainer		
Explain to you what your rights and responsibilities are whilst undertaking training		
Provide you with enough information on the administration and other procedures used in training		
Explain the company's and your responsibilities under Health and Safety at Work Act		
Discuss your training plan with you		
Give you the opportunity to question how you will learn		
Allow you to agree/disagree with your training plan		
Ask you if you understand his/her instructions		
Give you the opportunity to express your opinions about your training		
Encourage you whilst training		
Give you feedback, soon after completing a task		

Figure 2.18 Trainee checklist

Source: City and Guilds of London Institute 9293 *Direct Trainers and Assessors Award Assessment Handbook* (1990) CGJ34955 (M19) © 1990 City and Guilds of London Institute, London[6]

COACHING CHECKLIST

DID THE TRAINER:		COMMENTS:
Check with the trainee his/her existing skills and knowledge		
Establish the elements and units under discussion		
Encourage the trainees learning		
Correct trainees errors as and when they occur		
Identify strengths and weaknesses		
Coach/guide trainee as and when required		
Provide on-going assessment		
Involve the trainee in his/her own assessment		
Negotiate with the trainee his/her future training		

Figure 2.19 Coaching checklist

Source: City and Guilds of London Institute 9293 *Direct Trainers and Assessors Award Assessment Handbook* (1990) CGJ34955 (M19) © 1990 City and Guilds of London Institute, London[6]

ASSESSMENT CHECKLIST

DID THE TRAINER:		COMMENTS:
Remain as unobtrusive as practicable		
Allow the trainee to complete the task unaided		
Give clear information on assessment to the trainee		
Give accurate information on assessment to the trainee		
Put the trainees at their ease		
Ensure trainee understands the level of their attainment		
Explain clearly to the trainee when the standard has not been met		
Explain clearly what the trainee has to do to achieve the required standard		
Give feedback as soon as practicable		
Choose an appropriate environment for giving feedback		
Give feedback in a constructive manner		
Encourage trainee to ask questions		
Involve the trainee in their own assessment		

Figure 2.20 Assessment checklist

Source: City and Guilds of London Institute 9293 *Direct Trainers and Assessors Award Assessment Handbook* (1990) CGJ34955 (M19) © 1990 City and Guilds of London Institute, London[6]

The Assessment Checklist

A checklist favoured by some assessors when assessing trainer competence is given in Figure 2.20. The elements listed may be also used by trainers to check their own performance during induction.

A similar assessment checklist is provided in the Candidate's Pack issued to those who register for the latest City and Guilds 7281/12 Vocational Assessor Award.[7]

It may be possible to get a colleague to carry out the assessment or alternatively the trainer could ask trainees to go through the checklist with them. Video recordings of the induction may be reviewed and analysed and this technique is widely used for self-assessment purposes.

Notes

1   *People and Work,* MSC Training Services Division. London, 1979, pp. 2–6.
2   *Literacy and Numeracy – a guide to practice,* Training Agency, Sheffield, June 1989.
3   Ibid.
4   Figure 2.7 Source: *Working with unemployed people,* Careers and Occupational Information Centre, 1987 (see *Literacy and Numeracy,* Training Agency, Sheffield, 1989, p. 7).
5   Figure 2.8 Source: *Working on reading,* Careers and Occupational Information Centre, 1988 (see *Literacy and Numeracy,* Training Agency, Sheffield, 1989, p. 6).
6   'Assessment checklists are provided for use in collecting "performance" and "process" evidence by observation or discussion. Checklists are included for each of the contexts in which evidence is produced. (For assessment purposes in connection with the Award – Author's note).' Source: City and Guilds of London Institute 9293, *Direct Trainers and Assessors Award Assessment Handbook,* 1990, CGJ34955 (M19) © 1990 City and Guilds of London Institute, London.
7   See page 73, C&G7281/12 Vocational Assessor Candidate Pack. CGG 47302 D23 P92 © 1992 available from: The Sales Section, City and Guilds of London Institute, 76 Portland Place, London W1N 4AA.

CHAPTER THREE

PLANNING AND PREPARING TRAINING

Chapter coverage

Selecting the training strategy
The importance of planning
Training and assessment plan
Integrating training components
Designing a training and learning programme
Scheme of work
Training programme format
Understanding and practising effective training preparation
Plan of instruction – Checkout Operator
Designing a training session plan
Training session planning system
Preparing and planning training session plans
Checking and rehearsing
Assessing the session
Assessing the preparation of a job instruction

Selecting the training strategy

A **strategy** is a longer-term plan for success. **Strategic planning** is a process that involves thinking about the knowledge, skills and procedures involved in each task or operation where competence is to be demonstrated, and devising an outline programme that will allow trainees to meet performance criteria.

When planning ahead, it is advisable to analyse training needs or requirements and then select suitable strategies that will enable trainees to learn and to qualify for awards. Planning and organising training and assessment can be crucial to outcomes in the form of trainee attainment.

Strategic planning is a creative process that calls for an imaginative approach to providing training that stimulates learners while meeting their needs and those of employers. The form, content and timing of training opportunities requires good judgement and a sense of purpose that will promote a business-like approach to learning.

Planning may involve decisions about some or all of the following:

- Module content and performance criteria.
- Methods and activities.
- Duration of training and length of sessions.
- Timetable of activities.
- Allocation and briefing of trainers.
- Availability and preparation of resources.
- Assessment criteria and methods.
- Monitoring and evaluation of training and outcomes.

When compiling a training and skills assessment plan for a group or an individual trainee, the planner can bring together those elements essential to effective performance at work: skills, complementary or underpinning knowledge, attitudes and standards. The plan should also bring together in a logical order further education, progressive work-based learning and experience, skills testing and other forms of assessment.

Where the availability of suitable training opportunities is not known in advance, detailed programming of learning may not be possible. In some cases this is inevitable and that is why contingency plans should supplement the main plan. This will ensure that training is as effective as possible.

A well conceived outline training and assessment plan is given in Figure 3.1. This plan together with the record of achievement given in Chapter 9 is used in planning and organising training associated with the RTITB Modular Training Scheme.[1]

The importance of planning

The aim of planning training is to decide on the strategy and the means by which individual and workplace training needs may best be met. Performance criteria and detail of what is to be done and how best to do it can then be negotiated with learners and training providers.

A form of **planned training** that has been adopted by many trainers is the 'four-stage training cycle' – find out what the trainees need to learn and do and review performance criteria; design and plan learning sessions and agree with the trainees what is to be learned and when and how they will set about learning it; create a suitable learning environment, provide resources, prepare materials and equipment and carry out the training; continuously monitor what is going on during the programme and 'keep the train on the rails'; and finally evaluate performance, feeding back into the cycle corrections and improvements that will be used to improve later training. Overall effectiveness of the training programme will be validated by competent workplace performance of the learners concerned.

TRAINING AND SKILLS ASSESSMENT PLAN
LIGHT VEHICLE MECHANIC

TEST DAY NO	REF. NO	MODULE TITLE	YEAR 1 (AUG–JUL)	YEAR 2 (AUG–JUL)	YEAR 3 (AUG–JUL)
1	MV 014F LV 001A	Foundation Scheduled Servicing	▉ MCH		
2	LV 005C LV 114B LV 116B LV 118B LV 119C	Vehicle Fault Tracing & Tuning Spark Ignition CB Systems Spark Ignition Breakerless Systems Engine Cooling & Ventilation Systems Engine Cooling & Ventilation Systems	▉ MAY		
3	LV 105C LV 107B LV 213B LV 218D LV 301B	Exhaust Systems – Fitting & Fault Diagnosis Carburettor & Air Supply Systems Braking Systems – Remove, replace & adjust Braking Systems – Brake Pipe manufacture Vehicle Electrical Systems – Starter circuit		▉ OCT	
4	LV 201B LV 207B LV 304B	Suspension Systems Mechanical Steering Systems unassisted Vehicle Electrical Systems		▉ FEB	
5	LV 214C LV 221C LV 401B	Braking Systems – Condition Assessment Transmission Systems – Clutch & Manual Gearbox Vehicle Body Exterior		▉ APL–MAY / JUN	▉ DEC
6	LV 101B LV 102C	Engine – Removal replacement & adjustment Engine – Condition Assessment			▉ FEB ▉ APL–MAY
7	LV 108C LV 202C LV 208C	Carburettor & Air Supply Systems Suspension Systems Mechanical Steering Systems Unassisted			▉ JUN

NOTE

- The plan requires the training to be completed by the beginning of each of the 7 blocks above. The trainee will then be ready for skills testing in the following 3 month period.
- For illustrative purposes, this plan is based on the trainee starting in August.
- Each of the 7 blocks will require a full day for skills testing. Where possible, MV 014F and LV 0001A will be tested together on the same day but the facility to test them separately will be available.
- Skills testing will be provided locally and a quarterly programme will be sent to employers, YT Managing Agents, and ET Training Managers.

Figure 3.1 Training and assessment plan

Source: RTITB National Craft Certificate Guide: *Light Vehicle Mechanic*. © Road Transport Industry Training Board, Wembley, Middlesex

Trainers will need to demonstrate that their training provision has been planned so as to develop learners' potential to perform competently at work. Other key objectives would be to assist trainees to attain personal goals within their occupational area and to help create a more flexible workforce.

Integrating training components

When integrating the two important training components, activities and resources, the aim should be to arrange learning experiences that will allow trainees to achieve performance criteria. Teaching and learning approaches used should be compatible with the personal needs of trainees and with occupational needs.

Material that encourages transfer of training and which can be applied to working in a variety of contexts is of great value to learners. Those who may wish to redeploy skills they already own but may not be able to use at the present time can benefit from opportunities to rehearse their prior achievements.

Being able to adapt materials to the needs of different groups of learners and to integrate learning materials into the overall training programme is an important skill for trainers.

Designing a training and learning programme

Before a training programme can be produced it is advisable to consider a strategy that will be adopted for the training as a whole. This is where a design system can be of use. Figure 3.2 gives details of a layout that could be used as a basis for programme design.

The starting point for any kind of vocational education and training programme is the **occupation**. Extensive knowledge of the occupational area enables the trainer to derive lists of **relevant competences** and **job objectives**. It is the ability to achieve and demonstrate such competences that measures the effectiveness and outcomes of the training and learning programme. This is true whether the occupation be that of nursing, horticulture or construction. In the case of academic learning a syllabus may be the starting point.

Whatever the training may be connected with, it is likely that there will be a need to work towards the achievement of **work-related performance criteria** or to specified training and learning aims and objectives. Once these have been identified and negotiated the training and learning steps can be planned and session plans, assessments, trainee support, profiling and certification process developed.

Scheme of work

A **'scheme of work'** is a planning document that gives information about:

- The trainee group: previous experience, prerequisites and age range.
- The programme aims and objectives: broad aims giving direction and purpose backed up with performance criteria and detailed objectives.

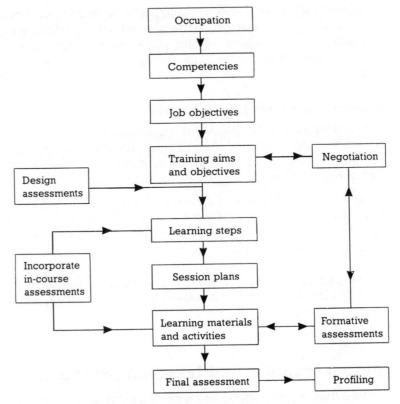

Figure 3.2 Designing the training programme

- Organisational factors: location, meeting times, duration, programme information, training content, sequence, availability of resources, aids and equipment, trainers and trainees involved.
- Methods of delivering training and making use of learning opportunities.
- Assessment and evaluation methods, instruments and feedback.

Trainers should be able to design a scheme of work that outlines in a logical sequence the way in which they and their trainees working together may best cover the work that is to be learned.

When drawing up the outline plan trainers will need to bear in mind the nature of the learning group; training content; performance criteria timing and duration of training sessions, reviews, guidance and assessment procedures.

Trainers will need to integrate their topic areas with those of other trainers and consider routes for progression to other jobs or levels.

Trainers may need to review the scheme of work with colleagues and trainees and if necessary modify the scheme taking account of any observations or suggestions made.

Trainers will need to use the scheme of work, monitor its suitability week by week and subsequently evaluate its effectiveness.

Trainers should revise and modify the scheme incorporating ideas for improvement that are collected during the monitoring and evaluation stages and, most importantly, take good account of trainees' criticisms and suggestions.

The scheme of work given in Figure 3.3 relates to motor vehicle mechanic training. It is based upon RTITB Module LV108C, a component of the training and skills assessment plan given in Figure 3.1. The module specifies tasks, operation and procedures to be completed by trainees. It remains for the training provider to work out with employers, trainers and trainees how associated education, training, skills testing and other assessments may be achieved. Writing sets of these documents can help providers to plan and organise adequately resourced and logically sequenced learning opportunities.

Training programme format

An alternative **training programme format** is given in Figure 3.4. Each step follows a logical sequence. The starting point is the writing of performance criteria or objectives that state in behavioural terms what the trainee is expected to be able to do as an outcome of the training. Then, a plan of instruction is laid out similar in form to the example shown in Figure 3.5.

Detailed training session plans such as that shown in Figure 3.8 may then be produced. The sample session plan has been written to cover an element of competence entitled: 'Preparing the Checkout Workstation' given in Figure 3.5, 'Plan of Instruction: Checkout Operator'.

The remaining steps follow conventional teaching and learning practice.

Understanding and practising effective training preparation

The way in which features of work activities are identified using functional analysis has already been discussed. The next stage is to draw up a training specification. Within industry and commerce a **training specification** is prepared after a job has been studied, its work content listed and skills needed to carry out the work identified.

The job is broken down into separate tasks and a sequence of operations is listed. Key break points and areas of difficulty are noted, together with details of standards, resources utilised, safety factors, inspection and quality assurance requirements. A **task analysis** that may be as detailed as necessary is then produced. The analysis itemises results obtained including the knowledge and practical skills involved in doing the job effectively and at the right standard. From the data recorded a training specification is written and an efficient learning programme is then designed.

Sheet 1

Charlton Marshall College

Lecturer

Course:	Light Vehicle Mechanics Stage Three (CGLI 381 Part 2 Year 2)	**Subject:**	Module IV 108 C Carburettor and Air Supply Systems	**Duration:**	Flexi-study option

Course: Light Vehicle Mechanics
Stage Three
(CGLI 381 Part 2 Year 2)

Subject: Module IV 108 C
Carburettor and Air Supply
Systems

Duration: Flexi-study option

Training location: Workshop and Training Room 21

Meeting times: Tuesday and Friday
0800–1700 hours

Trainees: Employed RTITB
registered and Govt.
Sponsored

Training module aims: The trainee will be able to demonstrate competence in the tasks, operations and procedures listed in this scheme of work and will be able to perform work involved in condition assessment and fault diagnosis to appropriate standards and tolerances.

Notes: Refer to Training Standards given in RTITB Post-Foundation Module IV 108 C.

Sheet 2

Carburettor and air supply systems – Condition assessment and fault diagnosis

Element	Task	Method	Resources	Notes
	Air supply			**Standards**
	Assess serviceability of:			Standards for the elements covered by this scheme of work will have been achieved when the trainee has demonstrated the skills and has performed the tasks to the prescribed standards and tolerances specified by the vehicle or system manufacturer and those required by the employing company
1	inlet manifold	Guided discussion	Specifications	
2	manifold heater	Examining spares	Variety of components	
	Follow systematic diagnostic procedures to identify faults causing:	Demo on running engine on test bed using diagnostic equipment. Follow with practice	Engine test bed Sun or Crypton analyser Data books	
3	loss of power			
4	rough slow running			
5	incorrect mixtures and emissions			
6	induction noise			All work to be carried out safely and in accordance with the Health and Safety at Work Act 1974
	Carburettor			
	Measure:			**Complementary knowledge**
7	fuel consumption	Demonstration and practice	Flowmeter Measuring cylinder Stop watch	Trainees must know how and why the specified components and settings deteriorate; the factors which affect their serviceability; the procedures for and methods of fault diagnosis
8	fuel pump pressure/vacuum		Pressure gauge	
	Assess serviceability of:	Practical activity inspecting components	Selection of components:	
9	carburettor		usable	
10	fuel pump		rectifiable	
11	pipes and hoses		faulty or scrap	
12	breather systems			

Figure 3.3 Scheme of work

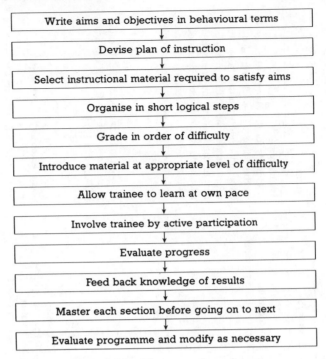

Figure 3.4 Training programme format

Trainees often experience greater difficulty getting to grips with learning essential underpinning knowledge associated with new concepts than with getting on and doing the job. Some seem to find academic learning carried out 'off-the-job' hard to master.

> **The trainer needs to put a good deal of thought into preparing a suitable training session plan and situation that will help trainees to learn efficiently, confidently and enjoyably.**

Integrating study skills and work-related activities is now, more than ever before, becoming an essential part of planned training and NVQ development work.

> **An organised approach with a definite purpose in view needs to be adopted when setting about the task of promoting work-related education and training.**

Such an approach is critically important to achieving integration through the design and delivery of short courses and **modules** of training and learning that are now becoming increasingly widespread.

The **training session planning system** shown in Figure 3.6 contains the basic elements involved in the production of a **training session plan** (also known as a **coaching plan**), while Figure 3.7 sets out some aspects for the trainer to consider when producing a plan.

Session number	Training element description	Training elements	Date completed Trainee initials
1	The job	Video: Role of checkout operator Job responsibilities	
2	Company policies	Uniform and appearance Hygiene Health and safety at the workstation Security	
3	Customer care	Standards of service Courtesy and attitude Offering information and advice on merchandise	
4	Checkout operation	Video: Checkout operator in action How to operate the checkout equipment: handling merchandise conveyor belts weighing scales operating the till handling money	
5	Preparing workstation	Opening up: (see Figure 3.8) assembling equipment collecting float checking float switching on signing on	
6	Serving the customer	Ringing-up Bag packing Receiving payment	
7	Closing the transaction	Giving receipt Checking change back Saying thank you Bidding farewell	
8	Closing down	Switching off Signing off Removing the money tray Tidying up	

Figure 3.5 Plan of instruction: Checkout operator

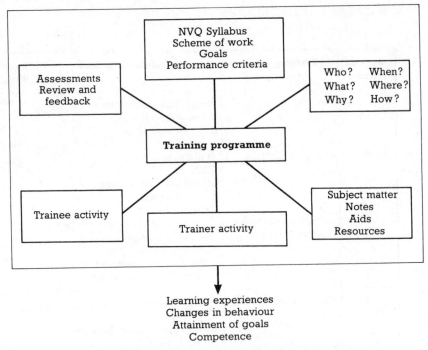

Figure 3.6 Training session planning system

Key factors

Analyse task skills, knowledge and attitudes.
Identify important elements.
Determine special skills involved.
Specify performance criteria.
Specify prerequisite knowledge required.
Set goals for session.
Include interesting content.
Relate new learning to prior knowledge.
Build on existing knowledge and skills.
Provide continuity.
Structure learning in logical sequence.
Integrate learning with occupational skills.
Encourage active learning.
Design training around trainees' needs.
Plan for maximum trainee involvement.
Resources: specify the real thing or suitable aids.
Specify training and learning methods to be employed.
Include question and answer sessions.
Provide for assessment of achievement.
Include frequent checks of learning.
Provide for early knowledge of results.
Share feedback.
Incorporate: note making; frequent summaries and reviews; recapitulation of important facts;
    final summary of session content; look forward and introduction to next session.
Set work for self-study.

Figure 3.7 Preparing a training session plan

Designing a training session plan

A **session plan** is based on specific performance criteria or learning objectives that describe how the trainee's learning needs and employer's training requirements will be satisfied. It amplifies the information given in a training programme or scheme of work.

Content should be structured in a logical sequence and details of methods, activities, learning aids, timings and checks of learning should be included.

Training session preparation involves three main stages:
- Collecting, selecting and preparing relevant subject matter.
- Preparing material and planning methods to be employed.
- Checking and rehearsing.

> Before starting work on a training session plan, due consideration should be given to the group of people wishing to learn. Their needs, job requirements, work content, resources and methods to be employed should be carefully considered.

Collecting, selecting and preparing
The **session aims** and **objectives** should be written down and should relate to the contribution the training will make to the trainees' achievement of competence. Sources of information should be explored and the structure and sequence of the session decided (see Figure 3.7).

Preparing and planning
The extent of the material to be used and methods appropriate to the content to be learned should be determined. Aids and equipment needed should be noted and subject-matter prepared. Session notes should be arranged in logical sequence and should contain: notes to assist instructing and learning, diagrams for the flipchart or overhead projector, key facts for trainees to take note of and details of practical work relating to specified performance criteria that will be practised. Worksheets and handouts should be prepared and resources organised.

The training session plan can then be drawn up and later used as a basis for guiding delivery by controlling the timing and content of the session. It should be written in a logical sequence and should provide a framework for development of the competence. A variety of activities should be included, together with checks of learning.

Making the most effective use of available time and resources results from working to carefully laid out session plans. However, it should be remembered that the plan is not set in concrete – everything should be negotiable during delivery.

> Trainers should plan the session so as to make the most effective use of available time.

The sample training session plan given in Figure 3.8 outlines the content and work methods chosen in relation to the element of competence to be achieved. Associated performance criteria have also been written.

The importance of trainees gaining the underpinning knowledge and skills required to achieve competence will be stressed by the trainer throughout the learning session. Checks of learning have been allowed for by including guided discussion and question and answer periods during the training session.

The assessor will probably ask to see training session plans and check them for evidence that training and learning methods have been sensibly chosen in relation to the trainee's occupational area.

The assessor will need to confirm that resources and materials to be used are adequate and suitable for their intended purpose

The assessor will seek opinion of trainees as to their part in negotiating and planning session content proposed in the plan.

The plan will be scrutinised by the assessor who will be looking for the inclusion of checks of learning and for opportunities for trainees to clarify doubts by asking questions.

Date: 4 May   **Time:** 0900–1130   **Location:** Training Room

Trainees:	Four new checkout operators
Element of competence:	Preparing checkout workstation
Duration:	150 minutes
Aim:	Trainees will be able to prepare the checkout workstation in accordance with Company procedures and policies
Performance criteria:	'Checkout closed' sign displayed Checkout clean and tidy Necessary equipment in place and ready for use Condition of electrical equipment checked Weighing scales checked for accuracy Conveyor belt operation checked Sufficient supplies of till rolls, credit card slips, carrier bags and paper bags available Credit card machine available Cash register plugged in, switched on and unlocked Opening readings recorded Cash tray with float placed in till drawer Correct till insert layout adopted Keyboard area tidy Basket tray slid out 'Checkout open' sign displayed when ready
Equipment:	Training Checkout set-up as per those in store / Four cash trays complete with float — Credit card machine / Supply of stationery / Till rolls / Calibrated weights / Carrier bags and paper bags
Assessment:	Trainees self-assess against check lists and performance criteria Workplace Trainer/Assessor assesses, accredits and records achievement before assigning trainee to store checkout
Note:	This Session Plan covers Element Number 5 of the 'Plan of Instruction for Checkout Operators' given in Figure 3.5

Figure 3.8 (cont.)

Time	Stage	Method	Trainee activity	Aids
0900	Welcome and intro	Talking		Checkout
0905	Experienced checkout operator in action in busy store	Video	Watching	Videotape Recorder Monitor
0915	Review video	Guided discussion	Question and answer	Review sheet
0920	Checkout layout Conveyor belts Hygiene Checking electrics Keyboard area 'Closed' sign	Demonstration with explanation	Question and answer Hazard-spotting	Check list Electricity at Work Regs 1989 Checking cleanliness
0930	Assembling equipment Basket tray operation	Demo with explanation	Watching Practising setting up Self-assess	Scales Credit card machine Stationery
0940	Checking scales	Demo with explanation	Watching Practising checks	Calibration weights Merchandise
0950	Plugging in and switching on Key procedures Recording opening reading Obtaining opening printed report Opening till drawer Inserting cash tray Signing opening report and placing in till drawer Closing till drawer	Demo with explanation	Watching Practising	Checkout Keys Ball point pen
1005	Review and reinforce training covered	Guided discussion	Question and answer	Check list
1015	Refreshment break			
1030	Introduction to handling money Need for float Till insert layout Checking float	Guided discussion Guided discussion Demo	Question and answer	Cash tray with money Layout-diagram Cash chart Four cash trays containing float

Figure 3.8 (cont.)

Time	Stage	Method	Trainee activity	Aids
1050	Loading cash tray to till drawer Display open sign	Demo with explanation	Watching Practising	Cash tray Till
1055	Carry out complete procedure	Monitoring process	Practising and demonstrating competence	All aids Record of achievement
	Assessing competency and checking underpinning knowledge and understanding	Observation	Question and answer	Check list
1120	Review key points and performance Look forward to next element	Guided discussion Negotiation	Active involvement	Check list List of performance criteria
1130	Session ends			

Figure 3.8 Sample training session plan – Checkout operator

Checking and rehearsing

Plays are rehearsed before the first night in order to ensure a flawless performance and to check lights and props. In the same way sessions should be rehearsed in order to check content and sequence and to try out resources.

Numerical examples should be worked out in advance to verify that no information is missing and that examples set are capable of solution. Instructing 'off-the-cuff' can go wrong!

Demonstrations and **experiments** should be tried out to make certain that equipment is complete and in good working order. **Timing** should be checked and a decision taken as to what could be omitted if time runs short and what supplementary material could be included if spare time becomes available.

Assessing the session

Trainers cannot hope to produce a perfect plan for every training session. In many cases the plan will have to be modified in the light of experience gained during the first presentation of training. As the session progresses (and if you remember and are not too pressurised to do so) actual timings should be recorded and a brief note made of any improvements that could be made in preparation, presentation, aids or methods.

The revised plan based upon consideration of the notes made will give a more realistic outline for use when the session is repeated.

Trainers may self-assess their session plan using the assessment sheet given in Figure 3.9 and rating the elements shown.

Rating Scale: **Score:**
Excellent   5
Very good   4
Good   3
Fair   2
Poor   1

Element	Rating	Remarks
Stating of performance criteria		
Logical development in suitable steps		
Variety of methods and activities		
Use of resources		
Adequacy of trainee involvement		
Checks of learning		
Feedback on achievements		

Figure 3.9 Training session plan assessment sheet

Assessing the preparation of a job instruction

Self-assessment and supportive consultative assessment with one's peers are two excellent ways of analysing and improving preparation of training. Reflection and review are of prime importance in any modern learning programme and this technique should be practised by trainers.

Aspects of the planning and preparation that could usefully be discussed include:

- Adequacy of preparation.
- Performance criteria and objectives specified.
- Context and relevance of the session to stated objectives.
- Logical development of the session.
- Evaluation of outcomes: checks of learning, test results, efficiency and effectiveness of planning in terms of learning achieved.

Notes
1   Source: RTITB National Craft Certificate Guide: *Light Vehicle Mechanic.* © Road Transport Industry Training Board, Wembley, Middlesex.

CHAPTER FOUR

PLANNING AND DELIVERING TRAINING

Chapter coverage

A systematic approach to teaching and learning
Management of learning
Training system
Adult learners
Counselling and guidance
Assessing needs of adult learners
Barriers to learning
Building confidence
Individual differences in adults' learning
Applying principles of learning to individual training strategies
Instructing for transfer
Assessing product skills
Assessing process skills
Instructing by demonstration
Practice session
Job instruction training
Comparison of job instruction methods
Job factors
Assessing the delivery of a job instruction
Assessing instructional techniques
Assessing the trainer at work
Observation checklist

A systematic approach to teaching and learning

Before starting a training session, trainers must know what it is that they intend to cover and to what standard. What the learners are expecting to learn and what they are expected to achieve must be negotiated. Trainers must know what the trainees are already able to do and the learning session must be designed accordingly. Instruction should be pitched at a level to suit trainee needs.

Trainers must have a clear picture of the elements of competence and related performance criteria around which the training plan has been developed.

The outcome of training will be that trainee performance will reflect what they are able to do as a result of taking part in the learning experience. Learning will be identified as '**a relatively permanent change in behaviour**' brought about by this experience.

Trainees will be able to demonstrate achievement of competence in certain elements.

The diagram given in Figure 4.1 shows training as a system. The input is a training session which depends for its success upon effective communication between trainer and trainees. During the session, trainer activity combined with that of trainees will hopefully produce a satisfactory learning experience for all concerned.

Management of learning

Training would be very undemanding if it simply involved pouring knowledge into empty bottles, however, when training people, every instructor encounters problems sooner or later. Coaching sessions can go wrong but good practices relating to the management of learning can go a long way towards avoiding pitfalls.

A trainer is responsible for managing learning and for using resources to the best effect. The aim should always be to arrange things so that trainees may learn efficiently and effectively.

Providing for flexible learning and training

The location and timing of training sessions and other learning opportunities needs to be acceptable to all concerned otherwise a poor response can be expected.

For colleges and training providers a flexible timetable should be implemented, adjusted to suit people with time constraints. Single parents and those who rely on infrequent public transport to reach the training centre are examples of those who may need help.

For adult returners wishing to update skills before taking up full-time employment, child care can be a problem. The provision of crèche facilities can greatly improve matters.

For people at work it may be more cost effective and beneficial to hold training and assessment sessions off-site or outside standard working hours. A negotiated commitment by participants is recommended. Some Training Providers provide an 'all-the-year-round' assessment service while others operate 'roll-on/roll-off' programmes of initial assessment and training. This means that if candidates miss the start of a course of education and training they have only to wait a short time for another intake to the course. They will not have to wait until the start of a new 'academic year' as was once the case.

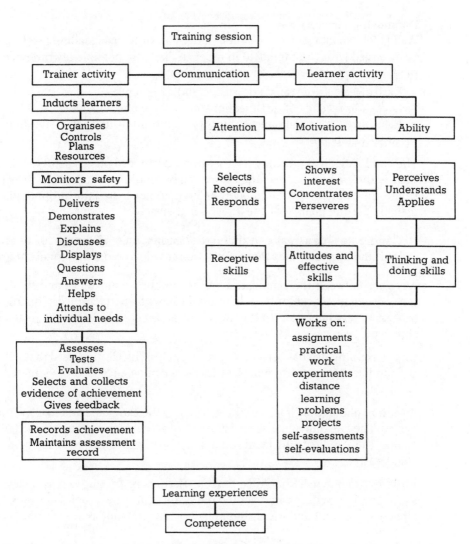

Figure 4.1 Training system

Considerable benefit to employers and staff can result from offering adaptable and variable facilities.

> The assessor will check on whether or not account has been taken of the trainee's preferred learning style and whether open learning provision and the use of work-based projects are available to learners.

Diagnosing learning need

Well before an assessment session is sought an **initial counselling** meeting should be arranged with the candidate in order to diagnose possible learning needs. The range of topics to be covered could include:

- Existing levels of skills, knowledge and experience.
- Level and recency of qualifications or profiles of competence.
- Relevance, scope and transferability of prior training and experience to proposed target competences.

The candidates will probably have a strong desire or hope to achieve something. That is their reason for seeking advice. They should be encouraged to talk about where they want to get and how they hope to get there and to think about how realistic are the goals that they have set themselves.

> Candidates can make training decisions only if they are aware of learning opportunities that exist in their preferred occupational category.

Any gaps between the candidate's present level of competence and the level and types of competences to be achieved will have to be identified. This **diagnostic process** is very important to the individual and it should neither be neglected nor skimped.

Once a **training gap** has been detected, an analysis of learning need that will enable the candidate to move from present levels of competence to those targeted should be made.

An **action plan** that will lead to the goal set by the candidate and to a NVQ award is agreed. Then an individualised programme of activities is negotiated and tailored to enable the candidate to learn what needs to be learned to meet performance standards.

Entry to programmes should be flexible. Barriers restricting access to assessment should be removed. Learners should not be made to repeat topics in which they are already competent and there should be no age limits for award of qualifications.

> The trainer/assessor will need to understand the role that guidance can play in assisting candidates to complete an action plan and be able to conduct guidance sessions.

Learning from work

The workplace is one of the better places to learn in, but it is also a place where those not involved in the learning process can adversely affect matters. Learners are capable of being physically or emotionally wounded or hurt by the mockery, contempt and criticism resulting from taunting by workmates.

Ridicule can remind some people of bad experiences at school and any suggestion of 'going back to school' can quickly put an end to a commitment to learning new things. High motivation can result from group working and the value of team problem solving should not be underrated when preparing people for assessment of interpersonal skills.

> There is a need for workplace trainers to develop trainee confidence by encouraging those concerned to take a fair measure of responsibility for their own learning. A heightened sense of achievement and job satisfaction will result.

> In order to secure co-operation and enhanced motivation the trainer should adopt a supportive attitude.

Distance learning

Distance learning is a means of widening and creating access to learning, training and the accreditation of competence. It is a relatively new national approach which places the emphasis on learning rather than teaching. Learning opportunities are tailored to meet the needs of individuals and employers.

Open learning provides opportunities for people to fill gaps in their education and training and to attain more qualifications and update their work-based skills after they leave school.

> Workplace trainers and assessors supporting trainees on open learning will need to find out what flexible learning is all about and become competent in tutoring and counselling. They may in some cases be required to write and adapt open learning materials to suit local conditions.

Adult learners

Adults like to be in charge of what they do. They usually know where they want to go but may need a hand in getting there. This is where consultation and negotiation on the content and mode of learning is the key to success. There is little doubt that they favour active involvement in their own learning.

> It may be helpful for the workplace trainer to think about how those members of the workforce seeking further achievements differ in their approaches to learning.

Some adults will have no study problems. Some will be highly motivated but their expectations may be beyond their reach. They may be over-confident and not eager to apply themselves to the training. Others will have poor retention levels and will quickly forget things.

Poor concentration will act as a barrier to learning new things. Some people may feel anxious when returning to learning while others may feel scared out of their wits. Confidence may be lacking and nervousness may restrict their activities.

Access to facilities and resources may be a problem as will finding the time to study and someone to lend a hand when help is needed. For these reasons provision needs to be made for the learners to work at their own pace and level using easy to follow learning materials with expert guidance on call.

Trainers will need to be able to put trainees at ease by establishing a rapport and adopting a caring attitude. The assessor will be looking for evidence of how trainers anticipate matters of concern for adult learners and how they allay fears and apprehension.

Counselling and guidance

Steps should be taken to actively involve people in decisions about their learning. The need for joint negotiation throughout the training and accreditation programme should be understood right from the start. Study guidance would include help for learners in deciding on learning methods and resources to be used, the level of trainer support needed, the rate of learning and how this will be regulated.

Workplace assessors should never forget that negotiation is a 'two-way' process.

Guidance and review should be available to all candidates for assessment. Giving guidance and advice to people is a very responsible and demanding duty. The services of someone who is able to support trainees and help them to identify their individual training needs and possible learning opportunities is essential to good morale.

Where action plans or personal training plans have been written it is helpful to review with trainees their progress in occupational areas and in achievement of elements of competence. The review encourages trainees to think about what they have done that was good and what they might do better. It also leads to thinking about progression and transfer of training to other tasks.

Discussion also serves to bring into focus difficulties which hold up progress and allows possible courses of action to be considered. Advice on where and how to move on is welcomed by some. But there are cases when it is advisable to refer the trainee to external agencies who may be better placed to handle the problem identified.

Assessing needs of adult learners

Adults have learning needs that vary considerably from those of the young. Whereas the young will depend upon the trainer for guidance and control and are unlikely to be self-directing, the industrial or commercial experience of adults and their life experience will cause them to expect to be treated differently.

Adults will have a wealth of experience to bring with them into the learning situation and they will be disappointed if they are not given credit for this or if their prior experience and competence is not utilised. They will expect to make use of new learning more or less immediately.

Trainees will expect their trainer to be in a position to help them to satisfy their learning needs. They will hope to gain from attending training sessions and will expect outcomes to make an important contribution to their future career prospects.

Methods may need to be revised and access to training adjusted to suit the changing pattern of provision now being encouraged to meet adult's expectations. Potential client groups, especially when comprising the adult unemployed, will contain people with a wide range of ability and attainment. It would be easy to stereotype trainees on the basis of very little knowledge but this must be avoided. Some will have a pretty good idea of where they want to go and how they are going to get there while others will need a lot of support.

This is where a sound knowledge of confidential counselling and sources of referral becomes critical to the success of the learning proposition.

As far as the actual learning processes are concerned, there is no doubt that both younger and older adults will respond much better to methods that encourage active involvement in their own learning. However, it is likely that the older trainees will make more fuss if they do not get what they want. Having introduced the topic perhaps readers will now be better able to focus their ideas on the handling of adult learners.

Study guidance is a priority activity for successfully matching needs to training provision. Given that this is the case the trainer and adult learner will both need to be committed to a process of consultation and negotiation of content and mode of learning.

Trainers should be able to demonstrate the bases for individual differences in learning and the problems that such differences can create during training sessions.

Regrettably, many people find it difficult to learn simply by waiting for suitable chunks of information to come their way and relying on their brain to do the rest automatically. Efficient learning calls for co-operation between the instructor and the trainee.

New knowledge is a result of real and tangible incidents linking in some way with experiences, knowledge, attitudes and concepts that have already been stored in the trainee's memory. The amount of knowledge and understanding already attained will influence the rate and capability to add subsequent learning.

Barriers to learning

Barriers and blockages to learning may be self-imposed or may result from past involvement with trainers. Some bad experiences in school, college courses or previous training may have coloured trainees' attitudes toward a return to learning. They may feel that they are getting too old to learn and fear that they may be made to appear dense relative to others. They may have physical impairment such as failing eyesight or hearing that would hold them back. They may feel that they have been out of the game for too long and out of touch with modern methods. There are countless reasons for fears and individual learning differences among trainees but whether a real problem exists or not, if the trainee thinks a problem exists then that trainee has a problem. Try convincing them that no problem exists! A good way of clearing barriers to learning is to ask each trainee to make a note of their perceived problems and to share their worries with a sympathetic trainer. The problems which such differences and fears can create in training are not insignificant, but nor are they insurmountable.

> When instructing people who have learning blocks the trainer should be aware of the fragile relationship that will initially exist and work hard at dispelling anxieties.

Building confidence

Being confident implies having a feeling of trust in those with whom one is involved, gaining self-assurance and fostering belief in one's own abilities.

Positive ways of building confidence in trainees are:

- Making them feel at home.
- Being friendly and open.
- Getting them to talk to you and using their names when addressing them.
- Agreeing with them what it is that they will be doing and to what standard.
- Explaining things carefully, moving from the known to the unknown.
- Taking your time and not rushing things.
- Anticipating problems and avoiding getting impatient when they are slow to grasp the point. Finding out whether or not a special learning need exists.
- Encouraging questions and rewarding those who volunteer answers.
- Teaching in small digestible chunks, giving plenty of practice and reinforcement.
- Delivering training in a logical sequence hooking each new piece of information on to the last piece.
- Avoiding jargon and trying to avoid being too theoretical.
- Using frequent checks of learning.
- Using objective type tests to evaluate progress rather than lengthy written tests.
- Turning their mistakes into valuable learning experiences.
- Asking them to take your word for it if the concept is particularly difficult to comprehend but essential to the session. Trying too hard to make them understand could be disastrous for their confidence.
- Where appropriate, using computer-based training programs of suitable level and with entry point at a proper level for the trainee and helping with accessing and exiting the program.
- Using mnemonics where applicable as an aid to learning.
- Giving advice on improving study skills and learning out of the workplace.
- Identifying transferable skills and building on their existing skill ownership.
- Breaking down the learning content into suitable parts such as memorising, understanding and doing, depending on the objectives set.

- Integrating theory and practice but taking it easy on the theory.
- Providing plenty of opportunity for learner-centred activities.
- Allowing them to go at their own pace.
- Negotiating learning objectives and agendas for action with individuals if possible.
- Instigating a study guidance and reviewing system.
- Offering information and advice when it is really needed.
- Encouraging self-evaluation and quality assurance practices.

Individual differences in adults' learning

Adult learners differ in their approaches to learning. Factors influencing learning include:

- Level of motivation and expectations.
- Retention level, long-term and short-term memories.
- Knowledge, skills, practical abilities and experience.
- Access to facilities, resources, time and support for study when away from the training provider's premises.
- Powers of concentration and problem-solving skills.
- Confidence level and capacity for learning new things.

Assessors may ask trainers to discuss what actions they would need to take in anticipation that some or all of their trainees may need help with aspects of learning listed above.

Decide how you could make it easier for trainees to cope with a return to learning and what you will need to do to facilitate this.

List some of the ways in which adults may differ from young persons in their previous experience and attitudes.

Prepare a strategy for assessing a trainee's suitability for the training opportunity you offer. Consider in particular: existing levels or skills, knowledge and experience; level and recency of qualifications or profiles of competence; relevance, scope and transferability of other training to the proposed training.

Applying principles of learning to individual training strategies

It is important to stress every skill that trainers teach. In order to promote the concept of **transferability** of skills and experience there is an increasing need for trainers across the whole education/training spectrum to become aware of and to practise **teaching for transfer**.

It is the prime responsibility of trainers to relate principles, theory and skills to the needs of commerce and industry as well as to provide education and training for the trainee concerned. There are, at present, some who disseminate facts and information without linking their output to 'whole work role' situations and the needs of employers.

Instructing for transfer

Trainees need to develop and become owners of new skills and concepts, to use them in a number of different situations and to recognise their applicability to a range of other contexts.

> Using techniques and strategies that help trainees to acquire transferable skills should be of considerable importance to the trainer.

How instructing for transfer may be promoted

Transfer of skills from one situation to another can be aided by designing it into the training programme. Skills that are learned in one specific occupation, sport or course offer the potential of transfer to other occupations, games or subject areas.

What is not so obvious is how trainers might teach for transfer and how to design transfer into everyday session plans. Instructing for transfer is not new. We have all been doing this to some extent since the day we started instructing. What is needed is a fresh look at what we have been doing and an increased awareness of the benefits that may accrue from designing education and training programmes that contain explicit aims and objectives relating to transfer. Then to deliberately use training strategies associated with promoting transfer.

A person operating a checkout in a store will not use manipulative skills in isolation from the numerical or the inter-personal skills needed to do the job. As well as recording the cost of items by pressing keys and calculating change (where necessary), the operator has to answer customer queries, overcome objections, remain pleasant and be able to open and close the encounter efficiently so as to maintain good customer relations.

With this in mind it becomes necessary to describe the assessment of two skills that feature in the encounter. The terms are: **product skills** and **process skills**.

Assessing product skills

A **product skill** can be demonstrated by a candidate and accurately assessed by the trainer or assessor using normal techniques for accreditation against performance criteria.

An example might be: 'After instruction the candidate will be able to type at a rate of 40 words per minute for a period of five minutes continuous using an IBM electronic typewriter and making not more than four errors'.

Performance may be observed and assessed fairly accurately against the criteria. But how the typist feels and whether or not he or she will be able to work consistently under pressure in an office remains to be seen, as it is untested.

> The acquisition of product skills can be demonstrated by precisely describable behaviour and can be assessed by observation and written or practical tests.

Assessing process skills

A **process skill** often cannot be precisely described in terms of exact behaviour as can be product skills. During training and work experience sessions few formal learning methods are used. Often no practical skills, testing or written tests are applied and there is no positive measurement of behaviour against carefully written specific learning objectives.

Performance can be described rather more subjectively by reference to instances of observed behaviour while candidates undertake such tasks as group activities relating to painting and decorating a room, setting up a campsite, or cooking a meal for a large number of people in a catering establishment. Individuals may be assessed by observing their performance in the workplace. The checkout operator is a good example of this.

> 'Process skills cannot be described in terms of exact behaviour but are demonstrated in a person's abilities in tackling problems, working with others on task-based activities and listening, counselling and persuading.' (FEU)

> Assessors may check process skills that are demonstrated by a candidate while working with others on a task-based activity that involves planning and communicating. Inter-personal and problem-solving skills that are encountered at the workplace during day-to-day routines may also be assessed.

Instructing by demonstration

A **demonstration** is a practical display or exhibition of a process that serves to show or point out clearly the fundamental principles or actions involved. Instructing by demonstration plays an important part in coaching and in the teaching of skills. A suggested sequence for planning and delivering a demonstration is given in Figure 4.2.

> The assessor will check that the trainer, when making a presentation, has placed learners in positions where they can observe the whole demonstration.

> The assessor will be looking for evidence of prior preparation including: relevant, current and accurate information presented in small steps and in a logical sequence; safety factors and hygiene matters researched and included during session; suitable resources available and checks of learning planned.

Practice session

A **practice session** should immediately follow a demonstration in order to reinforce procedures. When operator training, if the actual equipment is delicate or expensive, a cheaper simulator should be substituted for the real thing.

Sequence	Remarks
Preparation	
Plan demonstration	Include key factors
	Logical sequence
Obtain apparatus	Do not leave anything to chance
Rehearse demonstration	Perfect sequence and delivery
Delivery	
Lay out apparatus	Each element in correct order
Establish rapport	Create suitable atmosphere for learning
State aims	What you intend the learners to achieve by the end of the session
Show end-product	Establishes in learner's mind the need to participate
Demonstrate silently at normal speed	Repeat several times
	Allows learner to focus attention on process and arouses curiosity
Demonstrate at slow speed	Describe hand or body movements and senses involved
Ask learners to explain process	Learners think for themselves and are actively involved
Discuss safety aspects	Forewarns and creates awareness of inherent dangers
Ask for volunteer to attempt demonstration	Encourages competition
	Other learners asked to spot mistakes
Each learner attempts demonstration	Remainder watch and comment
	Teacher corrects faults

Figure 4.2 Instructing by demonstration

Learners learn best by doing. There is no substitute for practice when acquiring a skill. During the practice session, the trainer supervises the learner, giving individual guidance and attention when needed. Errors and omissions are spotted and corrected quickly. Bad habits and unsafe working procedures are difficult to unlearn once established.

After trainees have built up confidence they can concentrate on accuracy, style, rhythm, speed and quality. But watch for signs of boredom. Once learners have mastered a technique there is no further challenge. Move them on to another stage, but be careful not to confuse boredom with fatigue. Reward with praise whenever possible since this can act as a reinforcer. Aim to stimulate not to distress. Never blame a trainee. No-one deliberately sets out to make mistakes. Be positive. If there are difficulties look at your instructional method and try a new way.

> Trainers should ensure that any performance target set is within each learner's mental and physical capacity.

> Trainers will need to check underpinning knowledge and understanding of the skill being demonstrated.

During the observation the assessor will need to confirm that the trainer has prevented the trainee forming bad habits and is working safely while performing the task.

Feedback should be given when possible and the assessor will expect content to be constructive, helpful and supportive rather than destructive or highly critical.

Trainers should encourage trainees to review their own progress and to self-assess performance.

Job instruction training

'**Sitting by Nellie**' is an old-fashioned method of coaching where an experienced male or female worker who may be inept as far as coaching technique is concerned acts as a trainer. In some cases this method has worked well and many people have picked up skills simply by watching and copying. But there are weaknesses. Safe and efficient working does not always occur but bad habits are frequently acquired. Learners often cut corners while trying to imitate the 'instructor' and ambiguity and the lack of quality checking subsequently leads to poor learner performance. Work produced is often unsatisfactory.

The trainer should ensure that occupational standards relating to the tasks to be learned are known and understood by the trainee.

Training should be carefully planned and executed by qualified trainers.

Traditional method

Job instruction techniques have been developed which are widely used today. The traditional method of job instructional training involves the seven main stages set out in Figure 4.3.

The whole job is demonstrated and explained by a trainer while the learner observes. The learner then tries to emulate the trainer and endeavours to reach experienced worker standard. On the way, learning plateaux[1] are sometimes encountered which hold up progress. After a while the learner overcomes the difficulties and reaches the required standard.

The assessor will check that the trainer has:

- Monitored the trainee's performance.
- Maintained adequate guidance and supervision.
- Encouraged trainees to constantly check and correct their own mistakes.
- Promptly corrected errors that are not detected by trainees.
- Checked underpinning knowledge and understanding.
- Encouraged trainees to self-appraise and comment on their achievements.
- Given constructive feedback on performance and given direction on further development of competence appraised.

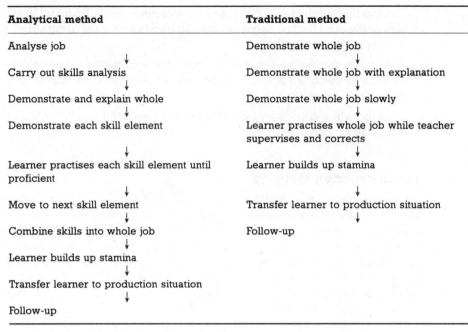

Analytical method	Traditional method
Analyse job ↓	Demonstrate whole job ↓
Carry out skills analysis ↓	Demonstrate whole job with explanation ↓
Demonstrate and explain whole ↓	Demonstrate whole job slowly ↓
Demonstrate each skill element ↓	Learner practises whole job while teacher supervises and corrects ↓
Learner practises each skill element until proficient ↓	Learner builds up stamina ↓
Move to next skill element ↓	Transfer learner to production situation ↓
Combine skills into whole job ↓	Follow-up
Learner builds up stamina ↓	
Transfer learner to production situation ↓	
Follow-up	

Figure 4.3 Comparison of job instruction methods

The analytical method

The **analytical method** is based upon a **task analysis** for the job concerned. The task is studied and broken down into logical steps and skills elements which may be demonstrated separately. The learners practise and master each element after which they are required to combine the individual skills into a complete job. Learners can better cope with complex or difficult steps using this technique. Time to reach experienced worker standard is usually shorter than by the traditional method. Holdups in learning are reduced or eliminated with consequent savings in training time, while the learners benefit by experiencing less frustration.

A closer look at the analytical method

Before preparing a job instruction plan, the job itself should be analysed and the following questions asked:

What is done?	When is it done?	How is it done?
Why is it done?	Where is it done?	Who does it?

Having established answers to these questions and agreed the method, a **task analysis** is carried out and skills involved identified. A **skill** is the ability, either innate or acquired by practice, which enables a person to perform a job expertly. The purpose of the task analysis is to separate job factors into their component parts, so that a training session plan can be devised and used to train people to perform their work effectively. Each factor is analysed under three headings:

- function
- knowledge
- skills involved.

The example shown in Figure 4.4 is the procedure for administering an intramuscular injection. It involves the nurse in carrying out a sequence of well-defined actions. In order to do this correctly, the nurse must learn the sequence, and the knowledge and skills needed to perform the task. Careful co-ordination of hand and eye movements ensures that the injection is skilfully administered and that the patient suffers the least possible discomfort.

Function	Knowledge	Skill
1 Clean hands	Effective handwashing Modes of infection	Wash and dry hands
2 Select drug for administration	Interpretation of prescription sheet (a) Indications for use of drug (b) Normal dosages and frequency (c) Side effects and contra-indications of drug (d) Routes of administration (e) Manufacturers advice for diluting drug Location of drug and dilutent	Read chart correctly Select drug and dilutent
3 Load syringe with drug	Location of equipment (a) Gauge length of needle (b) Size of syringe Recommendations for mixing drug Required dose Consequences of air emboli	Select and assemble needle and syringe Reconstitute drug with dilutent Draw up correct amount of drug Expel excess air from syringe
4 Identify patient	Location of correct patient	Check patient's name band and hospital number against prescription sheet
5 Administer injection	Sites for intramuscular injections Method for giving injection (a) Angle of needle (b) Consequences of needle entering blood vessel (c) Method of injecting large volume of drug	Select site for injection Swab injection site Insert needle Draw plunger back slightly Inject drug steadily Withdraw needle quickly Apply slight pressure to injection site with swab
6 Record drug given on prescription sheet	Recognition of layout of prescription sheet	Enter date, time and dose in appropriate place Sign chart
7 Dispose of equipment	Modes of cross-infection Location of disposal container	Place syringe and needle in Sharpax box
8 Clean hands	Effective handwashing Modes of infection	Wash and dry hands

Figure 4.4 Table of job factors: 'Administering an intramuscular injection'

Source: Gill French, Dorset School of Nursing

The advantages of carrying out a task analysis are that the following are identified:

- sequence of operations
- key elements of task
- hand skills involved
- other sensorimotor skills involved[2]
- necessary co-ordination of movement
- kinaesthetic senses involved[3]
- need for learning aids
- need for special exercises and practice
- estimate of knowledge aspects of task
- estimate of training time.

Assessing the delivery of a job instruction

Self-assessment and supportive consultative assessment with supervisors, assessors and trainees are excellent ways of analysing and improving presentation techniques.

Reflection and review are of prime importance in any modern learning programme and this technique should be practised by trainers. Whenever possible micro-training sessions should be video-taped and reviewed with other trainers.

Some of the instructional aspects to be discussed during evaluation of this type of delivery are given in Figure 4.5.

- Adequacy of preparation. Everything needed to hand, checked and ready to use.
- Performance criteria and objectives to be achieved understood. Learning tasks analysed and matched with workplace and awarding body criteria. Standard occupational category standards linked with relevant element of competence.
- Context and relevance of the session to stated objectives. Training area selected is suitable. Layout of resources matched to learner's needs.
- Logical development of the session. All critical learning features included.
- Prior learning and achievement assessed. Avoidance of trainee overload.
- Trainee group management and relationships. Learners put at ease. Ready and willing to learn.
- Body language, mannerisms and maintenance of attention.
- Delivery style, choice of words and way of saying what must be said.
- Understanding of performance criteria and methods employed to test knowledge and skills.
- Evaluation of outcomes: interest, practice time allowed, test results, efficiency and effectiveness of delivery in terms of trainee learning.

Figure 4.5 Assessing instructional techniques

Trainers will need to carry out on-going assessment of their instructional technique.

Note: A more detailed discussion of factors concerning the assessment of a trainer's performance during individualised job instruction training is given in Chapter 8.

Assessing the trainer at work

The assessor will check whether or not the trainer:

- Created a calm, safe and comfortable atmosphere for the learning session.
- Started trainees off with a learning task that all could easily master, thereby ensuring early success.
- Encouraged highly participative discovery learning by providing suitably graded work-related learning opportunities.
- Allowed the trainees to set pace of learning.
- Avoided overloading the trainees' recall capabilities by asking them to memorise lengthy procedures or too many facts and figures.
- Adopted a logical routine when instructing, thereby helping trainees to follow what the trainer was demonstrating.
- Where necessary varied the method of instruction and when the learners did not 'get it' the first time avoided unhelpful repetitions that could demotivate or frustrate them. Found another way and used short steps.
- Kept explanations brief.
- Called things by the same name every time it was necessary to talk about them. Did not confuse trainees by using a variety of terms to describe or label an object.
- Did not 'butt-in'. Avoided interrupting the flow of learning by intervening without real justification.
- Encouraged trainees to manage and monitor the correctness and quality of their own performance.
- Corrected remaining errors at the earliest possible opportunity.
- Allowed trainees to demonstrate mastery of one 'meaningful whole' element of learning before moving on to the next stage.
- Gave praise and credit for successfully achieving elements of learning.
- Allowed for plenty of practice to enable trainee to reinforce and strengthen new learning.

Observation checklist

A person that generates goods, services or products does so through a mix of **thinking** about what must be done in order to bring the product into being and employing some **method** in order to actually create it. These two are integrated to form the process or procedures and actions that produce the desired **outcome**.

Performance at work involves carrying out actions and doing things according to some pattern or with some definite purpose in mind. Such activities usually result in products inspected or otherwise evaluated.

Performance observation is a very important and useful method of assessing competence that involves **perceiving** what is seen. This involves assessors in becoming aware of what candidates are doing and coming to grasp and make sense of what is going on. Once a clear picture is obtained the assessors compare what is observed with physical standards or with criteria that exist within their minds.

OBSERVATION CHECKLIST

DID THE TRAINER:		COMMENTS:
Prepare an appropriate learning environment for the trainees		
Structure the session		
Use resources and materials suitable for the trainees		
Provide the appropriate level of training for the trainees		
Adjust training for individual trainees where necessary		
Encourage trainees to question their own training and learning		
Allow trainees to express their views		
Anticipate the trainees pace/level		
Maintain effective control and participation		
Encourage trainee participation		
Check trainees understanding		

Figure 4.6 Observation checklist

Source: City and Guilds of London Institute 9293 *Direct Trainers and Assessors Award Assessment Handbook* (1990) CGJ34955 (M19) © 1990 City and Guilds of London Institute, London

People differ in the way they see things. The assessor's opinion of a given performance may be at variance with that of the candidate due to the fact that opinion may well be clouded by past experiences.

What is perceived may depend to some extent upon what the assessor expects or wishes to perceive rather than what is actually observed. Assessors should be mindful of the fact that in truth, things may not always be as they appear.[5]

The Observation Checklist reproduced in Figure 4.6 was developed by the City and Guilds of London Institute for use when assessing elements of competence relating to their CGLI 929 Series of Awards. The checklist provides a basis from which to carry out an assessment of a trainer's performance with trainees while delivering training. The method of assessing being that of natural observation.

Notes
1   In a learning curve a 'plateau' is a period of no improvement preceded and followed by improvement.
2   'Sensorimotor skills' depend on connection between sensory and motor systems of the body. Sensorimotor tasks are multiple-response tasks where muscular movement is prominent. Riding a bike or playing a violin are examples.
3   'Kinaesthesis' which is also known as 'muscle tension' is the name given to the sensation by which bodily position, weight, muscle tension and movement are perceived.
4   'Assessment checklists are provided for use in collecting "performance" and "process" evidence by observation or discussion. Checklists are included for each of the contexts in which evidence is produced. (For assessment purposes in connection with the Award – Author's note).' Source: City and Guilds of London Institute 9293 *Direct Trainers and Assessors Award Assessment Handbook* 1990, CGJ34955 (M19) © 1990 City and Guilds of London Institute, London.
5   In the philosophy of Immanuel Kant (1724–1804), a German idealist philosopher, 'noumenon' could be thought of as: 'a thing as it is in itself, not perceived or interpreted, incapable of being known, but only inferred from the nature of the experience itself'. Source: *The Collins Dictionary of the English Language*, 2nd Edition, William Collins, Glasgow 1986.

CHAPTER FIVE

COMMUNICATION IN TRAINING AND ASSESSMENT

Chapter coverage

Establishing credibility

During training the purpose of communication is to help trainees understand what they need to know and do. The aim being to enhance their ability to perform tasks and to learn essential underpinning knowledge.

Trainers and candidates seeking assessment and accreditation leading to trainers' and assessors' awards will need to be able to demonstrate competence in communication skills.

Assessors will take account of some or all of the key factors highlighted throughout this chapter during observations of candidates in action during training sessions.

Effectiveness of learning will depend not only on adequate preparation of subject-matter but also on the way learners evaluate the trainer. If the trainer is seen to be credible, that is, capable of being believed, reliable and qualified by experience and ability in the task area, then the learners will recognise this. They will be keen to learn. On the other hand, if the trainer professes to be an expert and is seen by the learners to lack this expertise then it is less likely that effective learning will occur. Lack of co-operation and disruptive activities may well replace supportive and helpful behaviour.

A trainer is more likely to induce good attitudes to learning if credibility is high and that is why it is essential for a trainer to win the trainee's confidence and approval very early in the training programme.

Gaining attention

Learners need to be motivated before they will pay attention to what is going on in a training environment. Motivation comes in many forms. In the workplace, trainers and their trainees need to be aware of the importance of learning to them. They must have some financial, social or psychological need to learn if they are to learn anything.

Instructing, learning, assessing and being assessed involves **two-way communication**. Getting the desired result is not achieved simply by attempting to pass information from one to another. Some believe that it is sufficient to give the message and that the content will automatically be received and the intended outcome achieved. Unfortunately, all too often, this is not the case.

Communication forms the link along which information, opinions and attitudes flow. This requires active conscious thought and full participation on the part of assessor, trainer and trainees.

Poor communication leads to mistakes, misunderstandings and time-wasting. Inadequate communication can have a drastic effect on individual relationships. It can lead to bad feeling which spreads throughout the workplace resulting in low morale. Constant effort is required from all concerned to ensure that the flow of effective communication is maintained.

The ability to establish rapport goes a long way towards providing a good atmosphere for effective communication and learning. This is good for the workforce.

Words and **body language** can both play important parts in the communication process. Facial expressions, gestures and body language can take the place of or at least strengthen the spoken word.

Importance of body language

At first, it may appear that face-to-face communication consists of taking it in turns to speak. While a person is speaking the others are expected to listen and wait patiently until the finish before making any attempt to 'jump-in'. However, on closer examination, it can be seen that people resort to a variety of verbal and non-verbal behaviour in order to maintain a smooth flow of communication. Such behaviour includes head nods, smiles, frowns, bodily contact, eye movements, laughter, body posture, language and many other actions.

Non-verbal cues play an important part in regulating and maintaining conversations. During a meeting, speech is backed up by an intricate network of gestures which affect the meaning of what is said. In a learning situation all will at some time be moving their head, body and hands. These movements are co-ordinated with speech to make up the total communication.

Some movements repeated frequently are known as **mannerisms**. They are unplanned and are carried out quite unconsciously. Mannerisms can provide a source of amusement for others.

> **The facial expression of candidates for assessment provides feedback to the assessor. Their faces usually give a good indication of how they feel.**

Glazed or down-turned eyes indicate boredom or disinterest, as does fidgeting. Fully-raised eyebrows signal disbelief and when half-raised indicate puzzlement. Bodily posture adopted by people provides a means by which their attitude to the assessor may be judged and acts as a pointer to their mood during the assessment.

> **Assessors should be sensitive to the signals being transmitted by candidates. A working knowledge of the meaning of non-verbal signals will prove invaluable.**

Assessors and trainers talking

Hopefully, the outcome of talking and listening will be the exchange of knowledge, feelings and activities that promote co-operation. It is helpful to be always mindful of the language one is using. There is often a gulf between assessor and candidate or between trainer and trainees because some people tend to use language which is not readily understood by all concerned.

Technical terms and jargon (sometimes referred to as 'subject specific language') also produce barriers and hinder learning if used thoughtlessly and without adequate explanation. Trainees will imitate the trainer and learn to use technical terms without really knowing their meaning.

> **Trainers should ensure, as far as possible, that the meaning is being handed over as well as the words.**

Some practising trainers need to be far more careful about using words. They need to recognise the difficulties experienced by some trainees when they do not understand what is being said. A **store of words** commonly used in the workplace should be drawn upon and trainer talk pitched at the trainees' level. It is better to work at relevant tasks as an aid to learning backed-up by explanation, than to rely on words alone.

Encouraging trainee participation

Practice is one of the best methods of increasing a learner's word store and developing skills in the use of words. This can be achieved by getting trainees to attempt to put into their own words explanations of what they are doing when learning.

The trainer can help by carefully choosing the words used to introduce the training, by putting open **probing questions**, by seeking opinions and by making the most of what trainees have to say.

The type of question which gets a greater amount of trainee response is of the **open-ended** type where a number of different answers are often quite acceptable.

Reasoning-type questions also call for trainees to think aloud and to construct from memory a logically organised answer. **Observation-type questions** relate to demonstrations of workplace skills that trainees may watch and which require them to comment on. The type of questions described provide good sources of trainee activity. They are preferred to **closed questions** which have only one acceptable answer, or **naming questions** which invite an answer without requiring the trainee to know much about the topic.

> Trainers should encourage their trainees to talk about what they are doing and make notes in order to get the best out of a learning experience.

The importance of communication style

The four basic language skills a trainer/assessor needs are: reading, writing, speaking and understanding. Competence in each of these skills must be demonstrated when training or assessing.

> Trainers need to be able to 'correctly' pronounce words that they are using when working with trainees and must also be able to explain their meanings using several examples as and when required.

Deciding what is meant by the 'correct' pronunciation can be a problem. Custom and practice changes from county to county and regional or class dialects govern communication forms, particularly as different pronunciations are used by people from different parts of the country. However, the effect of searching for work, mobility and migration across the country is now reducing the once considerable differences between the 'standard English' of the BBC and the spoken word heard in closed, long-established communities.

When conversing in informal situations the language style will often be more familiar and less precise in its form and will include slang, local expressions and terminology picked up from the media.

Differences also exist between the spoken and the written word. The written word is governed by sets of rules – **grammar** – that have been derived over the years by experts who have studied language and the works of notable writers and speakers.

> **Trainers' notes, handouts and assessment instructions will need to be carefully written using words chosen with greater care than when telling trainees the same things.**

In the written form, words, phrases and sentences need to conform more closely to the rules of grammar. Short uncomplicated sentences made-up of words in everyday use are preferred to longer sentences containing many difficult words arranged in a complex form. These longer sentences are a 'turn-off' to learners and hinder their understanding.

> **For trainers to prepare written work in a form that they would use when talking to trainees would probably not be good practice.**

When new words, definitions and ideas are being introduced it has been proposed that trainees should first listen to the words, then read what has been spoken, and then, if possible, write down what they have read. This sequence is thought to improve learning but time, attitudes and context may well prevent its use.

When encouraging trainees to come out with their thoughts and ideas as an aid to learning, they could be taught to ask themselves questions, prepare in their minds possible answers and hold a silent 'conversation' with themselves. With practice, competence in putting things into words will then get better.

For trainees learning to use language, or to apply specific terminology to their subject, it is not enough to set about learning by heart a set of rules, or building up a bank of information by chanting or repetition.

> **Trainers will need to train learners to use what they have learned to solve problems and to communicate things about their work clearly and with insight.**

Trainees' vocabularies will vary with age, cultural and ethnic background and it will often be the case that the language of the classroom or workplace will be vastly different to that of the home. In practice, it will be found that each trainee has a **'language ceiling'**. Progress in learning beyond this level cannot be easily made.

> **Trainers should be aware of the limitations imposed by constraints in vocabulary and usage. They should help trainees to learn as much as possible by keeping within their language ceiling. Trainers have a duty when preparing and delivering material to arrange things so that the learners are able to learn in the most pleasant, efficient and effective manner.**

To expect a learner to be able to do something for which they are ill-equipped due to lack of language is unreasonable; to knowingly ask the trainee to do it is unforgivable.

If a trainer is unable or unwilling to recognise when a trainee has reached his or her limit and really is incapable of going on, the crunch will inevitably come. When it does, there will be no alternative but to go back and follow some form of remedial programme designed to correct the unfortunate situation.

Regrettably, a lot of damage will have been done. The trainee's motivation and self-esteem will have taken a hard knock and it may be difficult and time-consuming to put things right. That is, if it is still possible to do so.

Giving instructions

When giving instructions it is important to first ensure that all present are attentive and ready to share the information. No one should be writing, shuffling papers, working on something or otherwise distracted. It is no use talking to people if they are not giving their full attention to you.

Silence can be a very powerful weapon in a trainer's armoury. If a break in attention occurs due to a distraction, stop speaking, show firmness and control and wait for silence and attention to be restored. Then resume.

Trainers will need to monitor their group before starting to speak.

Using question and answer techniques

Perhaps one of the more important features of an assessment or training session is the **question and answer (Q & A) method** of confirming underpinning knowledge or of developing a subject (see Figure 5.1). The method is very useful when introducing technical awareness into a whole range of subjects. It provides a good background for the later development of ideas that result from carefully planned questioning. The outcome being to strengthen trainees' knowledge by encouraging them to contribute by relating their work experience to the discussion.

The 'Q & A' technique can be applied effectively to any topic and is used very effectively when training adults.

Starting the training session with questions

The use of a short question and answer session at the beginning of each training session can help in several ways. Questions can be used to arouse interest and curiosity, while at the same time allowing the trainer to determine the existing level of subject knowledge. No matter how complex the topic for discussion may be, a good number of responses will relate in some way to it.

Development of the trainees' abilities to think and ask questions should be encouraged, but there will be times when the trainer will need to help. Trainees' replies may need to be amplified in some respects and this can be done either by asking them for further clarification, or by asking others to enlarge on the statement.

Questioning techniques
- Use unambiguous language which is easily understood.
- Use questions which cover the subject step-by-step.
- Use also questions calling for considerable thought and longer responses.
- Put questions to the whole group – pause for up to five seconds – name person to respond. (Pose, pause and pounce. Some are opposed to the use of this technique on the grounds that learners may feel threatened and clam-up.)
- When choosing respondent be reasonably sure that the person chosen is likely to be capable of correctly answering the particular question.
- Repeat answers slowly (only if reinforcement is necessary) – can disrupt concentration.
- Give praise for correct response and redirect question to others for confirmation of their agreement and understanding.
- Involve all learners at some stage of session – do not rely entirely on those who volunteer answers.
- Encourage slow learners by cueing until correct response is elicited.
- Avoid irrelevant or trick questions.
- Questions with 'yes/no' answers have a '50/50' chance of being answered correctly by guessing and should be avoided.
- Do not answer your own questions unless you really have to.

Figure 5.1 Questioning techniques

Trainees will 'clam-up' completely if they are ridiculed or told that their answers are incorrect. In the event of making an error they will not wish to be embarrassed by the trainer. They will remember that there is safety in silence and the trainer may have lost them for a while.

During the assessment or training session
If questions and comments are encouraged to flow naturally as the session develops, the result will be greater participation. The thing to bear in mind at all times is that, in general, people learn most when they are actively contributing to the session.

Many trainee-generated questions are directly related to statements made by the trainer or other trainees, or to what they have heard or read about the topic. Wherever possible, the question should be broken down into a series of mini-questions and thrown back to the others, so that trainees formulate their own answers to the problem. If, after cueing, this ploy fails, the question will have to be answered directly by the trainer.

Questions may be asked by trainees because they are confused. The expression on an individual's face will signal bewilderment.

An observant trainer should never allow matters to reach this stage.

An able trainer will take steps to put things right before complete confusion exists. This can be done by repeating the subject matter more slowly or by putting it another way with a series of check questions injected at suitable break points.

With a more formal training style, key check questions should be thought out and recorded in the **session plan** well before the event. Planned questioning serves to stimulate, encourage and consolidate learning as the training session proceeds and creates self-confidence in the trainees, especially if they are rewarded for correct responses.

Concluding the training session
A prepared list of questions relating to the subject matter may be put to the trainees towards the end of the session. This enables the group to evaluate instruction and learning. It also serves to reinforce key points. Any difficulties apparent may be rectified there and then, and the session plan modified ready for the next time.

The use of **incomplete statements** by a trainer as a form of questioning requires little effort on the part of the learner. Be on your guard against this practice. Asking and answering questions can be quite stressful. When trainees are slow to give the answer you are looking for, the pressure comes on.

> **As a trainer you will be tempted to put words into the mouth of a learner who is unable to answer. When the question has been answered you are 'off the hook' and many trainers will go to great lengths to achieve this happy state.**

Responses required of trainees

Before communication may take place we have to be ready for it. If we hear our name, we look toward the speaker. If an intense light flashes, we look in its direction. In a training situation we pay attention when the trainer speaks. We try to take in information.

The main problem in gaining attention is that people are often preoccupied with what they are already doing. While this takes precedence, little or no effective communication can take place. To gain full attention, irrelevant things must be shut out so that the trainees concentrate only on those directed to them by the trainer. The trainees must learn to respond by reacting to what the trainer says or does. Attention involves motivation, while personality factors and nature of the task are also strong influences on trainees' behaviour in the workplace. The main aims of the trainer are to share with the trainees: skills, knowledge and experiences. Therefore, for successful communication, the trainees must be interested in what is being said and done. What they get out of it and the meaning they attach to it is determined to some extent by their needs and values.

> **The trainee's perception must coincide with the trainer's intended communication in order for it to be effective.**

Responding
To **instruct** is to attempt to teach someone to do something. The trick is to get trainees to **respond** to your instruction. No learning can take place without active responses from the trainees. Instruction can be said to have been successful if the trainer's actions result in the trainees getting out of the training what they need to learn.

Throughout the session the trainer's role is that of enabler, providing a framework of opportunities within which trainees can learn.

Attention peaks at the beginning of a training session. This is the time to outline the ground to be covered and to fuel the trainees' imagination and interest. Performance objectives should be spelled out and overall direction indicated. What the trainees will be able to do after the lesson should be agreed with the trainees, and if assessment is to be included, this fact should be indicated before learning commences.

The trainer should analyse the material to be covered in terms of 'previously learned material' and 'material to be learned'.

The means of obtaining the necessary trainee responses follows the usual form: introduce the task, get them involved, show, tell and get them to show and tell you. Check their understanding by asking questions, review and exchange feedback. Process and resources to be used should be explained to the trainees who should progress from the 'known' to the 'unknown', from the 'familiar' to the 'unfamiliar' and from 'simple' to 'complex'. Ample opportunities should be provided for the trainees to perform and practice the tasks. Correctly done work should be rewarded and knowledge of test results or performance on tasks should be 'fed-back' to the trainees as soon as possible. Increased motivation can often be obtained by relating material to the work situation or real world and by indicating the benefit to the trainees of successfully mastering the tasks.

Keeping lines of communication open

Words or phrases may be perceived differently depending upon circumstances in which they are spoken. A communication will be interpreted both in terms of the message and the context in which it occurs.

A **communication** is not just a collection of words. It comprises three elements: a measure of the communicator's feelings, the form and style of the message and an indication of the desired behaviour or response. The feelings expressed may include those of sincerity, dominance, hostility, irony, humour or sadness. The style may be technical or non-technical and the message may be formed in such a way as to produce a specific response.

The communication channel is opened by attracting the receiver's attention and is maintained by words backed up with non-verbal signals. These signals combine to convey the three elements of communication and the way in which the total communication is perceived governs its effectiveness.

Information is not merely transmitted and received, it is also interpreted. The message is frequently distorted as it passes from one to another. Barriers to communication will affect interpretation of content as will previous experience and personal values. The message taken in and meaning ascribed to it will govern the receiver's behaviour.

Effective communication results when a trainee's response corresponds with the trainer's intentions and vice versa. Communication failure results when a trainer's intention and a trainee's response are incompatible.

In order to avoid misunderstandings due to ambiguity, complexity or sheer volume of message content, feedback should be provided between the trainee and trainer to ensure that correct interpretation has been made. It is too late to shut the gate when the horse has bolted.

A second feedback link enables the trainee's response in terms of what is done to be compared with the trainer's intentions. This is particularly necessary in the workshop, laboratory or work placement as a means of checking that orders or instructions have been carried out effectively.

Imbalances

At college and while at work an imbalance exists. The learner sees that the person instructing possesses superior skills, knowledge and ability. As a master craftsperson, subject specialist or source of information and fountain of knowledge, the instructor may often direct or control learners. The learner engages in tasks set, supervised, monitored, assessed and evaluated by the instructor.

> **The instructor is a source of social reinforcement who holds the power to reward or punish the learner according to his or her assessment of the outcomes.**

Punishment may take many forms. Applying **sanctions** is not the only way to punish. Reprimanding learners in front of others and shouting impatiently at them is harmful and destructive to a relationship. A poor performance may result in criticism of an unhelpful kind, in which case a loss of esteem inevitably results and it will take a long time to repair the damage.

If the learner does well, praise and reward may be forthcoming. A constructive approach would be to fairly and calmly review with the learner 'what was good and what was not so good' about their performance.

Power is vested in the trainer's expertise and position within the organisation. The trainer should be aware of this imbalance in power and needs to take steps to reduce tension by providing a secure atmosphere within which learning will be encouraged. It is just not possible to simply 'pour-in' knowledge. Learning depends upon a healthy rapport existing between trainer and trainee and a commitment of both to achieving the desired outcomes of training.

> **Steps should be taken by the trainer to redress the effects of imbalance as early as possible. A warm, sympathetic and friendly attitude is recommended, backed by an enthusiastic approach towards the task of training and assessing.**

It is not always easy to breeze into a workplace training session brimming with energy and enthusiasm. Some trainees are more difficult to train than others. Sometimes the trainer has domestic worries, sickness at home, pressures and stresses brought about by the ever-increasing demands being made of staff outside the workstation.

But somehow or other the trainer needs to hide the negative attitude that is waiting for an opportunity to be displayed. Unhelpful trainees who lack sufficient motivation will quickly observe how one feels and will seize the opportunity to take advantage given half a chance. Committed trainees will feel unable to apply themselves to work that the trainer seems to be disinterested in.

Under normal circumstances, trainees should be encouraged to speak freely and if similarities between trainer and trainee are perceived these similarities tend to increase, resulting in better rapport and enhanced self-esteem for the trainee. The degree of familiarity should however be controlled. Elsewhere, as in some large hotels and restaurant kitchens, there is a power structure. There is a **pecking order** and control may be strictly enforced by those at the top. Some people still believe that familiarity breeds contempt and in the workplace like to distance themselves from others.

> The trainer should avoid sarcasm and should at all times be respectful to the trainees. A trainer's behaviour should be irreproachable and a model for the trainees to follow. Trainer talk should be uncontaminated with bad language even when interacting with trainees who adopt non-standard English as their norm.

Where opportunity exists, the trainer, being one of the most potent influences on the trainees, needs to seek every opportunity to correct communication styles as and when examples crop up in the workplace. Possibly the best way of introducing a positive attitude towards improving language and communications skills is to provide examples of good practice when instructing.

> Integrity and high personal standards will go a long way towards overcoming obstacles to effective communication with trainees and colleagues.

A checklist of communication skills

The checklist given below was at one time used in Youth Training.[1]

> The checklist may be helpful to assessors and trainers when planning, preparing or implementing training or assessment sessions.

Checklist

Planning, determining and revising courses of action
- plan the order of activities
- plan who does what and when
- plan all resources needed for a task
- plan the arrangement of elements in the job
- plan how to communicate for a given purpose
- plan how to find and present information
- diagnose a fault or problem
- plan for contingencies, hazards and difficulties that may arise
- plan how to deal with things that have gone wrong

Decision making: choosing between alternatives
- decide when action is required
- decide which category something belongs to
- decide between alternative courses of action
- decide how to make the best of an awkward situation
- decide on the best response when accidents or emergencies occur

Monitoring: keeping track of progress and checking
- check that a person is performing a task to standard
- monitor a process or activity
- monitor the availability of resources
- check the quality and condition of resources
- check written information
- monitor the safety of the environment
- notice that things have gone wrong and that action is required

Finding out information and interpreting instructions
- find out information by speaking to other people
- find out information from written sources
- find out information by observing
- interpret spoken instructions
- interpret written instructions
- find out the needs of other people in the workplace
- find out the facts about things that have gone wrong
- find out the needs of customers, clients or colleagues

Providing information
- provide information by speaking to customers, clients or colleagues
- provide information in writing and by means of tables and diagrams
- provide information by demonstrating to other people
- provide information by answering questions in the course of the job or project
- provide information to others by explaining about problems that have occurred

Working with people
- notice when to ask other people in the workplace for help
- ask others for help
- notice the needs of others and offer help
- react appropriately to requests from others
- discuss with others how things are to be done
- react appropriately to complaints from others
- converse with others in order to establish or maintain an appropriate relationship
- notice where people behave exceptionally and whether action is required

Writing competence objectives

The checklist given above provides a basis on which to negotiate and write a set of competence objectives that may be used to assess the effectiveness of trainees' communications and hence to yield information for performance, assessment and recording or profiling purposes.

Main features of competence objectives

The main features of using competence type objectives are that:
- Tasks that trainees will be able to do are listed and available to all concerned.
- The objectives are unambiguous and understandable to trainers, assessors, trainees, employers and others.
- Trainers and trainees using the objectives can assess whether or not the outcomes have been demonstrated.
- The objectives are usually written in occupational terms or at least as clearly recognisable activities.
- Checklisted competence validated by assessments of 'can do' outcomes are readily marketable to employers.

Note
1   Source: *Core Skills in YTS (Part 1)* MSC, September 1984.

CHAPTER SIX

MONITORING SAFETY

Chapter coverage

Monitoring workplace safety
Fire, accident and emergency procedures
Accidents
First aid
Good housekeeping and hygiene
Welfare
Workplace hazards and risks
Health and safety in the workplace
Health and Safety at Work Act, 1974
Electricity at Work Regulations, 1989
The Protection of Eyes Regulations, 1974
COSHH assessments
Assessing safe working in laboratories
Assessing health and safety in sport
HSE publications

Monitoring workplace safety

Fire, accident and emergency procedures

A **safe workplace** affords security and protection from harm. Somewhere that is virtually free from danger. But it is well known that no working environment is completely safe. Familiarity can breed contempt and this can increase the vulnerability of staff to the risk of injury.

Before assessing occupational training outcomes it is necessary to carry out a thorough safety inspection of the working environment in which candidates will demonstrate achievement of competences that the assessor has been asked to accredit. It has been suggested that a suitable assessment method would be **guided-discussion** between the assessor and each candidate, backed up by examination of records and **observation** of the occupational training environment.

Safety policy statements, employer's liability or public liability insurance certificates, fire, accident and emergency procedures should be up-to-date, accurate, complete and clearly displayed in a noticeable and prominent position that allows easy access to all.

Fire prevention

Unwanted fires can break out because someone has been careless by adding fuel to the two other ingredients required to ensure combustion, namely: heat and air. Any combination of the three will result in fire.

Fire prevention must be a high priority for all trainers, particularly when trainees use electrical power or handle flammable liquids, gases, wood, paper and other combustible materials. Even when care is taken, volatile materials, heat sources, powders and appliances can start fires. Being negligent, discarding cigarette ends and behaving thoughtlessly can add unnecessary risk.

Fire drills

Fire action notices shall be displayed giving details of alarm systems, assembly and evacuation procedures. In the workplace a means of raising the alarm when a fire breaks out should be provided. There should also be a fire escape route and fire-fighting equipment.

The assessor may ask the candidate and trainees to state the actions to be taken to raise the alarm (for example by hitting the fire alarm button) and when the alarm sounds. A suitable list might be that given in Figure 6.1.

When alarm sounds
- Close windows
- Switch off power
- Get out
- Close door
- Follow escape route
- No running
- Use emergency exit
- Go to assembly point
- Report to supervisor
- Do not re-enter premises

Figure 6.1 Immediate actions

Fire extinguishers

A **fire extinguisher** is a portable device for putting out fires. It usually consists of a canister with a directional nozzle that is used to direct a spray of water, chemically generated foam, inert gas or powder onto a fire.

Serviceable fully maintained fire extinguishers relating to existing hazards should be available in the workplace. Documentation relating to the servicing of fire fighting equipment should be to hand in case the assessor asks to see the evidence.

Assessing fire-related aspects

To estimate a candidate's ability to react effectively to a fire the assessor might ask such questions as:

> Given that all reasonable precautions have been taken and yet a fire breaks out; what action would you (the candidate being assessed) take when:
> - the establishment's fire alarm is sounded
> - a fire occurs in his or her workplace, classroom or laboratory
> - called by trainees to the scene of a fire
> - asked to classify and report a fire
> - asked to supervise evacuation of a complete area?
>
> What do you know about fire fighting equipment and other things relating to fires including:
> - alarms   - escape notices
> - blankets   - escapes
> - buckets   - exits
> - classification   - extinguishers
> - doors   - hazards
> - drill   - prevention?
>
> For your workplace, classroom or laboratory sketch a plan and on it note all references to fire precautions, fire-fighting equipment and escape routes.
>
> How do you check that all the equipment is serviceable and are you able to demonstrate that you are competent to use it?
>
> How do you make sure your trainees know what to do in the event of fire?

Accidents

An **accident** is an unforeseen event or one without apparent cause. Accidents occur unintentionally or by chance but can result in injury or death. Details of all incidents where injury, no matter how trivial, is caused must be reported and recorded in an accident book kept in the workplace.

> Current accident books shall be available for inspection by the assessor. Any accidents reported shall have been entered in the record book, investigated, analysed and remedial action taken.
>
> Trainees must know to whom the accident must be reported.

Accident prevention is an essential part of a workplace trainer's job. The number of damage accidents, minor injuries and near misses might suggest to the assessor that sloppy accident control exists in the workplace.

> The assessor could ask candidates about any action that they have taken or intend to take to prevent a recurrence of any accidents reported.

Assessing accident procedures

When assessing accident procedures candidates seeking accreditation of competence will probably need to demonstrate that they are able to:

- Describe what to do and take appropriate action if there were an accident in their location.
- Call an ambulance or enlist the aid of some other person to do so.
- Get hold of a qualified First Aider.
- Specify the locations of First Aid boxes and the nearest sick room.
- Manipulate patients into the recovery position and cover them.
- Take appropriate action if the patient has received an electric shock and is still in contact with the power source.
- Indicate where a 'phone connected to an outside line can be found daytime and during the evening.
- Specify what information should be given when reporting an accident by 'phone or runner.
- Describe how to contact the patient's parent, guardian, relative or friend.

A schedule of actions that would need to be taken to meet the needs of such emergencies in the Candidate's own workplace could be produced for inspection. This documentation would serve as evidence to back statements made by candidates when the assessor is assessing competence.

First aid

The object of **first aid** is to provide immediate medical assistance in the event of an accident or emergency. It is essential that first aid boxes in the charge of a trained first aider are clearly identifiable and accessible. The first aider should be readily available during working hours. Boxes must contain all specified resources. Related checklists of contents should be available for inspection. Additional boxes must be provided for staff working off-site.

First aid procedures

All trainees and trainers must be aware of the procedure to be followed if they sustain an injury.

```
First aid procedure:
- Assess injury
- Call first aider
- Give treatment or
- Call ambulance
- Report to supervisor
- Enter in accident book
- Complete 'form of record'
- Follow company reporting system
```

Figure 6.2 First aid procedure

Trainees must know where and when to go for first aid.

Workplace supervisors could be asked to describe how they have checked and ensured a safe working environment for the candidates. Alternatively, it may be the candidates that will need to be able to do this for themselves or for their trainees.

Before assessment begins the assessor will need to be satisfied that candidates are aware of their role in ensuring that regulations relating to the Health and Safety at Work Act are being complied with. Candidates should be able to demonstrate a working knowledge of those factors applicable to their own sphere of operation.

Good housekeeping and hygiene

Hygiene is concerned with the maintenance of the health of people working. Good housekeeping in the workplace promotes clean and healthy practices among the workforce.

Occupational hygiene is concerned with the identification, evaluation and control of environmental health hazards that may arise in the workplace. Personal hygiene and good housekeeping both have an important role to play in protecting health. Working with materials, machines and processes can result in the release of potentially harmful agents such as dust, liquids, gases, chemicals, radiation and toxic substances. These agents give rise to situations in which people are unable to work effectively and may result in **occupational diseases**.

Skin complaints such as dermatitis are often caused by contact with an irritant. They are a major problem that can be overcome or reduced by preventing contact with skin sensitising materials. Workplace and personal cleanliness together with the use of protective clothing and **barrier creams** serve as precautionary measures that may reduce the risks of disease when working with particular substances.

Adequate skin cleansing facilities such as an ample supply of hot and cold water, nail brushes and clean towels should supplement the use of effective barrier creams.

When monitoring the workplace, the assessor will be looking for evidence to confirm that those factors relating to good housekeeping, hygiene and welfare listed in Figures 6.3 and 6.4 are available and in use.

Candidates must be familiar with hygiene-related aspects of the environment in which they and their trainees operate. The assessor will seek evidence that trainees will be/have been given adequate hygiene training before they commence work.

The assessor will check with trainees their understanding of the importance of good housekeeping and hygiene to themselves and other workers.

Check:
- Floors and passage ways are unobstructed, well lit and have level surfaces.
- Oily or wet patches are cleaned up.
- Stairs and landings are well maintained, handrails are provided and there are no obvious defects.
- Work areas are clean and tidy.
- Storage facilities are not overfilled and are adequate for the materials. Tools, boxes, waste materials are not left lying around.
- Floor coverings are in good repair.
- If smoking is allowed, there is a designated safe area, e.g. away from flammable materials.
- Remember to look for hazards above, below and at eye level.

Figure 6.3 Good housekeeping

Check:
- There is adequate lighting and heating.
- Sufficient toilets and washing facilities with both hot and cold water are available and kept clean.
- Where required there are separate toilet facilities for men and women.
- Separate areas are available for eating.
- There are facilities for the disposal of food, food papers, etc.
- There is appropriate provision for drying and storing clothing.

Figure 6.4 Welfare

Workplace hazards and risks

The **hazard** presented by a substance or situation is its potential to cause harm or exposure or vulnerability to injury, loss or damage. Some substances can cause harm by breathing them in, getting them on your skin or swallowing them. Potential hazards should be identified, evaluated, assessed and controlled. They should be eliminated or reduced. If remedial action is needed this should be dealt with immediately, if practicable, but in any case before assessment of competence in the workplace can commence. The **risk** from a substance or process is the likelihood that it will harm you when in use.

> Candidates for assessment will need to be able to describe and apply proper precautions so that the risk of any person in their charge being harmed by even the most hazardous substance can be adequately controlled.

Within the context of the candidate's workplace the assessor will probably question trainees to check awareness of the hazard presented by a substance they have been trained to understand. And also that they have sufficient knowledge of rules and procedures relating to other dangerous substances, machinery, lifting heavy or awkward objects, hygiene and housekeeping.

For each of the hazards listed above candidates will need to demonstrate that they have given trainees suitable training and that the trainees know:
- what the risks are from using it
- how these risks are controlled
- precautions that they must take when using it.

Workplace checklists

An example showing the form of a **workplace checklist** that may be helpful to trainers when assessing their workplace and the systems of work used in it is reproduced in Figure 6.5. While the checklist applies to painters, many of the concepts are transferable to other occupational areas.

Protective clothing and equipment

Overalls, waterproofs, wet suits, high visibility clothing, safety harness, lifelines, safety helmets, gloves, safety footwear, eye protectors and breathing apparatus should be worn whenever necessary.

Watches, rings and jewellery should not normally be worn when working. Loose clothing and ties must not be worn when there is a chance of them being caught up in rotating machinery.

Protective clothing provided must fit the wearer and all equipment must be maintained in good condition and must be used in accordance with regulations or company policy.

- Has your employer made an assessment of the hazards related to the painting processes – including any preparation work?
- Have steps been taken to substitute less harmful substances, e.g. water-based paints?
- Are safety data sheets available from manufacturers and suppliers?
- Have occupational exposure levels been identified?
- Are control techniques used other than protective clothing and respiratory equipment, e.g. exhaust ventilation?
- Is the local exhaust ventilation for dust and/or fumes regularly examined and tested?
- Are vacuum cleaning or wetting techniques used to keep down dust?
- Has the right protective equipment been provided for the hazards to which you are exposed?
- Is your protective equipment kept in a clean state and properly maintained?
- Are washing or shower facilities available to enable you to keep clean and prevent you taking substances home on your body or clothing?
- Is health surveillance carried out and are the results of any medical examination provided?
- Is suitable first-aid equipment available?

Figure 6.5 Workplace checklist

Health and safety in the workplace

Health and Safety at Work Act, 1974

The Health and Safety at Work Act received the Royal Assent on 31 July, 1974 and it provides a comprehensive system of law covering the health and safety of people at work. Since the Act was introduced workplace trainers and trainees and teaching and non-teaching staff in further, higher and adult education have been affected by its implications, and the legislative framework provided by the Act has had considerable influence and effect on day-to-day operations in the workplace or college.

The Act covers all staff employed in an establishment, all trainees, students, visitors and contractors, and it gives statutory protection to anyone who is present on the site (see Footnotes 1–4).

The Act comprises four main parts:
- **Part 1** is concerned with health, safety and welfare in relation to work
- **Part 2** relates to the Employment Medical Advisory Service
- **Part 3** amends the law relating to building regulations
- **Part 4** deals with various and general provision.

The Act is concerned with:
- **securing** the health, safety and welfare of persons at work as described in Part 1 of the Act
- **protecting** persons other than persons at work, against the risks to health or safety arising out of, or in connection with, the activities of persons at work
- **controlling** the keeping and use of explosives or highly inflammable or dangerous substances
- **preventing** people acquiring, possessing or illegally using such substances
- **controlling** the emission of noxious or offensive substances from any area.

Figure 6.6 Health and Safety at Work Act, 1974

Basic obligations of employers

Employers (including Local Education Authorities and college managements) have a duty to ensure that their activities do not endanger anybody. They have an obligation to provide, **so far as is reasonably practicable**, for employees and other persons, the specified processes and resources listed in Figure 6.7.

To provide:
- healthy and safe systems of work with safe plant, machinery, equipment and appliances all of which are maintained in good working order
- safe methods for use, handling, storing and transporting materials, articles or substances
- healthy and safe working environments including premises with adequate amenities
- adequate instruction and training for employees including such information and supervision by competent personnel as is necessary to ensure the health and safety at work of employees.

Figure 6.7 Obligations of employers

Basic obligations of employees

Quite apart from any specific responsibilities that may be delegated to them, workplace supervisors and teachers have a legal obligation, as do all employees in industry, commerce or elsewhere (except domestic service) under Section 7 of the Health and Safety at Work Act, 1974; namely, to take care of their own health and safety as well as that of trainees, students and of any person who may be affected by their acts or omissions.

To:
- cooperate with their employers so far as is necessary to perform any duty or comply with any requirements imposed as a result of any law that may be in force
- make themselves familiar with and conform to any statement of Safety Policy or Safety Code of Practice issued by employers, college principals or governing bodies
- avoid the possibility of commiting criminal offences due to putting the health and safety of themselves or other persons at risk
- conform to safety instructions issued by employers, principals or governing bodies and share their responsibility for safety, health and welfare
- report any hazard, accident or dangerous occurrence to their immediate superior and to their safety representative, whether or not physical injury has occurred
- use and ensure that employees, trainees or students use the appropriate protective clothing, equipment and safety devices at all times and ensure that any such equipment or devices are maintained in a safe working condition
- comply with improvement notices or prohibition notices that may have been served on them as employees
- comply with the duty not to interfere with or misuse things provided pursuant to any of the relevant statutory provisions
- set a good example to trainees, students, colleagues and the public in their approach to Health and Safety matters.

Figure 6.8 Obligations of employees

Assessing duties and responsibilities of trainers

Assessors will need to be able to monitor the safety of the working environment whether this be at workplace trainer or trainee level.

> **A workplace trainer or teacher must ensure that trainees are carefully briefed about safety arrangements in normal work environments and when in unfamiliar surroundings.**

Examples of such situations might be:
- new starters joining the company
- trainees on work experience attachment
- newly enrolled students beginning a college course
- trainees relocated to another workplace or site
- when practicals or work commences in laboratories and workshops
- in any other novel situation.

It is essential that the trainees shall know:
- the fire exit route
- the location of the nearest first aid box

- the location, uses and methods of operation of fire extinguishers in the vicinity
- content and application of accident and fire regulations
- what to do in the event of an emergency.

When trainees are undergoing training or work experience the workplace trainer assumes responsibility for providing a safe working environment. When students are on the register the teacher is in charge and must accept responsibility for all aspects of safety and control of the environment in which work is taking place. Any activities that the trainer is expected to supervise should be inherently safe. If a situation arises where any aspect of work is judged to be hazardous to the health or welfare of trainees, such work should stop immediately and a report be made in writing to management.

Since the workplace supervisor or teacher is ultimately in charge in a workshop or laboratory, other support staff, whilst being helpful, can only offer advice to the trainer or trainees. The 'buck' stops with the supervisor or teacher. It is the trainer who is responsible for ensuring that trainees are properly instructed and it is the trainer who is responsible for trainees operating machinery or processes safely, not the technician or other support staff. It is the trainer who must ensure that no request is made of trainees or others to undertake operations that are or may be hazardous.

Burden of proof

In any proceedings for an offence under any of the relevant statutory provisions consisting of a failure to comply with a duty or requirement, Section 40 of the Act lays the burden of proof on the accused. It is usually the employer who will be required to prove that it was not reasonably practicable to do more than was done to safeguard employees or other persons injured or otherwise disadvantaged by a contravention of the Health and Safety at Work Act, 1974.

Electricity at Work Regulations 1989

The Electricity at Work Regulations, 1989 requiring precautions to be taken against the risk of death or injury from electricity while at work came into force on 1 April 1990. The Regulations that are additional to the Health and Safety at Work Act, 1974 enforce compliance with duties concerning work activities on or near electrical equipment.

Where trainees are working on or with charged or live equipment there will be a risk of injury due to the inherent danger present when current is flowing. Action must be taken to prevent injury resulting. Trainees must not undertake any work where technical knowledge or experience is necessary to prevent danger or injury unless they possess appropriate knowledge or experience or are adequately supervised.

Inspection and repair work subject to the Regulations must be carried out only by **competent persons** so as to ensure safety.[5]

- electric shock
- current leakage
- faulty insulation
- arcing causing burning
- ultra violet radiation
- smoke inhalation
- overheating cables
- overloaded conductors
- meltdowns and fires
- explosions
- microwave (RF) burns

Figure 6.9 Sources of injury

Trainers are required to take all reasonable precautions to prevent danger and the risk of injury to themselves or their trainees.

Trainers may expect to be adequately briefed by those who allocate responsibilities for supervision. Although where risks are low verbal instructions may in some cases be sufficient, written instructions giving details of safe working procedures may be called for. Assessors will check with candidates and their trainees that they understand and properly apply verbal or written instructions and working procedures.

Inspection and repair work subject to the Regulations must be carried out only by competent persons so as to ensure safety.

It is the duty of trainers and trainees while at work to co-operate with employers to enable any duty placed on those employers by the provisions of the Regulations to be complied with.

The Protection of Eyes Regulations, 1974

An employer must provide approved eye protectors to each person engaged in hazardous processes (specified in the Regulations) in a workplace and to those where there is a risk of injury to their eyes from the employer carrying on such processes. Others who are not employed in the workplace but who may likewise be at risk should also be issued with eye protectors.

Approved eye protectors, shields or fixed shields are required where processes such as welding, abrasive wheel dressing, grinding, forging, casting, fettling, chipping of metal and machining are involved.

Everyone who is provided with eye protectors or shields must take care of them and make full and proper use of them while carrying on the processes specified in the Regulations.

Loss, destruction or defects in the eye protectors or shields provided by the employer must be reported immediately to the employer or his agent.

COSHH Assessments

The Control of Substances Hazardous to Health Regulations, 1988 (COSHH) introduces a new legal framework for controlling people's exposure to hazardous substances arising from work activities. The impact of COSHH regulations will be felt by every concern from the multinationals to small jobbing workshops. There are over 40 000 substances that are classified as being very toxic, harmful, corrosive or an irritant, and practically all will be covered by COSHH regulations.

Evaluation of health risks in the workplace will have to be made and records will have to be maintained on assessments, implementation and testing of control measures for at least five years from the date they were made. In the case of health surveillance, records have to be kept for at least 30 years.

An essential requirement is for employers to make an assessment of the health risks created by the work and of the measures that need to be taken, as a consequence, to protect people's health and meet the requirements of the **COSHH Regulations**.[6]

From 1 January 1990 no work that is liable to expose anyone to substances hazardous to health may be carried on unless a 'suitable and sufficient' assessment has been made. The responsibility to make an assessment rests with the employer and cannot be delegated, although the task may be given to some other competent person with the authority and ability to perform assessments.

> **If assessors of competence in the workplace think that hazardous substances might be present in the environment where the candidate for accreditation is employed, it would be reasonable for them to ask to see the 'Record of COSHH Assessment' and check that the employer's assessment has been recorded.**

Questions could be asked about:
- how the decisions about risk factors were made
- what precautions to limit such risks have been taken
- the detail with which assessment has been carried out
- the dissemination of information to those who need to know about the risk
- the circumstances under which the assessment might need to be reviewed.

COSHH assessment sheets

A number of different assessment sheets are in use and two of these are reproduced in Figures 6.10 and 6.11. Figure 6.10 shows an assessment of **'Hazardous Substances in Construction'**. The HSE gives this as an example of how an assessment sheet may be laid out under the headings: **substances, health risk, jobs** and **controls**.

The example given in Figure 6.11 is laid out somewhat differently using the headings: **hazardous substance, nature of hazard and risk,** and **control**. Prevention and control methods are listed under the 'control' heading.

Risks: SK – skin   I – inhalation   ENT – irritant eyes, nose, throat   SW – ingestion

Substances	Health risk	Jobs	Controls
Dusts:			
Cement (also when wet)	SK. I. ENT	Masonry, rendering	Prevent spread. Protective clothing, respirator when handling dry, washing facilities, barrier cream
Gypsum	SK. I. ENT	Plastering	
Man-made mineral fibre	I. SK. ENT	Insulation	Minimise handling/cutting, respirator, one piece overall, gloves, eye protection
Silica	I	Sand blasting, grit blasting: scrabbling granite, polishing	Substitution – e.g. with grit, silica free sand; wet methods; process enclosure/extraction, respirator
Wood dust (dust from treated timber, e.g. with pesticide may present extra hazards)	I. SK. ENT	Power tool use in carpentry, especially sanding	Off site preparation; on site – enclosures with exhaust ventilation; portable tools – dust extraction; washing facilities; respirator
Mixed dusts (mineral and biological)	I. SK. ENT	Demolition and refurbishment	Minimise dust generation; use wet methods where possible; segregate or reduce number of workers exposed; protective clothing, respirator; good washing facilities/showers. Tetanus immunisation
Fumes/gases:			
Various welding fumes from metals or rods	I	Welding/cutting activities	Mechanical ventilation in enclosed spaces; air supplied helmet; elsewhere good general ventilation
Hydrogen Sulphide	I. ENT	Sewers, drains, excavations, manholes	All work in confined spaces – exhaust and blower ventilation; self contained breathing equipment; confined space procedures
Carbon Monoxide/ Nitrous Oxide	I	Plant exhausts	Position away from confined spaces where possible; maintain exhaust filters; forced ventilation and extraction of fumes
Solvents:			
In many construction products – paints, adhesives, strippers, thinners, etc.	I. SK. SW	Many trades, particularly painting, tile fixing. Spray application is high risk. Most brush/roller work less risk. Regular exposure increases risks	Breathing apparatus for spraying, particularly in enclosed spaces: use of mistless/airless methods. Otherwise ensure good general ventilation. Washing facilities, barrier cream

Risks: SK – skin   I – inhalation   ENT – irritant eyes, nose, throat   SW – ingestion

Substances	Health risk	Jobs	Controls
Resin systems: Isocyanates (MDI:TDI)	I. ENT. SK. SW also Sensitisation	Thermal insulation	Mechanical ventilation where necessary; respirators: protective clothing, washing facilities. Skin checks, respiratory checks
Polyurethane paints	I. ENT. SK. SW	Decorative surface coatings	Spraying – airline/self contained breathing apparatus: elsewhere good general ventilation. One piece overall, gloves, washing facilities
Epoxy	I. SK. SW	Strong adhesive applications	Good ventilation, personal protective equipment (respirator; clothing) washing facilities, barrier cream
Polyester	I. SK. ENT. SW	Glass fibre claddings and coatings	Good ventilation, personal protective equipment (respirator; clothing) washing facilities, barrier cream
Pesticides: (E.g. timber preservatives, fungicides, weed killers)	I. SK. ENT. SW	Particularly in-situ timber treatment Handling treated timber	Use least toxic material. Mechanical ventilation, respirator, impervious gloves, one piece overall and head cover. In confined spaces – breathing apparatus. Washing facilities, skin checks. If necessary biological checks. Handle only dry material.
Acids/alkalis:	SK. ENT	Masonry cleaning	Use weakest solutions. Protective clothing, eye protection. Washing facilities (first aid including eye bath and copious water for splash removal)
Mineral oil:	SK. I	Work near machines, compressors, etc. mould release agents	Filters to reduce mist. Good ventilation. Protective clothing. Washing facilities: barrier creams. Skin checks
Site contaminants: e.g. Arsenic. Phenols: heavy metals: Micro organisms, etc. e.g. Weil's disease, tetanus, hepatitis B	I. SK. SW	Site re-development of industrial premises or hospitals – particularly demolition groundwork and drain/sewers	Thorough site examination and clearance procedures. Respirators, protective clothing. Washing facilities/showers; Immunisation for tetanus

Figure 6.10 Hazardous substances in construction COSHH Assessment Sheet

CONTROL OF SUBSTANCES HAZARDOUS TO HEALTH REGULATIONS [COSHH] - ASSESSMENT

Hazardous Substance	Nature of hazard and risk	CONTROL – Prevention and control measures
CDD7 (Concentrated dish washing detergent)	Corrosive – causes severe burns	Store separately from routine cleaning products. Avoid skin contact.
OVSOL (Spray-on oven cleaner)	Corrosive – causes severe burns	Immediate action if swallowed, inhaled, skin or eye contact or splashes clothing. (Refer to Data Sheets in Health & Safety file in Manager's Office.)
PHDD (Powdered heavy duty detergent)	Non-hazardous. But prolonged use will de-fat the skin	Avoid prolonged contact. If product enters eye wash with plenty of water.
LHDD (Liquid detergent for heavy duty hand dish washing)	Prolonged contact will de-fat the skin	Refer to Data Sheet for action if swallowed, skin or eye contact, or inhalation of spray or vapour.
GLASDER (Glass washer detergent)	Non-hazardous but avoid contact with neat product.	Refer to Data Sheet for action if swallowed, skin or eye contact.
RINADD (Dish washing machine rinse additive)	Prolonged contact will de-fat skin	Avoid prolonged contact. Refer to Data Sheet for action if swallowed, or skin or eye contact.
GLAD (Glass washer rinse additive)	Prolonged contact may de-fat skin	Avoid prolonged contact. Refer to Data Sheet for action if swallowed, or skin or eye contact.

Health surveillance	Implementation of control programme
Check frequently for rashes Protective clothing to be worn (as applicable)	To be supervised by Food and Bar Manager. Head Chef: Head Bar person: (Dish washing and oven cleaning). (Glass washing)

Training need	Monitoring programme
No member of staff will use any cleaning product unless they have been instructed in its correct use, and the precautions to be taken in its handling and use	Frequency 3 monthly (or if health problem occurs – immediately).

Assessment carried out by .. Anita Marple ..   Date .... 7 December ..

Figure 6.11 Alternative COSHH Assessment Sheet

There is also space on the sheet for notes on:

- **Health surveillance** where details of the close observation and supervision that may be necessary may be recorded.
- **Implementation of control programme** where the management of the hazard and how to achieve the limitation of risk is specified.
- **Monitoring programme** where frequency and mode of ongoing reviewing of the hazard is recorded.
- Where staff development **training needs** are noted.

Candidates will be expected to be familiar with COSHH and be able to relate the Regulations to their own working environment and that of their trainees.

They will be required to identify and specify those hazardous substances that are handled or are present in the workplace and produce the relevant assessment sheet.

Candidates must be able to satisfy the assessor that they have informed, instructed and trained their trainees in the risk involved in handling the substances and the precautions to be taken. The assessor will seek confirmation from the trainees.

Assessing safe working in laboratories

Workplace trainers responsible for laboratories will need to be aware of the potentially hazardous conditions and dangers that exist. Some of these are:

- Over a period of time, materials will have been accumulating that may not be in regular use; large stocks of little-used resources may be held; quantities of flammable chemicals may exceed the permitted allocation or be incorrectly stored; and incompatible materials, poisons, gases or other dangerous chemicals may be stored unsafely. All of these promote a potentially dangerous environment.
- Disposal of chemical waste will present problems concerning: washing down sinks, disposal by burial, burning or other methods.
- Practical work in laboratories will always be subject to physical hazards and hazards associated with chemical, electrical and mechanical processes and the use of power tools and appliances.

Health and Safety Executive Inspectorate have horrifying tales of the bad state and organisation of some laboratories. Some have been so bad, and have contravened so many regulations, that the Inspectors have photographed them as almost unbelievable examples. In every one of these cases, a qualified trainer was in charge.

As the person in charge, the workplace trainer will have tacitly accepted responsibility for all aspects of safety relating to training sessions held there. Bearing in mind some of the points given in the text above, confirmation of whether or not it is free of hazards could be satisfied for each factor by repeatedly asking the question: 'Is it safe?'

The assessor when assessing the trainer will need to determine, using structured discussion and observation techniques, whether or not the environment is safe. In preparation for the visit and as a normal course of day-to-day work routines the candidate will need to be able to demonstrate that a comprehensive check of the laboratory and working environment has been carried out.

Assessing health and safety in sport

Reducing the probability of injury or accident during physical education, swimming and games activities must be an important item on the minds of many trainers. Every kind of sporting activity has inherent risks and it is impossible to remove every aspect of danger from the material and physical requirements of sport. Trainers may also have to cope with trainees' self-imposed dangers such as exhaustion, strained muscles and raised blood pressure due to violent or inappropriate exercise patterns.

Think about the gymnasium, swimming bath, playing field, court, playground, or changing rooms; the range of physical education equipment that you and your trainees use including: the floor, trampoline, beams, vaulting equipment, ropes, weight-lifting apparatus or that equipment specific to your specialism; and the chemicals, lotions or preparations associated with the sport.

In order to assess safe working skills relating to physical education and games, trainers and trainees seeking accreditation of achievement will need to demonstrate the ability to:
- survey the risks and dangers associated with resources and group members
- review methods and facilities with a view to confirming that trainees are not being exposed to unnecessary risk
- produce an action plan for reducing dangers and improving safety aspects of the operation.

Notes

1   A booklet containing a list of HSC/E publications is available from the Health and Safety Executive Library and Information Services Unit, Broad Lane, Sheffield, S3 7HQ. The booklet gives details of publications produced by the Health and Safety Commission and the Health and Safety Executive since 1974. HMSO also produces a number of leaflets and titles catalogues on selected titles and themes.
Workplace trainers and assessors will find the information invaluable when monitoring the workplace environment in the context of health and safety. By conforming with Regulations and making use of the advice outlined in the publications the candidate for assessment will be better able to demonstrate achievement of competence in this important area of responsibility.

2   The booklet: *Mind How You Go* which is available from HSE is intended to supplement safety rules and training for your workers such as those on Government-sponsored training schemes. Common causes of accidents and their prevention are described. It is recommended that all people going to work for the first time should receive a copy.

3   It has been recommended that all supervisors and trainers who have direct responsibility for Youth Training trainees be issued with a copy of the booklet: *Health & Safety on YT – Guidance for providers of training, education and work experience*, Employment Department Training Agency, Sheffield, March 1989.

4   For those concerned with monitoring health and safety on Government sponsored schemes please refer to the booklet: *A Good Start To Assessing Placement Safety*, Employment Department Group Training Agency, Sheffield, 1989.

5   See: *Memorandum of Guidance on the Electricity at Work Regulations 1989*, Health & Safety Executive, HMSO London, 1989.

6   *COSHH Assessments*, HMSO London 1988.

CHAPTER SEVEN

ASSESSING KNOWLEDGE, SKILLS AND EVIDENCE

Chapter coverage

Assessing prior learning and achievement (see also Appendix A)
Purpose
Procedure for accrediting prior learning and achievement (APLA)
Claiming achievements
Claims
Training and learning gaps
Checklist of supporting evidence
Assessing underpinning knowledge and skills
Knowledge-based assessment
Skills-based assessment

Assessing prior learning and achievement

Purpose

The purpose of assessing **prior learning (APL)** and **prior achievement (APA)** is to enable people to obtain credit for competences they already have. Achievement that has been recognised and accredited can be used to enhance career progression. It can assist people to gain access to continuing education and training. Adults can 'call-up' and apply a wealth of skills and knowledge based on past achievements when the need arises and it is in everyone's interests to accurately record and accredit competences that have developed over a period.

Learning has been defined as: 'A relatively permanent change in behaviour that occurs as a direct result of experience'. **Prior learning** is learning that has taken place previously. It may be knowledge intentionally gained by study or instruction, or it may have occurred informally as a result of watching television, reading or interacting at work or elsewhere with people, places and things. Becoming skilled and competent can result from the experience of doing things and does not necessarily depend upon the outcomes of formal instructional processes.

One of the problems with the accreditation process is: 'spotting the difference between experience and achievement'. The formal terminology for this is **'differentiating between . . .'** It can be likened to evaluating a salesperson working on commission who knocks on hundreds of doors but who makes no sales. Industrialists do not normally reward people for making great effort but they do reward people who get tangible results. The same goes for candidates seeking awards – it is **achievement derived from experience that is accredited, not the experience itself.**

A candidate may well have had a wide range of experiences but an achievement is something that has been accomplished – something successfully completed.

> In the case of prior learning, assessors will need to compare with relevant performance criteria what candidates say they can do. They will review reliable evidence of competence before an award can be made. Awards will not be made for work experience alone.

Competence of assessment team members

Employers may have a core of trained staff engaged in the assessment process.[1] The Personnel Officer may head up a team of accreditors backed by professional counsellors and administrative staff. Alternatively it will probably be a line manager with one full-time or part-time accreditor, an owner or consultants from educational and skill training centres.

> Assessment of Prior Learning Counsellor/Assessors will need to be credible and competent in skills such as:
>
> | | |
> |---|---|
> | icebreaking | asking questions |
> | drawing out | counselling |
> | listening | reviewing |
> | managing silence | mentoring |
> | reflecting back | clarifying |
> | advising | summarising |
> | target setting | prescribing |
>
> A responsible assessor/counsellor needs to consult with candidates and adopt a sensitive attitude to their views.
>
> Counselling should be available from staff with whom people from ethnic minority groups can also relate in order to demonstrate equal opportunities for all.
>
> It is the assessor/counsellor's duty to provide a secure atmosphere in which consultation may take place.

Candidates can be sensitive to the language and terminology used by counsellors. A general complaint being that: 'They use posh words that nobody can understand'. (The assessor/counsellors use specialised language or jargon.)

Inadequate communication leads to misunderstandings, mistakes and time-wasting that results in poor cooperation. Constant effort is needed to keep things moving and to establish a healthy rapport and a good atmosphere to work in.

Occupationally-specific assessors will need to have expert knowledge of the processes and resources involved in the creation or manufacture of goods or services in the workplace. They should also understand the principles of experiential learning[2] as applied to the accreditation of prior achievement and learning and be able to:

- Negotiate with candidates or otherwise design suitable and acceptable assessment processes.
- Encourage and promote self-assessment techniques where applicable.
- Interpret performance criteria and be able to communicate content with candidates.
- Assess areas of weakness by direct observation and give advice on how to master related difficulties.
- Sift through portfolios and select evidence of experience and achievement.
- Validate knowledge and skills against checklists of competences.
- Evaluate and compare equivalence of formal qualifications and confirm transferability of prior learning claims to new learning opportunity.
- Rigorously check and validate informal evidence of previous learning.[3]
- Evaluate currency of skills claimed.
- Process documentation relating to candidates' accredited prior achievement with awarding bodies or other interested parties.
- Justify decisions made to candidates and to senior assessors.

Administrative support

Supervisors have enough on their plates without the added responsibility of handling paperwork that may be associated with the accreditation of prior learning and competence in the workplace. While it has always been a role of the 'person-in-the-middle' to carry out unofficial workplace training and staff development, the formalisation of training and accreditation of competence has added another layer to an already stressful supervisor's workload.

Managers and staff development officers should be seen to be encouraging staff to come forward for accreditation.

Administrative support and organisational systems should be in place to help the workplace trainer and assessor and also supervisors to make a success of vocational learning and training for NVQs.

Monitoring officers

Monitoring officers and **training co-ordinators** play an important role in planning and delivering induction sessions. During the induction, trainees are given guidance about training programmes they will follow and information about assessment, recording and relevant qualifications. The officers identify training placements and arrange for counselling and guidance support where required. They review progress during practical training with reference to personal training plans and monitor arrangements for work-based projects. Trainee achievement is recorded in their National Record of Vocational Achievement (NROVA)[4], National Record of Achievement (NRA)[5] or elsewhere by monitoring officers who liase with awarding bodies. They also establish and maintain systems for handling trainee assessment and certification.

Procedure for accrediting prior learning and achievement (APLA)

In the case of a college it may be necessary to market the assessment and accreditation facility so that clients in industry and commerce will know what is on offer. There will always be a work-based or performance-related assessment element in courses or training relating to award of NVQs so that college staff and other training providers will need to be qualified in order to participate as workplace assessors.

Workplace assessors will respond to calls by management to assess certain staff or will otherwise arrange with individuals an assessment schedule.

When a request for APLA is received it will be necessary to arrange an initial meeting between the candidate and a trained APL assessor/counsellor. During the meeting, agreement may be reached about the need to:
- Discuss what units of competence or qualifications are available that relate to the Candidate's experience.
- Reflect on prior experience.
- Identify learning related to claims and how demonstrated – described in precise performance terms.
- Collect evidence relating to prior achievements.
- Assemble a portfolio of experiences.
- Arrange assessment for accreditation.

This 'evidence' can then be used to support claims made for the accreditation of prior achievement.

In some cases the Candidate may feel confident enough to come to the first meeting armed with their NROVA, NRA or with a portfolio of material or file that could include indirect evidence, but this is infrequent.

Evidence of prior achievement
Evidence to support claims of prior achievement could be drawn from:
- Work experience in the occupational setting.
- Non-occupational, self-motivated learning outside the workplace.
- Incidental learning from peer groups or from the social environment.
- Previously unassessed or unrecognised achievements resulting from any form of intentionally planned learning, such as: 'in-house' company training, external courses and open learning packages.

Assessment of evidence will normally be made for elements of competence against related performance criteria, so that a task is carried out under prescribed conditions to specified standards.

For more information about the assessment of prior learning and achievement, turn to Appendix A.

Claiming achievements

Claims

Given a checklist of competences relating to the qualification sought, the candidate would quite likely be overwhelmed if asked to identify and give evidence of achievements claimed. The road to accreditation is not easy to travel alone.

The assessor using a better approach would arrange to meet with the candidates and give a general outline of the process of evaluating evidence and assessing achievement.

The meeting will serve to help the candidates review where they are now and where they hope to be later. Any claims to prior achievements and newly acquired skills can be discussed and guidance given as to how to set about selecting and gathering supporting evidence.

Self-evaluation by reflection

Being **reflective** is characterised by quiet thought or contemplation. It involves settling down for a while to recall what has happened at work and to think about what went well and what went wrong. Through this process one is able to identify areas where improvement can be made and to note new things that need to be learned in order to get on.

Future **competence-based** and **performance-assessed** skills may be targeted for attention by reflecting upon relevant experience gained in the workplace. Such reflection and evaluation will form the basis for producing an action plan that will help trainees progress in their chosen occupation.

Training and learning gaps

Probable outcomes of meetings of candidate with assessor will be the identification of achievements that will be assessed and also gaps in knowledge and skills that will need to be filled. This may involve college services and support or further experience at the workplace. This in turn will require decisions to be made about the **mode of study**.

The old system of annual enrolment for courses at colleges is now obsolete. It is being replaced by a more customer friendly provision. The **flexible curriculum** approach involves modularisation of courses, roll-on/roll-off enrolments, extended college year, tutor-supported open learning and individualised learning opportunities outside the classroom.

Having taken on board the necessary updating the next stage involves the assessor who will evaluate the candidate's evidence of achievement against performance criteria.

Unless the right level of competence can also be proved, successfully completing a course will, in itself, mean little or nothing in terms of gaining a NVQ.

Mastery must be established and this means that the assessor needs to be sure that the competence can be demonstrated in novel or unfamiliar circumstances. Evidence in support of the claim must relate directly to the competence being assessed.

Supporting evidence

The assessor may ask searching questions concerning information provided in support of the candidate's claims. This is often referred to as '**authenticating**' or '**challenging**' the evidence. It may be that the assessor's probing will lead to a request either for further evidence of achievement or for a direct demonstration to confirm competence.

Although irritation and annoyance may result from such a request it is comforting to know that the award will be current and valued by employers, and that standards and credibility will be maintained.

On the other hand, a qualification may be awarded without necessarily taking and passing a course of training at all. If candidates can show that their performance meets the definition of competence specified by the relevant Industry Lead Body they will deserve an award.

Checklist of supporting evidence
- Assessment procedures.
- Checklisted core skills integrated within vocational activities with indication of opportunities for skill transfer.
- Counselling and guidance.
- Debriefing trainees.
- Diary record of experiences and training.
- Discussion of teaching and learning procedures underpinning the demonstration of competence.
- Induction programme.
- Log book completion.
- Micro training sessions.
- Minutes of discussions and meetings.
- Negotiated learning agendas.
- Observation by assessors and supervisors.
- Profiles and skills attainment checklists.
- Residentials and participation in teamworking.
- Review of a case study involving individual trainee contact with candidate.
- Review of materials and resources.
- Schemes of work.
- Self-appraisals and assessments.
- Students' learning agendas.
- Submissions – course or others.
- Supervisor's observations and reports.
- Trainees' Report.
- Trainee/tutor profiling sessions.
- Training programmes – teaching and support materials and learning strategies.
- Video-tape recordings of tutor with trainees at work.
- Work-based assignments and projects.

Figure 7.1 Checklist of supporting evidence

Diaries

A **training diary** is a personal record of daily events such as work experience, off-the-job learning, appointments, problems encountered and overcome, reviews and observations. It can also be used as a record of training activities.

During a specific period entries might include detail of:

- The type of work undertaken.
- Working skills learned.
- Other knowledge and skills learned.
- Tools, machines, equipment and other resources used.
- Other workplace-related tasks where knowledge and skills gained and tools and equipment could be used.
- Outside work uses of newly acquired competence.
- Quality of work produced and processes involved.
- Attitudes of supervisors and other workers towards the person compiling the diary.
- Who benefitted from the work outcomes.
- How the type of work carried out has helped with learning and understanding of related performance criteria.
- What the next move should be.

Reflection is important and the diary is helpful when recalling experiences during reviews and discussions with the trainer or assessor during formative and summative assessments leading to accreditation. It provides a means of recording feedback and notes of discussions with the assessor.

When used as a basis for self-assessment the diary provides an opportunity for reflection and identification of how training skills and opportunities might be improved.

> **Several meetings with the assessor will be needed. Summative assessment will result in the accreditation of competence against performance criteria that make up an element of competence.**

Log books

Log books may be used to:

- Provide a record of the training received.
- Provide a source of reference which may be of use later in the trainee's career.
- Help develop written communication skills and express understanding of work performed.
- Provide the training supervisor with a means of assessing the trainee's progress and achievements.

The Lead Body representative may also need to examine the log book, together with completed skill and training specifications and records of progress before awards may be made. It is the trainee's responsibility to record details of tasks carried out in the log book and keep it up-to-date. Entries should be made regularly and examined and initialled by the workplace trainer or supervisor. The work will be checked by the supervisor using performance criteria to ensure that the trainee has reached the required standard of skill.

Job numbers should be entered in the training specification against the item covered. This enables an assessor to validate performance against the job. The two specimen entries shown in Figure 7.2 are examples of production and maintenance type tasks. Entry 1 is related to turning skills and includes reference to work standards and safety precautions. Entry 2 refers to electronic equipment wiring and assembly and is an assessed Phase Test.[6]

Case study
Case studies are records of real-life situations involving trainees or other members of staff. The study may be presented in the form of a written, tape recorded or videoed account of some incident or series of incidents. When used with the client's permission to record counselling or guidance sessions the nature of involvement would be recorded with notes of process outcomes, referrals, advice given, support offered and reviewing procedure adopted.

Due to the sensitive nature of some counselling sessions and the need to preserve confidentiality it will not always be possible to video a candidate in action. This is where the written or tape recorded case study can be used to good effect referring to the client as Mr, Ms or Mrs X.

Assessors will refer to case study content and will establish how the study was developed, managed and evaluated. Features of the study and outcomes will be reviewed and outcomes discussed.

Practical work
Work-based learning is gaining knowledge of some work role and acquiring skill through practising work-related activities. Knowledge can result from a structured learning programme and also by experience. Where possible, tasks, work content and experience should be adjusted to suit the needs of trainees as well as fitting in with work-provider needs. Work experience should be integrated with off-the-job training provision. Outcomes should be recorded in terms of what it is that the trainees can do and how they performed against prescribed performance criteria.

Practical work and the preparation for it can yield many kinds of evidence. Some kinds of associated evidence are listed in Figure 7.1, a checklist of supporting evidence.

Work-based projects
Work-based projects can be structured around work activities that are carried out in a commercial or industrial environment. The design of projects is negotiated with employers, trainers and 'off-the-job' providers, with the learner at the focal point of attention and interest. Trainees will obtain first-hand experience of how a business operates and will: develop enterprise skills; improve ability to communicate, think and solve problems; set and achieve goals; work in groups and realise the value of team spirit; identify creative potential and recognise previously unrecognised skills. All of this work-related experience will serve to develop their sense of responsibility and promote greater self-confidence. It will tend to further their personal career development. Learning opportunities and work-role combine to produce results that are relevant and useful to the trainee and to the work provider. Some of the outcomes will normally lead to the accreditation of elements of competence.

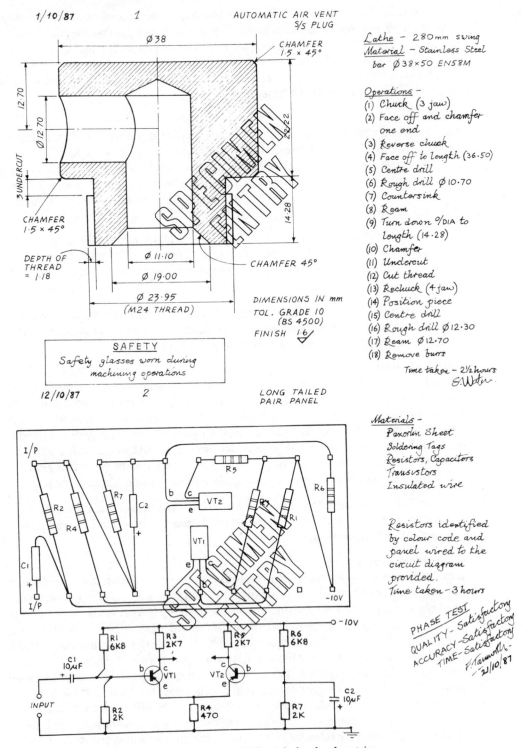

Figure 7.2 Sample log book entries

Source: The Engineering Training Log Book (MS02) published by EITB Publications, Stockport[6]

The candidate will need to show that work-based project aims and objectives negotiated with trainees are valid and that they relate to training programme content.

Does the project:
- Contain aims that relate to the training programme?
- Specify performance criteria?
- Integrate essential skills within vocational context?
- Provide opportunities for trainee to learn underpinning knowledge relating to skills and competence sought?
- Encourage quality assurance awareness?
- Allow for self-assessment and review?
- Provide for the feedback of outcomes to Employer and Assessor?
- Provide for monitoring and evaluation of process and outcomes?
- Give opportunities for amendment to suit changing needs of learners?
- Lead to achievement of competence?
- Serve as evidence in support of claims to competence?

Figure 7.3 Work-based project checklist

Observation

Micro-training sessions recorded on video provide excellent feedback on performance to assessor, candidate and trainees. This evidence is an invaluable source of back-up to 'live' demonstrations observed by the assessor.

> The assessor will need to observe the candidate at work. Trainers seeking accreditation of competences will need to be in routine day-to-day contact with their trainees and other staff. They should be performing normally without having made special arrangements simply because the assessor will be in attendance.

> Trainees seeking accreditation of competence will need to be working with clients or other trainees and members of the work force. There should be no 'stage-managed' performance on a 'one-off' basis. This would be invalid and the trained assessor would be quick to spot the charade.

Mentors

A 'mentor' is a fellow worker or friend. A person who has already been through the assessment and accreditation process and who can offer advice.

Mentors will often be in daily contact with candidates who are preparing for assessment and hence will be on hand to give support should this be needed. They are probably the best people to provide sound counselling and guidance as they will have shared the same sort of experiences, worries and problems met by potential candidates.

> The assessor will need to have access to mentors if they are to serve as a source of 'evidence' as to the candidate's ability to perform competently at the workplace.

Triangulation

A useful method of assessing claims for accreditation of competence is the method of **triangulation**. This method allows several interpretations of the same performance to be offered by a number of observers. The value of this approach lies in the possible combinations:

- assessor/candidate/trainee
- assessor/candidate/mentor
- assessor/candidate/countersigning officer
- assessor/candidate/other candidate model.

Assessing underpinning knowledge and skills

Knowledge-based assessment

It has been suggested that in order to be competent, a person must have the ability to successfully perform occupational work or work-related activities and to demonstrate the skills, knowledge and understanding that underpin performance in employment.

The assessment of knowledge and understanding is not always an easy matter to deal with. While **multiple choice tests** and **computers** can be used to reliably test specific elements of **knowledge**, assessing less well-defined **process skills** will probably take much longer and involve subjective value judgements.

The performance of employment-related work activities in the workplace involves different degrees of complexity of thinking. Skilled working embraces many levels of thought, concentration, reasoning and imagination.

> The assessor will need to be able to assess knowledge and understanding at several levels but in each instance only as far as the current performance criteria and assessment requirements are concerned.

In some instances there will be an emphasis on **remembering** facts without the need to understand what is **recalled**. But at an elementary level of understanding candidates would also need to be able to explain what they are doing when using recalled information.

When it comes to drawing on knowledge of a given concept and relating what is known to a different but somewhat similar situation there could be problems for the candidates. Being able to correctly apply basic principles calls for a higher level of understanding.

When given a problem candidates begin to think about it and will turn it over in their minds. While doing this they will probably try to break down the problem into its basic elements. To be able to do this requires a yet higher level of thinking – that of **analysing**. The candidates will, however, need to sort out the bits and pieces and bring to bear knowledge of many concepts and much experience in order to come up with a feasible solution. This level of thinking is called **synthesising** and is applied to many instances of planning work procedures.

Probably the highest level of thinking and understanding takes place when **evaluating**. This involves making judgements about the value or worth of a proposed solution, appraisal or comparison. It also operates when monitoring the quality of work processes and products in order to check that performance meets with the employer's standards.

> **The assessor will need to establish the degree of knowledge and understanding underpinning the performance of employment-related work activities. This could involve the assessment of the candidate's knowledge and thinking ranging from simple recall to evaluation.**
>
> **When assessing understanding the assessor will often use the method of guided discussion based on a series of well-thought-out probing questions.**

In the case of prior learning, candidates who have skills and knowledge gained from employment and life experience will have collected and assembled a portfolio of evidence to support their claims of achievement. Before seeking an assessment session each candidate will need to have learned, absorbed and thoroughly understood the information and procedures contained within their portfolio.

> **The assessor will take into consideration evidence held in the portfolio, NROVA or NRA but may also require the candidate to undertake written, oral or practical assessment tasks before being willing or able to confirm achievement claimed.**

Skills-based assessment

Skills may be joined together in a variety of ways in order to perform a **task**. As tasks involved in the day-to-day **work role** of a person are many and varied then it follows that a competent worker needs to own and demonstrate many different skills.

The task analysis given in Figure 7.4 that covers the operations, skills and complementary knowledge involved in painting a wall could be used for assessment purposes. Unlike the procedure for administering an injection given in Figure 4.3, which involves a sequence of well-defined actions, the painting task may be approached in a number of different ways. The important feature being the listed skills that together with complementary knowledge helps the trainer when planning and delivering training. It also helps the assessor to focus on key features of the demonstration and to frame subsequent questions when confirming underpinning knowledge.

Using the **NVQ Assessment Model** reproduced in Figure 7.5 allows for the assessment of **performance-related** evidence of competence as well as essential **underpinning knowledge**. It can be seen that the model embraces several different methods of collecting evidence of skill ownership:

– The method of **natural observation** in the workplace where the assessor quietly watches routine and complex activities and forms an objective opinion (or tries hard to assess) whether or not the candidate is performing to the level specified in the performance criteria.

Operation	Skill	Complementary knowledge
Preparation		
Inspect wall	Observation and recording	Identification of defects
Assemble tools and equipment	Lifting and transporting	What is needed
Repoint brickwork	Mixing mortar Handling trowel	Sand/cement ratio Form of pointing
or		
Repair rendering	Hacking defective surface Filling cracks Using chisel and club hammer Handling float Scratching-up Levelling surface	Selecting tools Exterior grade filler Keying for final coat
Remove mould, moss or algae	Mixing and applying wash	Fungicide wash Sterilisation features
Remove flaking paint	Using of scraper and wire brush	Correct tools
Remove powder from surface	Using masonry cleaning brush	Stiff-bristled brush needed
Mask off window frames and drainpipes. Cover paths, etc.	Applying masking tape Laying out plastic sheet	Risk of splashing
Apply stabilising solution	Applying solution	Binding characteristics of solution
Measure-up areas to be painted	Measuring areas with steel tape Checking spreading rate Calculating paint needed	Reading dimensions Numeracy
Obtain paint		Batch numbers for uniformity of colour
Performing Work		
Positioning ladder	Lashing and securing	Ladder drill Location and easy reach Support
Fix buckets and attachments	Attaching to ladder	Wire hooks and amount of paint in bucket
Select roller and brushes	Inspecting condition Using rollers and brushes	Coverage and loaded weight
Apply paint	Coating wall to standard required Starting in right place Blending edges	Working in sections Knowing where to start Before paint dries
Final inspection	Checking completeness and assessing quality	Specification and contract requirements
Cleaning-up		
Clean brushes and equipment	Cleaning and rinsing equipment	Cleaners and their application
Recover, inspect and stow equipment	Checking condition	

Note: Eye protection and safety equipment should be worn in accordance with The Health and Safety at Work Act (1974) and Company policies.

Each operation should be monitored and assessed for quality and correctness.

Figure 7.4 Task analysis – painting a wall

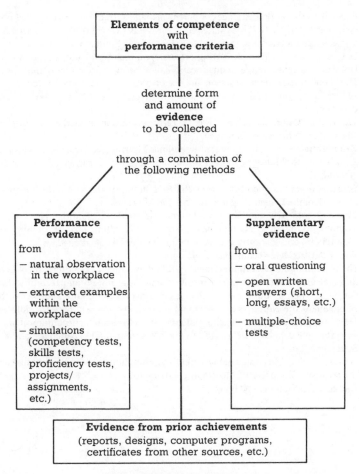

Figure 7.5 NVQ assessment model

- The method of **extracting examples** from the workplace where **products** are examined and the processes and skills involved in their production are reviewed and questions designed to confirm competence claimed are asked.
- The method of observing, reviewing and assessing **simulations** in the form of **competency tests, skills tests, proficiency tests, work-based projects and assignments** and the like.

Using a combination of the methods outlined above together with supplementary evidence gathered from prior achievements and knowledge-based assessments, the assessor will be able to accredit achievement against performance criteria or elements of competence.

Notes

1   The City & Guilds of London Institute's 7281 Series comprises a number of competence-based awards for skills assessors, vocational trainers and assessors, APL advisers, internal verifiers and external verifiers. The qualifications are based upon Training and Development Lead Body (TDLB) Standards and most of the units are in the NVQ Level Three in Training and Development which is

relevant to the work of staff development managers, training providers and other human resource developers. The C&G 7281 awards build on the earlier C&G 929 series which replaced a trainer/assessor qualification often referred to as the 'WTAA'. Similar new awards are offered by Pitman, RSA, LCC and other bodies representing professional, technical, craft, clerical and service occupations. Holders of the new range of qualifications will be qualified to train and assess others.

These registered trainer/assessors may be operating in the field of government sponsored training such as Employment Training and other initiatives, or they may be working in any area of industry or commerce.

The HCTC 'CaterBase' scheme was an early innovation in workplace assessment of competence where such skills were demanded.

2 **Experiential learning** is defined as: 'open-ended learning activities incorporating a range of skill and knowledge demands, the opportunities for developing particular capacities not being clearly determined'.

Source: *Developing social and life skills* FEU London 1980 (see: *A guide to work based learning terms* FESC, Coombe Lodge, Blagdon, Bristol 1989 © HMSO.)

3 **Informal evidence** may include: letters and testimonials from past and present employers, assignments, reports, photographs, certificates of attendance at training events, courses and conferences, and anything else that cannot be directly accredited.

4 The NROVA is described on page 164.

5 The **National Record of Achievement (NRA)** draws together information obtained from formal and informal assessment and is the result of planning, review and recording between student and teachers. When a young person changes or leaves school, enters further or higher education or employment the NRA acts as a **personal summary** of a young person's skills and abilities.

The NRA contains records of achievements within the school curriculum, qualifications and credits, an employment history, details of other achievements and experiences, and a 'Student's Personal Statement'.

Source: 'National Record of Achievement – Information for Schools and Colleges', The Employment Department, Group N705, Moorfoot, February 1991.

6 Source: EITB Training Log Book.

CHAPTER EIGHT

ASSESSING COMPETENCE

Chapter coverage

Qualifications
Vocational qualifications
National Vocational Qualifications (NVQs)
Terminology
Occupational competence
Assessing and recording competence
Assessing and accrediting NVQs and SVQs
Role of assessor
Role models
TECs and LECs
Modes of assessment
Assessment in the workplace
Designing assessment procedures
Life experience credits
Assessing candidates
Workplace training and assessment
How to assess competence
The assessor in action
Preparing to assess
Direct observation
Safeguarding standards
Reviewing portfolio of evidence
Collecting evidence
Selecting evidence
The candidate in action
Barriers
Attitudes
Guided discussion
Skills testing
Trial by pre-test
Test administration
Skilled performance
Certification
RTITB skills testing

Qualifications

Vocational qualifications

A **vocation** is a specified occupation, profession or trade. The word vocation is sometimes used to describe a calling or urge to follow a certain career or to do a particular job. **Vocational guidance** may be provided by the Careers Service or by trained interviewers who may be able to help people find out what kind of work may best suit them. Psychological tests can help get suitable people into vacant jobs.

Working out what would best suit someone is fine but an employer will need to be fairly sure that the applicant can do the job available before taking them on. They will want to know what knowledge, skills and experience the person has. They will want some kind of proof. This is where vocational qualifications can come in handy.

A **vocational qualification** is a statement of competence befitting the employment concerned. Vocational qualifications come in many forms and awards have been made by over 300 bodies including the City and Guilds of London Institute (CGLI) – an examining body for technical and craft skills. Others who award vocational qualifications include: the Royal Society of Arts (RSA), the Business and Technician Education Council (BTEC), the Scottish Vocational Education Council (SCOTVEC) and industrial and commercial training bodies such as the Construction Industry Training Board, Hairdressing Training Board and Hotel & Catering Training Company and the London Chamber of Commerce and Industry Examinations Board.

A need to rationalise qualifications

Before 1990 in the United Kingdom there was a very wide range of qualifications in use. Employers were confused when confronted with application forms giving details of certification and qualifications from schools, colleges, HM Services and establishments overseas. On top of that there seemed often not to be any connection between what certificates implied the holder could do and what the person could actually do in a working situation!

Little or no credit was given for prior learning that had been achieved in day-to-day working or in domestic situations. 'Doing' skills described during interviews without back-up evidence counted for very little, neither did accounts of what applicants claimed went on in their firm.

Book learning was valued more than work experience or the application of skills and knowledge in a real world situation on the shop floor. Now, at long last, all that has changed for the better. The ability to apply skills in the workplace and to demonstrate occupational competence is valued.

National Vocational Qualifications (NVQs)

In 1986 it was publicly recognised that something needed to be done quickly to sort out the qualifications mess. With this in mind, the Government established **The National Council for Vocational Qualifications (NCVQ)**.

The Council quickly realised that the existing system of qualifications needed to be rationalised, that is, to be made more straightforward and acceptable by all employers across the nation and hopefully within the European Community (EC).

They also saw that the best place for the demonstration and assessment of skills and knowledge is the workplace, where performance 'on-the-job' can be evaluated and accredited.

National standards for each job competence or skill are being certificated in the system of **National Vocational Qualifications (NVQs)**. An NVQ framework has been created covering all occupations and significant areas of employment. The main features of NVQs are that they are **employment-led**, **competence-based** and logically arranged in **levels**. Awards show what it is that the owner actually can do and to what standard. **Profiles of competences** are now being issued by a wide range of educational and training establishments and employers now understand and accept NVQs as valid evidence of competence.

Employment and promotion prospects are improved and status is given to those who hold these awards. The NVQs are recognised within whole industries and not just locally. It is these pieces of paper, the proof of demonstrated and accredited competence, that help an employer decide whether or not you will get the job.

Through the National Certificate, the major certifying body in Scotland is SCOTVEC.

The NVQ Database
Each year more than 150 bodies award several million vocational qualifications covering different occupational areas and levels of competence. With such a range to choose from the task of career planning is not easy. Choosing the right qualification to pursue that matches an individual's need can be facilitated by having recourse to the **NVQ Database**.

The Database provides details of the components, structure, level and content of each qualification and when accessed provides a valuable source of up-to-date information to learners, study counsellors and training providers.

Using the Database
The software which runs on IBM PCs or 100 per cent compatibles operating under MS-DOS Version 2.11 or later is user-friendly and information may be accessed in four ways:
- by classification according to industry, occupational training category and subject
- by NVQ level
- by Awarding Body
- by title of qualification.

Methods of assessment of competence may also be accessed.

Other developments planned included automatic links to training opportunity databases, access to career advice and training planning facilities and details of local training provision.

The NCVQ provide information about the Database.

Terminology

Competence

Being **competent** is being capable. To be competent a person needs to have sufficient and suitable skill, knowledge and experience to consistently perform to specified standards the work related to role or occupation. **Competence** is the name given to the state of being legally competent or qualified to carry out your chosen work. A surgeon would be competent and qualified to operate whereas a butcher would probably not be.

Being able to demonstrate skills in a single instance does not necessarily mean that skilful working could be maintained continuously or from time to time over a long period. Being competent requires a person to be more than someone who can put on a well-rehearsed display of behaviour. It involves owning skills and being able to transfer them to many other situations. In other words it calls for flexibility and adaptability at work, an aptitude for planning of work and problem-solving and for using those occupational skills needed to do the job.

NVQs are certified statements of units of competence that have been demonstrated at the right standard in a given occupation.

Occupational competence

Four main features of **occupational competence** to be assessed are:
- personal effectiveness
- competence in a range of occupational skills
- competence in a range of transferable core skills
- ability to transfer knowledge, skill and experience to novel situations.

Being **personally effective** is being able to get things done properly and without a lot of fuss. It embraces the ability to successfully deal with clients' needs and to interact well with the many grades of staff employed in the workplace. It involves being productive and working efficiently. Being able to solve problems, getting yourself organised, creating a good impression and getting results of the right quality in a reasonable time – these are the outcomes of an effective person.

Occupational skills are the skills, standards and practices associated with a particular occupation or job whereas vocational area skills are skills that have been picked up by sampling general areas of training, work experience or other employments.

Being competent in **transferable core skills** means that a person would have knowledge, skill and experience in:
- language (reading, writing, speaking and listening)
- numeracy (calculation, measurement, graphical work and using tables of data)
- manipulative dexterity (handskills, picking and placing, moving things around)
- problem-solving
- interpersonal relations
- computer literacy (being able to use computers – not necessarily as an ace brain would)

Transfer is a term relating to applying knowledge or skills that learners bring with them to a new learning situation or to their work. Experience gained during past encounters can be used to speed things up.

Statement of competence

Statements of competence form the basis from which assessment procedures, recording and certification are drawn. The statements list units that describe elements of competence, with schedules specifying performance criteria. They include any behaviour, conditions and standards that must be met when demonstrating the competence being assessed.

Unit of competence

A **unit of competence** is the smallest sub-division of a key area of work that can be separately certificated as a credit towards the award of an NVQ. Each unit is split up into a number of **elements of competence** each of which will have at least one **performance criterion**.

Programmes of training leading to NVQs will be based on learning objectives derived from statements of competence.

Element of competence

An **element of competence** is a subdivision of a unit of competence. It is the smallest portion of competence that can be achieved toward the award of an NVQ. Each element will be stated in behavioural terms with performance criteria clearly specifying standards to be achieved and any conditions under which the demonstration will take place.

Performance criteria

Successful achievement of an element of competence will be recognised when the candidate meets the standard given in clearly stated **performance criteria**.

Emphasis should be placed on the 'performance' requirements of employment when assessors are assessing the candidate's demonstration of achievement.

Lead Industry Body (LIB)

The **Lead Industry Body** is a group formed to represent an occupational family, a sector of industry or commerce or a specific area of employment. It is required to work out and list acceptable competences and performance standards for those working in an assortment of jobs, firms and situations within the occupational area.

Some Lead Bodies together with related training organisations examine the skill and training requirements of a particular subdivision of industry or commerce and monitor provision of resources for meeting the needs revealed.

Assessing and recording competence

Assessing and accrediting NVQs and SVQs

A systematic approach similar to that shown in Figure 8.1 will be needed for assessing achievement. The process normally adopted involves the trainee, student, learner or other person seeking confirmation of achievement described as the candidate, the teacher or trainer providing training, the assessor or observer carrying out the assessment and a countersigning officer validating the maintenance of standards.

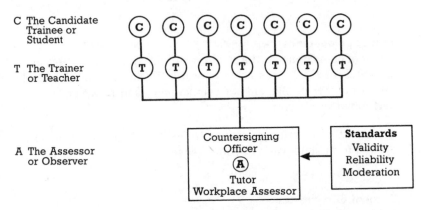

Figure 8.1 Assessing and accrediting NVQs and SVQs

Role of assessor

Assessors and workplace trainers will probably perceive their roles differently. Personality traits of individuals will vary considerably as will workplace conditions, so that a number of different styles will be evident. There is no hard and fast role model to adopt but it has been suggested that a formative and supportive role often promotes co-operation and collaboration between parties to the assessment process.

Role models	
Recommended	*Not recommended*
Advisor	Cross-examiner
Colleague	Detective
Counsellor – giving advice and help	Inquisitor
Consultant	Interrogator
Evaluator	Know-all
Mentor	Martinet
	Punisher
	Teller

Figure 8.2 Role models

To:
- Arrange a meeting with candidates for the purpose of advising and negotiating proposals for the accreditation of their skills.
- Establish rapport and build supportive relationships with candidates and others involved at the workplace, college or school.
- Maintain contact with other assessors and with candidates and employers.
- Promote good working practices and help to maintain occupational standards.
- Assist candidates by helping to arrange opportunities to achieve competences not available within their own workplace.
- Agree and communicate minimum standards in respect of performance criteria for each competence claimed by candidates.
- Link performance criteria to the method of assessing competence.
- Confirm existence of a skill or competence that has been demonstrated on a 'can-do' basis related to performance criteria.
- Debrief candidates after assessment and help them to build confidence and better understand their achievements.
- Monitor accreditation and certification process where applicable.

Figure 8.3 Role of assessor

TECs and LECs

In 1993 there were 82 employer-led Training and Enterprise Councils (TECs) in England and Wales and 22 Local Enterprise Companies (LECs) in Scotland. The TECs and LECs brought together managers of enterprise – people from industry, commerce, education and the Civil Service, who by using initiative and in consultation with others, would move the population closer to the Government's goal of a '**competent society**'. A highly skilled workforce that could: 'compete with the best and win' being the ultimate objective.

The TECs and LECs in cooperation with employers and training providers are able to provide training opportunities designed to meet identified national and local needs. The outcome of resulting training is often assessed and certificated to NVQ or SVQ standards.

By defining the skills, knowledge and understanding needed to successfully perform in an occupation, representatives of industry contribute directly to developing training and qualifications that reflect the needs of employment.

Benefit is cascaded using the link between training and certification provided through NVQ and SVQ awarding bodies. Flexibility in training provided within this qualification framework enables members of the workforce to realise their full potential and to learn in new ways.

Modes of assessment

The type of assessment method used will be matched to the particular competence being accredited. The guiding factor will be the need to properly validate the candidate's claim to ownership of given elements of competence.

Confirmation of competence may derive from a mixture of: **assessed prior achievement**, **observation of performance** at work or in simulations, and **supplementary evidence** such as written work and tests or face-to-face question and answer sessions.

Assessors will need to be able to determine just what it is that defines competence in a certain instance. There will often be a need for candidates to supplement demonstrations of performance with technical or other knowledge and an understanding of underlying principles or reasons for doing things the way they are done.

Assessing competence for NVQs

Assessment outcomes will be based on the performance requirement specified in the statement of competence. Separate units of competence or performance will be assessed and open access to accreditation and certification will be made available.

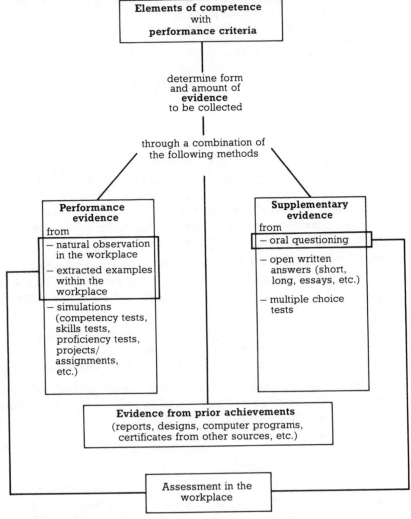

*Figure 8.4 Assessment in the workplace using the NVQ assessment model

*Assessment in the workplace should include live observation supported where necessary by guided discussion with the candidate and others. Examination of products and supportive documentation may also be needed.

The duration, manner and way of learning and training should be flexible and there should be no fixed period of study nor set attendance at college or elsewhere leading to qualification. Learning will be encouraged and validated both '**on-the-job**' in association with employers and '**off-the-job**' in colleges or with other training providers.

If a person can provide evidence of prior achievement and performance at the right standard then units of competence should be awarded.

> **Methods of assessing competence will need to be tailored to enable accumulation of units to occur and should embrace prior achievement and all relevant elements of performance at work.**

Unlike the old style of course structure where it could take several years for a person to qualify for the award of a certificate, within NVQ and SVQ, provision is made for the assessment and recording of separate units of competence. Repeating all subjects because someone has 'failed' the course is now virtually a thing of the past.

Assessment in the workplace

Performance-based assessment involves candidates in demonstrating competence when working.

'In general terms, **assessment in the workplace** means the collection (and evaluation) of evidence on the performance of an individual against agreed objectives and criteria, carried out within workplace premises.'[1]

This statement is beyond doubt and Miller gives examples of supportive quotations:

- 'Wherever feasible, having due regard to safety and cost, the basis of assessment should be performance in the workplace.[2]
- 'The ability of an individual to perform in the work role is the primary requirement of an NVQ and this should be reflected in the assessment . . . As a general rule assessment of performance in the course of normal work offers the most natural form of evidence of competence and has several advantages, both technical and economic.[3]

When it is not possible to gain access to the workplace for diagnosis of training need or assessment and accreditation procedures an alternative is to negotiate the use of further education and training providers' facilities. Counselling staff and work-based learning opportunities can be found in most colleges. Many have hairdressing and beauty therapy salons, food preparation and food service operations, travel and tourism agencies, training offices and information technology centres, community caring and special needs units, construction training and assessment centres and agricultural, horticultural and floristry units located on working farms. It has been found that in many instances college resources are more up-to-date than those found in some commercial enterprises.

Assessing and recording achievement

A systematic approach for ensuring that the prescribed assessment procedure is followed should be adopted.

> Assessors should be in day-to-day contact with candidates and their own skills and knowledge should be continuously updated.
>
> Where more than one assessor is involved in accrediting competence a uniform standard needs to be maintained. With this in mind it will be necessary for those concerned to meet regularly in order to monitor process and outcomes. The candidates will expect that a fair and reliable system is in use.

Competence-based accreditation systems should be flexible and allow assessment of achievement to take place 'in-house' or 'off-site' depending on circumstances.

> The workplace assessor will normally accredit skills 'in-house' with external validation provided either by an Accredited Centre or using national moderation. In some cases an assessor from an examining body will be used. Alternatively, a consultant or outsider with extensive skill or knowledge in a particular field, who is also a qualified workplace assessor, will undertake the assessment. Further education staff qualified as assessors may be used 'off-site' or in simulated work experience situations.

Designing assessment procedures

Responsibility for the design, quality, validity and reliability of assessment leading to certification of units of competence will rest with the awarding body or their appointed agent.

> Assessors will need to satisfy themselves about the quality of the assessment system to be used by the training providers and their staff.
>
> Assessment of achievement will be made using evidence collected that confirms performance 'in-line' with criteria that clearly specify what is to be demonstrated and to what standard.
>
> It is also necessary to maintain an assessment record showing all achievement in occupational training.

Problems encountered

Experience may be limited and candidates' performances inhibited when either oral or multiple choice knowledge tests are thought to be key parts of an assessment. The realism and benefits to be derived from exploring the competence from a number of practical and theoretical viewpoints may be lost. Teachers and trainers may offer only a limited and controlled training content. Rote learning that stresses recall and memory only and thereby limits understanding, may be resorted to. The preparation of model answers in anticipation of the right questions being asked may be recommended to anxious learners by trainers who may feel that they need to get results.

Formative and summative assessments

Modern training practice is more client-centred than in the past. Assessments and reviews often take the form of reflecting on training outcomes during subsequent counselling and guidance sessions and debriefings. Democratically agreed achievements are then recorded on **profiles** or **competence checklists**.

Informal assessment

Informal assessment is giving feedback needed by trainees so that they may be able to assess the effectiveness of their own performances. This will include discussion about strengths and weaknesses and what they will need to do in order to master the skill and knowledge that is needed to meet performance criteria.

Formative assessment

Formative assessment is an ongoing process designed to improve training and learning by reviewing outcomes and progress. Feeding back to the training provider information from assessments or negotiations with trainees enables problems to be overcome.

Summative assessment

A summative assessment is made at the end of a training programme in order to determine the overall effectiveness of training and learning outcomes. It can also be used during the **assessment of competence**.

Life experience credits

Experiential learning is defined as: 'learning through experience rather than through study or formal instruction'.[4]

The assessment stages specified by Norman Evans[5] are:

- identify 'life experience learning' by allowing learner to reflect on experience and review outcomes with accreditor
- relate elements of such learning to course objectives
- verify behaviour using 'can do' evidence of learning
- measure degree of learning
- evaluate against competence objective or other standard
- accredit and record previous learning

The **draft specification** given in Figure 8.5 is intended only as an aid to discussion and identification of relevant experience during the reflection-and-review session.

What to assess	How learned	Evidence of learning	How assessed	Accredited by

Figure 8.5 Draft specification – recognising 'life experience' credits

Assessing candidates

Workplace training and assessment

What is involved?

Employees can benefit from working towards clear goals specified in competence objectives, from meeting performance criteria and from understanding what is involved in achieving a finished job of the right quality.

Before undertaking training, trainees will need to get a clear picture of what it is that they must be able to do to become competent. They will need to accurately interpret related performance criteria. They will need to know what knowledge and skill to apply to the situation and how to acquire it.

Skilled performance demonstrated in the workplace by a competent person provides a realistic standard for trainees to strive for. Trainees should be encouraged to aim for this standard and to monitor their own achievement against the specified criteria throughout their course of training and later while building on the skills during normal working.

Before the assessment session commences, trainees seeking accreditation will need to be quite sure of what procedures and process will be involved. They will need a little time to settle down and let information given by the trainer/assessor sink in. Time should be allowed for questions and clarification. The trainees should feel at ease and well-disposed to the task and to the trainer/assessor before they need to demonstrate achievement of the competence in question.

> **The assessor will need to be convinced that before the workplace trainer/assessor's assessment of trainee's achievement begins they have succeeded in putting at ease those seeking accreditation.**

> **Trainees will need to know what is involved in the assessment. Information given by the workplace trainer/assessor will be assessed for accuracy and clarity. Explanations and instructions given should be unambiguous.**

> **The assessor could ask those being assessed to describe their interpretation of the performance criteria and particularly the standards specified.**

Why achieve?

The main incentives for building on existing skills and developing new ones are the resulting opportunities for enhancing job satisfaction and seeking career progression.

The more interested workers become in having their knowledge, skills and achievements formally recognised by the award of NVQ, SVQ or other qualifications, the more attention they will devote to the matter. If they are to learn new things and gain new skills, the accreditation of competence in their job can serve as a powerful motivator.

There are many and varied motives for seeking to achieve new competences. In some cases competence in the workplace may lead to a better job or, say, the opportunity to work and travel abroad. A waitress may be given her own workstation. Doing a task faster, more effectively and expertly could lead to better pay, better tips or praise and encouragement from employers and clients. There are also many private reasons for learning that relate to challenge and the need to master things. Often these things are known only to the learner. They have been described as **intrinsic motivators**.

If the effort involved in collecting evidence of achievement and gaining useful qualifications can be seen to improve future prospects then people will be more likely to overcome any resistance and take the plunge.

> **The assessor will confirm that training sessions and related performance criteria are designed to form a progressive sequence of learning opportunities compatible with the learners' action plans.**

When should assessment take place?
When is the best time for assessment? This will depend on individual circumstances. In a busy kitchen perhaps a less hectic time of day might be better than during peak service times. Some days of the week are quieter than others. Is there a best time? Probably not. Assessment sessions will need to be negotiated but outcomes should be reliable. It should not make a lot of difference to results if assessment had happened at a different time.

Assessment may take place at any time. **Prior learning** may be assessed as and when the need arises or during **induction and initial assessment**. New learning can be assessed during or on completion of training or after some learning experience, but preferably when demonstrating competence at work.

Continuous assessment is thought to have advantages over 'one-off' terminal examinations or trade tests. It is an on-going assessment of trainees throughout the entire training programme, in contrast to **terminal assessment** that takes place only at the conclusion of some courses. The purposes of continuous assessment outlined in the *IMS User's Guide* are:

- to encourage student involvement and motivation
- to monitor and provide feedback on progress
- to help in shaping the student's future learning on the scheme[6]

The aim of the vocational trainer is to provide the trainee with a profile of assessment that ranges over the whole set of training objectives or performance criteria and may also include information about unintended learning. This gives a better picture of overall performance. It indicates '**what the trainee "can do" or "has done"** ' rather than '**what the student knows how to do**'.

Finding the time to sort things out with the workplace trainer/assessor so that normal work activity is assessed rather than a one-off performance specially orchestrated for the assessment is likely to be valid and to yield reliable results.

> **The assessor will check to ensure that the candidate is ready for assessment and that action plans have been updated accordingly.**

Where to assess

The workplace is an excellent place to assess achievement. This is where the trainee normally works and where the right atmosphere exists. The smells, sounds, heat and lighting is that of the working environment, the pressures and stresses of work and other staff are there. It would probably make a difference if training and assessment takes place somewhere other than the workplace. Different results will be achieved. While simulated work experience is next best to the workplace, somehow both trainer and trainee feel a little uncomfortable knowing that they are acting out roles rather than getting involved in the real thing.

> Assessment should preferably take place in the workplace and be structured around units or elements of competence agreed with the candidate.

Who is involved?

The candidate concerned is the main player but the concept of training and accreditation of competence becomes a shared value among the workforce if positive and useful outcomes result.

Workers need to know what the accreditation of competence is all about, what's in it for them and how it can help them progress and develop fully their latent abilities. If candidates can be briefed carefully about preparing for the assessment and can come to realise that the process will be non-threatening, their attitude towards being assessed by a person from the same workshop, kitchen, office, salon or college will be more positive.

> Workplace trainers, assessors and countersigning officers hold the key to success – the ability to build trust and good relationships with the staff.

How to assess competence

Today a wider range of assessment methods is used than in the past. More assessment techniques are accepted as valid when assessing achievement in the workplace than was sometimes the case. Meeting candidates' personal needs is now becoming an even more important consideration than before. This calls for greater flexibility and the necessity to match method to individual need.

Methods such as the **informal observation and assessment** of candidates performing their day-to-day duties at the workplace are now accepted practice. **Self-assessment** where candidates are **learning by 'doing'** and are invited to assess their progress is encouraged. **Review of performance against criteria**, or some other form of instrument backed by discussion with the assessor, is now often used. In this way workplace activity and learning derived from experience is linked with assessment.

Sometimes, a more closely defined approach known as **structured assessment** is used. The candidate will perform set tasks at different levels of complexity and the assessor will assess each element of performance against specified criteria or checklists. Alternatively, the candidate will perform normally at the workplace and the assessor will assess outcomes against performance criteria. Ownership of underpinning knowledge and skill may become evident during the candidate's demonstration. If further confirmation is needed this can be negotiated afterwards during a logically structured review.

In some cases awarding bodies may require candidates to achieve an agreed standard when undertaking **standardised tests**. **Skills testing** is an example of this method of assessment.

> Foremost in the minds of candidates and assessors must be the duty to maintain quality, validity and reliability within any system of assessment and accreditation. These requirements are not easy to maintain due to the wide variety of skills to be assessed when candidates present their demonstrations.
>
> As accreditation confirms the existence of skills and gives credit for them, the methods agreed by assessor and candidate are critical if subsequent awards are to be credible.

Assessment model

A model that shows how the assessment of achievement against a set of performance criteria could be carried out is given in Figure 8.6. There is no one system that will meet every assessment requirement but many of the factors relating to the process and practice of assessing achievement are included in the model. Possible links between participants are shown.

It is well known that assessment is a collaborative activity. The candidate and assessor each has a different role and responsibility but depend upon mutual co-operation in order to carry out a satisfactory demonstration and assessment of achievement. Throughout the whole process there is a need to communicate, to negotiate, to support and to give and receive feedback.

The assessor in action

Preparing to assess

It is not possible to accredit elements of competence purely on the strength of candidates' claims that they 'know it', 'can do it' or 'have done it all before'. The candidate's knowledge, understanding and skill relating to the competence being assessed cannot be taken for granted. If it does not occur naturally in the **products** or through the **performance** provided as **outcome and process evidence**, it should be separately drawn out.

A number of things need to be sorted out with candidates before assessment of achievement can be undertaken. Some of these are listed in Figure 8.7.

> Assessors undertaking the assessments will need to liaise with the candidate and have worked through those items listed in Figure 8.7 before the actual assessment sessions can take place.

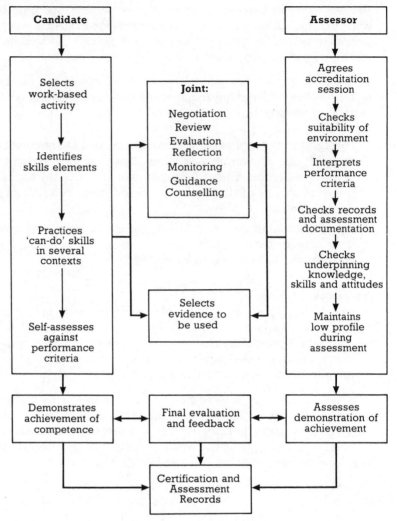

Figure 8.6 Assessment model

- Select check-listed skills to be accredited.
- Agree method of assessment for each element of competence.
- Agree frequency, duration, location and context of demonstration of achievement.
- Select and review evidence to support candidate's claim for accreditation of prior learning.
- Agree arrangements for the accreditation of all skills achieved by candidate.
- Plan a review and evaluation session to agree progress against performance criteria and to negotiate action plan.
- Arrange assessment sessions.
- Prepare to carry out actual demonstration and assessment of achievement.
- Plan form of review and feedback session.

Figure 8.7 Preparing for assessment

Negotiating assessment procedures

It would be unreasonable for an assessor to suddenly appear at a firm intending to assess some aspect of a person's performance at work. While it is desirable to assess competence under normal working conditions such an intention would be tactless and ill-conceived.

In the case of workplace staff seeking a recognised trainer qualification it would be useful for the assessor to arrange a preliminary meeting with each candidate. A suggested approach is shown in Figure 8.8.

The assessor will need to contact candidates registered for the Award and arrange a first meeting during which key features of the assessment process may be discussed. The meeting affords an opportunity to establish credentials and to give candidates confidence in the assessor's capability to fairly assess them. A sympathetic understanding attitude may also be established. Once the ice has been broken the assessment process may be explained and agreed.

In the case of workplace trainers and assessors, it is likely that the elements of competence to be demonstrated would be listed and that assessment would comprise a mix of performance-related activity and an evaluation of evidence. The roles of key participants in the assessment process, i.e. the candidate, the trainee and the assessor, would be clarified and then a programme of visits agreed.

An **assessment plan** giving details of elements to be assessed, target date and context for assessment, evidence to be presented and other relevant action agreed can be negotiated by candidate and assessor (see Figure 8.9). The form shown in Figure 8.10 can be used as a checklist during the assessment.

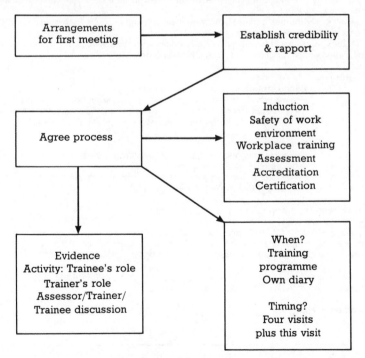

Figure 8.8 Preliminary meeting – assessor with workplace trainer

Vocational Assessor
Assessment Plan

WB&T

Walklin Books & Training

Candidate name: David Jon (Ben) McKaigg

Unit D32 Assess candidate performance

Element D323

Objective: To assess the Candidate's ability to collect and judge knowledge
evidence to support the inference of competent performance

Target date for assessment: 23 June 1994

Context for assessment:

Ben McKaigg will be in his normal work role, that of a Driving and Maintenance Instructor , Assessor and Examiner operating a training and assessment system in a realistic work environment within the Driving and Maintenance School.

Assessment methods:

In my earlier role of Staff Assessor I observed Ben McKaigg conducting oral questioning sessions while he was assessing candidates when he was achieving his C&G9293 and C&G9292 Awards. I monitored the appropriateness of the questions he asked by cross referencing content with the Candidate's assessment specifications. Ben and I will now reassess the related performance and APL evidence.
I will examine Ben's list of written assessment questions forming the basis of his oral questions put to the candidates.
Ben will justify the use of the checklisted questions and describe how his usage of the questions meets all the D323 Performance Criteria.
I will seek supplementary evidence of Ben's competence by asking him oral questions using my own checklisted written questions and judging his responses.

Evidence:

Performance:
Ben will provide written evidence relating to sessions that he conducted when he was using oral questions from a preset list and judging the candidate's responses.
Ben will also present records of assessor devised written questions.

Supplementary:
Ben will answer questions on the underpinning knowledge relevant to D323 (As listed in the assessment specification).
He will also explain how the assessment arrangements maximise access to candidate's according to their individual needs. [Pc (f)]

Other relevant information and action agreed:
Ben is claiming credit for prior achievement of Unit 32 (Elements D321, D322 & D324) and Unit 33 complete due to his C&G9293 and C&G9292 Awards recently obtained. He will present and discuss two sets of occupational area checklisted questions used by him during previous assessments observed by a qualified Staff Assessor when qualifying for his C&G9293 Award.

He will assemble his C&G7281/12 Evidence File using current evidence and relevant evidence previously presented (re:C&G9292/3 Awards).

Candidate signature: _____   **Assessor signature:** _____

Figure 8.9 Assessment plan

WB&T

Walkin Books & Training

Element Collect and judge knowledge evidence to support
D323   the inference of competent performance

Candidate _____

Performance criteria	Was this met? Yes No	Assessment method Observation Product	Comments
a) questions are selected to provide sufficient evidence to infer competent performance across the range	☐ ☐		
b) questions are justifiable in relation to potential performance	☐ ☐		
c) the inferences of competent performance can be justified	☐ ☐		
d) preset tests are correctly administered	☐ ☐		
e) questions used are clear and do not lead candidates	☐ ☐		
f) appropriate arrangements are made to maximise access for candidates according to their needs	☐ ☐		

Figure 8.10 Candidate assessment checklist

A range of assessment procedures may be suggested when the assessor contacts the candidate to agree assessment details. The candidate will be encouraged to put forward ideas of how best to demonstrate achievement while the assessor will already have available a basic checklist from which a mutually agreeable method might be chosen. If the assessor and candidate can agree the method so much the better.

Direct observation

It has been suggested that before starting an observation the assessor should agree with the candidate what is involved in doing the work and what will be assessed. What is happening during the assessment will govern the viewing position used by the assessor. In general it is recommended that a low profile should be adopted so that the assessor is as unobtrusive as possible.

In-company trainers normally give good notice of the proposed dates of assessment and agree main job responsibilities with the employee involved. While only those performance criteria relating to the claim for achievement of competence will be directly assessed, the trainer will be ever mindful of the need to maintain company specified standards.

> There can be no hard and fast rules for observing candidates at work since each occupational area will need a different approach that covers relevant features.

Observing cashiers

Observing a cashier at work provides an example of how the assessor might approach an assessment. In the case of a store, it would be essential for the candidate to adhere to company policies and procedures throughout the assessment. Customer care and service must be maintained at the highest level commensurate with the role.

Other features to be checked during the observation would be the candidate's dress and appearance, personal hygiene, usage of equipment in compliance with the Health and Safety at Work Act, 1974 and security of cash. The cash register and weighing scales must be operated efficiently in line with company policy and a sufficient knowledge of those commodities and produce sold by the company should be demonstrated.

> More specific criteria to be observed would include the candidate's skill and underpinning knowledge of 'front-end' or 'customer service point' tasks.

Bag packing procedures are an example. The assessor would check that the candidate had selected the correct size of bag for the item purchased. All soaps, powders and washing-up liquids should have been placed in one bag and not mixed with foodstuffs. Tops of bleach and detergent bottles should be tightened before packing. Fresh fish should be packed separately due to its strong smell. Red meat is packed apart from poultry. Bags should neither be over-filled nor too weighty. When packing bags both hands should be used. A framework should be formed using boxes and tins with glass and more fragile items placed in the centre for protection. Weight should be evenly distributed with delicate items on top. Strong brown paper bags may be offered to customers in place of plastic carrier bags and this practice is becoming more popular as the 'green revolution' spreads.

All these actions can readily be observed by the assessor.

Cheque handling is another example. Here the cashier will be observed carrying out set procedures when customers wish to pay by cheque. Visual checks should be demonstrated. Checks will include:

- cheque is payable to store
- dated correctly
- amount in words and figures agree
- unexpired cheque guarantee card produced
- cheque signed in cashier's presence
- signature on cheque and card agree
- alterations initialled.

Other competences that the cashier will be required to demonstrate include tasks such as till operating involving the use of 'hand on keyboard' and 'change selection and giving'. The trainee cashier may also be observed dealing with spoilage, damaged packaging or leakages; making customer refunds; cleaning the checkout and conveyors; using the intercom and operating procedures for calling the supervisor.

All of these operations may be observed by the assessor and evidence of underpinning knowledge determined by asking relevant questions.

Safeguarding standards

Personal hygiene and good housekeeping each play an important role in controlling health hazards in the workplace. Staff, such as checkout operators or cashiers who have direct contact with the public and who may be handling foodstuffs, have a duty to maintain the highest standards of cleanliness and personal presentation.

They should have a sufficient knowledge of the Sale of Goods Act and be able to take appropriate action in cases of customer inquiry or complaint. While at work and especially when using equipment at the checkout they will need to comply with the Health and Safety at Work Act, 1974, the Electricity at Work Regulations and other occupationally specific legislation.

Checkout operators are in a vulnerable position. They are probably the most important point of contact with shoppers and as such need to be seen to be safeguarding customers' interests as well as company standards.

The assessor will check with those seeking accreditation of competence their understanding of the importance of good housekeeping and hygiene to themselves, their employers and most importantly to the customers.

Candidates for assessment will need to be able to demonstrate safe use of equipment and approved switching 'on'/'off' procedures.

Workplace trainers and assessors will need to confirm that candidates are able to comply with current occupationally specific legislation.

Company trainers will check that cashier performance meets the standard set within store.

Reviewing portfolio of evidence

Collecting evidence

Knowing how to collect evidence is an important aspect of the candidate's preparation for accreditation. Evidence that could be provided in support of certification includes: a portfolio of experiences and related achievements, previously awarded certificates, assessments, testimonials, references and samples of work.

Selecting evidence

Strategies employed by assessors in order to identify skills could include:
- analysing with an individual, supporting evidence of competence or a record of learning from experience stated in performance terms
- arranging 'skill tasters' and accrediting those elements meeting performance criteria
- evaluating hobbies, interests and voluntary work carried on outside the company
- identifying strengths and resourcefulness by jointly reviewing with individuals their prior learning and experience.

The assessor will need to be able to identify and select evidence to be used when assessing an individual's achievement.

Reliability of evidence

The content of a candidate's portfolio of evidence should be valid and reliable. It should relate to the competence being claimed and the evidence should be **current**. Candidates will need to show that they are still competent and up-to-date.

Before accrediting a competence the assessor will need to be satisfied that supporting evidence produced by the candidate is authentic and not intended to mislead.

Assessors will review the candidate's portfolio of supporting evidence and are unlikely to take evidence submitted on its face value. The evidence will be challenged by asking systematic questions or by seeking confirmation from sources of evidence.

Indirect evidence

Indirect evidence is spoken or written evidence that cannot be validated by direct observation. Claims of expertise or skills exercised in previous employments may need to be confirmed by the employer concerned. The transferability of prior achievement to the performance against criteria being assessed would need to be established. Relevant documentation would also be evaluated.

Direct evidence

The **currency** of knowledge and skills can be proved by the candidates giving demonstrations with explanation of elements of competence claimed. Seeing is believing. Observing candidates' normal work routines while working alone or with other staff, backed by asking check questions, can bring to light evidence of understanding and competence. Similarly, evidence of achievement can result from reviewing with the candidate performance of work-related activities.

> **Assessors will assess the currency of evidence. They will challenge evidence of underlying principles and establish extent of the candidate's knowledge and understanding by asking questions and by observation.**

Where a candidate's capability does not meet the standards given in the performance criteria there will be a need for guidance. Discussion should centre on what action may be taken to promote progress towards achievement of the competence sought.

> **Correctly specified performance criteria are the key to assessment of competence. When assessing achievement only valid criteria should be used.**

> **The candidate will need to demonstrate the achievement of competence a number of times over a period of time. Each repetition is part of a formative process leading to the accreditation of achievement.**

> **The assessor of achievement must carry out reliable assessments.**

The candidate in action

Barriers

When people are in a state of mental distress or anxiety, assessing them in the workplace becomes difficult and can cause inconvenience and discomfort to all concerned. It is hard to deal with troublesome situations that may arise causing further worry, upset or annoyance. Every effort should be taken to avoid this kind of problem.

> **Anything that the assessor can do to reduce or relieve feelings of apprehension, embarrassment or distress caused by the impending assessment should be done.**

> **Workplace trainers, assessors and countersigning officers hold the key to success – the ability to build trust and good relationships with the staff.**

Attitudes

The candidates' attitudes toward the assessor will affect the way they perceive the assessment process. If the reader happens to have an assessor role try to put yourself in the place of those you will be observing. How would you feel? What kind of atmosphere do you promote? What is the general tone or mood of your contribution to the process?

If you are a candidate for accreditation of achievement what is your attitude towards someone reviewing your performance? Do you think you are being made to 'jump through hoops'? How do you feel about answering questions about your work? Can you accept advice, give and receive feedback or seek help and guidance?

All parties to the accreditation process will need to work at building a co-operative and supportive relationship.

Guided discussion

Active participation in a guided discussion about the achievement to be assessed is a good way of getting candidates to talk. The assessor and the candidate will learn something from one another. Each will have something to give and to get out of the session. Once the ice has been broken candidates will be more inclined to take the assessor through demonstrations of their achievements while telling and showing what they can do.

Some types of assessment demand that the candidate performs work normally without any contact with the assessor. If this is the case the assessor will remain unobtrusive and will not help, hinder or otherwise distract the candidate.

Assessors must be able to:
- **listen attentively**
- **think clearly**
- **summarise fairly**
- **express themselves impersonally**
- **avoid arguments.**

Candidates preparing for assessment will need to liaise with the assessor and have worked through those items listed in Figure 8.7, 'Preparing for assessment', before the actual assessment sessions take place.

Process skills and product skills will be assessed over a period of time in a range of contexts associated with daily work role.

Skills testing

Object of skills testing

Validation of competence is an important element of training. The object of **skills testing** is to allow candidates wishing to demonstrate the accomplishment of a skill or series of skills to do so under test conditions. The tests will enable manual proficiency involving cognitive and motor skills gained from training and experience to be assessed against performance criteria and validated by comparing performance with objective standards. Achievements are then certificated by approved awarding bodies.

Form of tests

Tests are normally practical in nature involving some form of physical or manipulative skills. Paper and pencil tests are also used but these are often restricted to **naming** or **identifying** tools or objects. Where equipment or tools are very large or too numerous to display, diagrams showing numbered tools would be provided together with a checklist of tools. The candidate would enter the numbers from the diagram against the checklisted tool names. In engineering, the same sort of test would be applied to naming such things as electrical components or locking and locating devices. Here, the numbered components would be fixed to a board and candidates would mark the number of the item on a checklist of components.

Test design

Test parameters are worked out and agreed with representatives of the occupational area concerned. Test authors would liaise with employers, training providers and competent staff working for the various concerns and a test specification would be worked out. It may be that it would be either too costly or too inconvenient to provide actual production or test specimens as test items. In such cases simulations would be used. In the case of spray painting, perhaps a roll of suitable paper could be substituted for, say, the side of a van. It would be possible to check the painted paper for runs, even coating and other features. Imperfections or faults could be detected reasonably well and it would not be necessary to provide large numbers of vans or metal sheets as test specimens.

Literacy and language

Literacy is the name given to the ability to read and write and to use language proficiently. With this in mind it becomes necessary to consider the likely level of spoken and written language available to the test user group. Allowance for those candidates who cannot read or write well or who have English as a second language must be made if the skills test is to yield reliable results across the entire client group.

It is the level of practical skill that is being tested and not the candidate's skill in translating into meaningful terms what is actually being said or written in the instructions or test material. Being proficient in knowledge of and usage of language should not be necessary for successfully completing the skills test. Using rhetoric that could adversely affect understanding of what is to be done during the test should be avoided. Instructions should be clear and unambiguous. But candidates should understand technical terms relating to the skill being tested.

In some cases it would be desirable for the tester to read out the instructions when, for example, the candidate is dyslexic or word blind. (Dyslexia is the name given to the state of impaired ability to read. It is not caused by low intelligence.) Unbiased translators or other non-interested parties may, on occasion, be called upon to read test instructions. Testers may ask candidates to 'Shout-up' or 'Call us' if they do not understand the written words. They would, for instance, explain that the word 'unserviceable' means: 'In its present condition a component is not fit to satisfactorily perform its intended purpose. It may or may not be capable of repair.' Candidates often think that the word means: 'incapable of being repaired' and that the word 'serviceable' means that the component can be repaired.

The tester could assume that candidates had been taught the concept together with job specific language and that they should know its meaning. However, this is sometimes not so, but testers will be careful to avoid giving anything away.

> **The aim of the skills test is to confirm that candidates can do the task. That is why the candidates present themselves for assessment.**

Wherever possible, candidate responses to test items concerning a skill should be in the form of 'ticks in boxes' or written measurements on the test paper. Where written answers associated with skills tests are required, either short-answer or multiple-choice questions could be used. However, this form of response may not be suitable when testing clerical or secretarial occupational skills.

Numeracy

Being **numerate** is being able to use numbers, particularly in arithmetical operations. Some people are not very talented when it comes to dealing with figures. They have problems in reading or writing numbers and in counting. Carrying out adding, subtracting, multiplying or otherwise calculating things or solving numerical tasks can be difficult for many.

For these people it may be necessary to provide facilities that will enable them to demonstrate skills other than those that rely heavily on being numerate. Alternatively it may be possible to arrange the test such that sections involving numeracy are separated from those that do not contain numerical elements.

When testing elements of numeracy, such as measuring that underpins some demonstrations of skill, it is advisable to print a range of response choices on the answer paper. The candidate is asked to tick the correct answer or alternatively to enter the measurement together with the unit of measurement in a box provided. It may be necessary to print on the candidate's paperwork, dimensions such as length and mass (and weight) using Imperial measure as well as the SI system of units now employed for most scientific and technical purposes. There remain many people employed by companies who use one or other or both systems and in order to be fair, the candidates may need to have a choice of units and measuring instruments.

In many disciplines numeracy is an important part of the task and it is necessary for the candidate to have the ability to measure and carry out arithmetic operations competently. Basic numeracy is often evaluated during job selection or at the initial assessment stage.

Skills test authors

Standards departments of companies, examining bodies and training providers set standards for all training and assessment activities. **Test authors** are often highly trained, qualified, competent and experienced within the occupational area in which they operate. They are also competent in test writing and many are able to write across disciplines. Some will have developed their skill **experientially** over quite a long period.

All must be conversant with the latest products, processes and practices within their test writing area.

Selecting test areas

Test authors work from **modules** that contain details of training **standards**, complementary or **underpinning knowledge**, safety requirements and a training specification listing task, operation or procedure. They are asked to design assessments that will form part of the conventional process of evaluating skills and knowledge of a subject or outcomes of training.

Observing the process

Before attempting to write a skills test based on existing procedures it is desirable to observe and record the complete task or activity prior to its analysis, diagnosis or interpretation. The whole process should be carefully recorded from start to finish using skilled workers operating at **experienced worker standard** as the model on which the skills test might be based. The procedures should then be broken down ready for further examination using natural break points in activity as the start and finish of each element.

Critically examining content

A checklist of possible areas for testing is very useful when analysing a task or activity. Main areas that might be examined are: the sequence of events, the handling of materials, movement of workers and use of machinery and equipment. Questions asked would include:

- 'Who does it? How? Why? When?'
- 'What is done? How? Why? When?'
- 'What resources are involved? How? Why? When?'

What can be tested

Product skills can be tested by observing the candidate's performance and examining the outcomes of work. Some process skills can be assessed and these would include:

- A planned, orderly, clean and tidy workmanlike approach while performing the task.
- Observance and demonstration of safe working practices.
- Effectiveness and efficiency of performance to identified and stated standards.
- Application of basic principles.

In a manufacturing context a candidate operating a lathe or machining centre would be able to machine and present for examination a car brake drum. All features of the drum could be checked against the drawing (blueprint) and a decision made about operator competency. Underpinning knowledge would be assumed as it is not easy to directly assess knowledge called upon during the production process without careful questioning.

What cannot readily be tested
Examiners may be somewhat detached and with skills testing they may assess or mark only what they can see, measure or touch. While it is possible to form an opinion as to whether communication skills are well developed, some process skills are not easy to assess; these include:

- Performance as part of daily work routine in the employer's premises.
- Attitudes towards employers or their representatives.
- Handling clients.
- Interpersonal skills at work.
- Team working and some group problem-saving activities.

Devising and designing test format
Examining boards set performance criteria for competences to be tested. All elements of a module or unit are tested and assessed. Results may be fed into a computer which then outputs to employers or candidates a readout in the form of a report or **rating sheet**. Some skills testing centres provide very detailed reports that specify errors, each graded in degree of seriousness. The report contains careful analytical evaluations of errors made and grades the error according to some predetermined scale. Frequency of incidence of the error is also recorded. This information, together with other data obtained from test results and observations, can be used to inform the candidate, employer, skills auditors and planners of the outcomes and quality of training within the occupational area. Successful candidates who achieve performance criteria may receive a record of achievement giving details of the modules or, in the case of NVQ, element and unit credits.

> **Rating sheets may be of considerable interest to employers who will be able to base remedial or further training on the detailed test information provided.**

Trial by pre-test

Skills tests should be tried out and 'proved' before offering them for general use. Where possible the first trial could be carried out by testers and support staff employed by the test author's organisation. Where this is not possible, qualified people engaged in the trade or service should be consulted and advice sought about the **validity** and **feasibility** of the proposed **test content** and procedures. HM Services or other institutions might be prepared to trial and verify the tests and provide valuable feedback. Otherwise, pilot groups should be formed to try out the test.

It must be possible to carry out the test within the time allowed or within manufacturers' standard timings (where applicable). However, a **contingency** time allowance may be added to allow for stress or test nerves and where unfamiliar equipment or tasks are involved.

Test **reliability** and **consistency** are key requirements of test performance and comparison of one group of similar candidates with another, perhaps from a different region, would need to yield broadly similar results before the test could be deemed dependable.

Test centres would subsequently be set up with a standard range of equipment similar to that used in the pre-test trials. Precisely the same test materials and documentation would be provided for the use of test administrators, testers and candidates.

Test administration

Individuals applying for skills testing are normally allocated a reference number that is used for test purposes. Names are not used so as to maintain confidentiality and to avoid bias or discrimination. Candidates to be tested are likely to be nervous and ill-at-ease when testing takes place in strange surroundings. It takes time to get to know where things are and to settle down, so time should be set aside to calm these fears.

Before tests commence candidates should be briefed about the test format, conditions and operation. Safety aspects should be highlighted and candidates should be instructed to dress in protective clothing, put on their safety shoes and generally get themselves prepared for the actual test. During the candidates' briefing, the importance of carefully reading the test instructions should be stressed. If candidates do not understand the instructions or if they suspect a component or other resource is missing, so that the task cannot be accomplished, they should call the examiner.

> Candidates must understand what is to be done and what is required of them otherwise test results will not be valid.

Signals are given at the start and finish of test periods when **timed tests** are involved. Where a group of candidates is to be tested on a number of elements, benches would be set up ready for the different tests. If the same time is allowed for each, a bell will sound and candidates will start the test. The bell would ring again after the allowed time and candidates would move to another work station and commence the next test. Examiners would then check and mark the work done, whether or not the test had been completed. Results would be recorded.

> Test invigilators and examiners should be trained and competent in preparing and supervising tests.

> Before the tests commence, examiners should check test facilities and set-ups and ensure that everything is ready as per the prescribed test criteria documents.

> Test instructions should be read or presented to the candidates in clear and concise language.

> Invigilators must not intervene when candidates are making errors.

> Validators need to ensure that the skills tests cover those skills needed by the trade and by candidates and that they are the same for all candidates.

Installing the skills test

After pre-testing and evaluating the outcomes of the test trials, corrections and changes are made before the skills tests are put into general use.

Maintaining the tests

Continuous **monitoring** of outcomes is demanded in order to retain the effectiveness and efficiency of the skills tests. Feedback from users and their sponsors is one of the most reliable indicators of test performance and post-test evaluations normally yield valuable comment on candidate's and employer's perceptions of the tests. A programme of sampling, monitoring and evaluation of all candidates' performances carried out by the testing centre is also necessary.

If test results seem to be fairly consistent and within projected targets then there are likely to be no serious problems. If, however, one test item fails consistently then alarm bells should ring. Something will probably be wrong either with the test design, its administration, the examiner's assessment or recording system.

Some training providers have been known to do their own thing rather than keep to the contract to teach a certain module containing specified performance criteria. The candidates are entered for skills testing and a high percentage fail certain elements. The provider complains about the poor results only to find that they have worked to their own syllabus and failed to cover module performance criteria and properly prepare the candidate. This is an example of the: 'Did not change last year's training provision to meet current module content' syndrome.

Candidate perception or criticism of the skills test may not always be entirely reliable. This may not be intentional. They may be over anxious and fail to read the instructions or heed the test administrator's advice. On one occasion, before starting a practical test concerned with checking for engine oil leaks, a tester read out all the instructions slowing down and stressing only important words. These key words were reproduced in bold print on the candidates' instruction sheets: '**You may start the engine if you wish**'. The tester then told them to pay attention to the bold printed parts.

The first candidate either did not read the bold print or did not remember to start the engine – neither did any of the others. They all failed – they did not diagnose a leaking oil filter because the defect would only come to light when the engine was running and the oil pressure built up.

Candidates who fail a test may blame the tools or test conditions. A drill might break while drilling a hole prior to tapping a thread. The candidate may be afraid to speak up and ask for another drill or simply not bother to tell the tester about it and leave the job unfinished. Others adopted a 'bolshy' attitude and say that they were unfairly treated or that trick questions were used or that the teacher's attitude was unhelpful. There are also those who are so familiar with similar tasks that they do not read instructions and miss requests to write down certain test findings and hence lose the marks and fail.

> In order to improve matters the tester will need to establish a rapport with the candidates. Encouraging remarks should be used, like: 'If you break a tool ask us for a replacement. We want you to feel that you are being fairly treated. No one is out to fail you. There are no trick questions. If in doubt, ask. We are here to . . . etc'.

Where things break down or components will not stand repeated stripping and reassembling or when test equipment fails during field use, the test specification or resources will need to be re-examined and replaced if necessary.

Monitoring may also be carried out by test operators, standards people, training boards and examining bodies.

Test outcomes

Product skills can be evaluated. Testpieces and concrete examples of work can be examined and fairly dependably assessed. Measurements and observations recorded during tests can be compared with prepared checklists of key factors and nominal dimensions with tolerances shown.

Process skills may not easily be fully evaluated since it may not be possible to observe all that is done in order to produce a particular product and what is involved may not lend itself to objective assessment.

Planning aspects can be assessed by looking at the way the candidate sets up for the job: the orderly layout of tools, utensils and resources needed and the logic of the methods adopted to do the work entailed.

Safe working procedures can be checked as work progresses.

Pressure

Commercial demands for quality work, often to be performed under pressure, together with the need to work productively 'on-the-job', demands skilful working techniques. Skills tests are timed and carefully structured so as to ascertain and test the accuracy of work performed under a certain amount of time constraint, thereby reflecting commercial practice. Work is set and marked under near ideal test conditions that reflect as nearly as possible the real job.

Skilled performance

A **skilled worker** is recognised by a consistently smooth, continuous, relatively effortless and error-free performance.

Computer printouts or other records of performance outcomes can be of value to skill owners, to employers and training officers and in a wider sense to the industry itself. Skills testing yields valuable labour market information that serves as accurate data for industrial workforce planners. At employer level test results help to establish just what competences staff can be expected to apply in the workplace.

Test results will show up strengths and weaknesses in training programme design and implementation. Where test outcomes are significantly different from those expected it is likely that something has gone wrong during the candidate's training and preparation for the test.

Where skills tests are carried out by external examining bodies often no post-test discussion or review between assessor and candidate takes place. This is unfortunate, although necessary sometimes, due to the method of testing and assessing adopted. In such cases performance profiles or results may subsequently be made available, but remedial work to bring candidates up to scratch is left to the employer or training provider to sort out.

Certification

Delays in getting results and in certification can be expected after skills testing has been carried out by some external agencies. Strict rules and procedures govern the operations of the more formal awarding bodies and feedback may be directed to centres for testing and assessment, examiners, sponsors and moderators rather than directly to candidates.

In the case of workplace assessments a more informal atmosphere generally exists. Feedback is immediate and there is an opportunity for assessor and candidate to ask questions of one another and to review outcomes.

Where employers are paying for the skills testing they will normally receive the test report direct. Well organised companies will then arrange to review with the candidate the outcomes of testing recorded in the report. This procedure motivates the trainee to look at what needs to be done to get up to scratch and if the report is good encourages greater effort towards career development and the acquisition of more skills.

RTITB skills testing

Skills testing is the main form of candidate assessment used by the Road Transport Industry Training Board and the Board requires that trainees should be independently assessed.

Skills assessment is available to all trainees and bookings may be made through the Board's Regional Offices.

Notes
1   Candace Miller, 'Assessment in the Workplace – Quality Issues' in *Competence & Assessment*, Issue 9, Employment Department Training Agency, Summer 1989, p. 15.
2   Training Agency Technical Advisory Group Guidance Notes.
3   NCVQ Information Note 4.
4   *Review of Vocational Qualifications in England and Wales*, MSC/DES, London, April 1986.
5   N Evans, *Assessing Experiential Learning*, FEU/Longman, London 1987.
6   *Training for Skill Ownership in the Youth Training Scheme*, IMS, Brighton 1983, p. 51.

CHAPTER NINE

FEEDBACK, RECORDS AND CERTIFICATION

Chapter coverage

Occupational aspects

Occupational qualifications

Before discussing the role of providing feedback on performance and achievement it could be helpful to consider the link between occupation and qualifications. Today different levels of NVQs, training and experience are needed in order to be competent in a certain job. The **skill level** owned by individuals will obviously affect their position within the **Standard Occupational Classification** which is described below. This skill level will in turn probably affect their position in society.

Occupational areas

An **occupation** is an area of employment requiring a common set of competences. An individual qualified in an occupation would be capable of practising in a variety of jobs, companies and locations where the competences are required.

An **occupational area** is a broad category of work or profession. Within each area there are a number of jobs. A list giving some of the job skills to be found within engineering and hotel and catering occupational areas is shown in Figure 9.1 (see also: SOC and Footnote 1).

Sales	Engineering	Hotel and catering
Buyers and purchasers	Electrical	Accommodation servicing
Importers and exporters	Electronic	Advance reservations
Merchandisers	Foundry practice	Assistant cook
Window dressers	Maintenance	Bar service and cellar work
Sales representatives	Marine	Call order cookery
Sales assistants	Mechanical fitting	Cashier
Van salespersons	Mechanical machining	Food preparation and cookery
Telephone sales	Pattern making, moulding	Food service
Check-out operators	and modelmaking	General kitchen work
Forecourt attendants	Vehicle body practice	Hotel reception
Market traders	Welding and fabrication	Licensed trade catering
Scrap dealers	Metal forming	Linen keeping
Commodity brokers	Auto engineers	Portering

Figure 9.1 Range of job skills within groups

Standard occupational classification (SOC)

'Accurate and comprehensive occupational classification is essential for identifying occupational trends and developments in the labour market to enable the effective planning and implementation of relevant employment and training programmes. This is all the more important as the pace of technological progress increases and occupational skills change.'[1]

The **Standard Occupational Classification (SOC)** resulted from collaboration between the **Employment Training Group**, including the **Training Agency**, and the **Office of Population, Censuses and Surveys**. It attempts to develop a single, standard classification to replace existing incompatible classification systems.

SOC is designed to cover all paid jobs now performed by 'economically active persons' in Great Britain and there are nine major groups.

The structure of SOC is 'hierarchical' which means that each group is arranged in a graded order. Each group relates to the general nature of qualifications and training and experience needed for competent performance. Two main criteria are taken into account when classifying the occupation: **skill level** and **nature of work activities**.

Major groups

---

1   Managers and administrators
2   Professional occupations
3   Associate professional and technical occupations
4   Clerical and secretarial occupations
5   Craft and related occupations
6   Personal and protective service occupations
7   Sales occupations
8   Plant and machine operatives
9   Other occupations

Figure 9.2 SOC – Major groups

The nine major groups are further divided into 'sub-major groups', 'minor groups' and 'unit groups'. Full details of SOC are available from HMSO Publications.

As there are several hundred unit groups any attempt to explain the whole thing to trainees would probably be a recipe for disaster. But the example to illustrate the classification given in Figure 9.3 would probably be of some interest.[1]

Major Group 5	**Minor Group 50**	**Unit Group**
Craft and	Construction	**502**
related occupations	Trades	Plasterers

Figure 9.3 Example of Standard Occupational Classification

Major Group 5 covers occupations whose tasks involve the performance of complex physical duties which normally require a degree of initiative, manual dexterity and other practical skills. The main tasks of these occupations require experience with, and understanding of, the work situation, the materials worked with and the requirements of the structures, machinery and other items produced.

Most occupations in this major group have a level of skill commensurate with a considerable period of training often provided by means of work-based training programmes.

The other criterion taken into account in SOC is the '**nature of work activities**' such as typical aspects of the job excluding status but including use of tools, materials and equipment. For example, the SOC describes the occupation of plasterer (Unit group 502):

'Plasterers apply plaster and cement mixtures to walls and ceilings, fix fibrous sheets and cast and fix ornamental plaster work to the interior and exterior of buildings.

- Mixes or directs the mixing of plaster to the desired consistency.
- Applies and smoothes one or more coats of plaster and produces a finished surface, using hand tools or mechanical spray.
- Pours liquid plaster into mould to cast ornamental plaster work.
- Measures, cuts, installs and secures plaster board and/or ornamental plasterwork to walls and ceilings.
- Covers and seals joints between boards and finishes surface.
- Checks surface using line, spirit level and straight edge.'[1]

It would be useful to explain to trainees how things are developing and how different levels of qualifications, training and experience are needed for competence in a certain job and how their 'skill level' will affect their position within the SOC.

Trainers will find 'Standard Occupational Classification' Volume 2 helpful when writing performance criteria, describing competences, carrying out a job analysis or devising job descriptions.

Feedback

Feedback defined

In industrial terms, the 'feedback' concept applies to linking a system's outputs to its inputs, thereby monitoring what is going on and keeping the system under control. In a training context, feedback provided by various methods of review and assessment gives information about the learner's progress.

Being able to give and receive feedback is an important skill for trainees, trainers and assessors.

Receiving **positive feedback** about learning outcomes and achievements is good for learners but **negative feedback** given skilfully can also aid learning.

The trainee, trainer and assessor will need to be able to share their perceptions of the good and not so good aspects of the demonstration of achievement.

Giving and receiving feedback

Feedback may be obtained during performance reviews where learners are able to find out just how well they have done. They are able to compare and verify with the workplace assessor their outcomes against performance criteria. Where there is a need to do better, they can discuss how they could go about reaching the standard required.

In some cases feedback is immediate, as in the case of a waiter who spills soup in a customer's lap.

> Here, the assessor would be able to comment on the process that led to the failure and offer advice on how to avoid a repetition in the future.

Even when the assessment confirms that criteria have been met, feedback can be valuable in that constructive criticism and review encourages the development of a healthy rapport and confidence.

The value to learners of 'self-referenced' feedback is recognised as being of great value. It is what the learners say, think and do about their 'achievements' or 'failures' that really counts.

Feedback given in a thoughtless manner is unhelpful. Candidates will know when they have not done well, there is no need to tell them. They will resent being at the sharp end of an assessor's tongue. No good will come of destructive criticism which may distress the person on the receiving end or leave them with feelings of worthlessness.

It is much better to encourage people by telling them that they are doing something competently. So when giving feedback, start with positive comments. Strengths should be highlighted and built upon before any negative comment is introduced.

When a candidate is denied the accreditation of achievement due to some shortcoming it may be essential to offer negative feedback. If this is the case then negative factors should be identified but shown to be capable of being converted into positives. Judgements should be avoided, as should statements likely to cause a defensive stance and hostile responses. Turn the weakness into a strength by suggesting alternative approaches that could be adopted by the candidate to overcome the problem.

> Assessors should avoid telling candidates that: 'They are good instructors.' or 'Will go right to the top'. Anything that is said can only represent opinion and not indisputable fact.

> Assessors should 'own their feedback'. They should accept responsibility for what they say to candidates. They should ensure that their comments are understood by candidates and that what is said is a personal judgement, valid only at that time and made under the prevailing circumstances.

> If when giving feedback the assessor can start by recounting some of the good aspects of the candidates' performances they will better appreciate what follows. There will be a greater probability that subsequent supportive criticism will be well received and will be acted upon.

Listening
Hearing is not listening. **Active listening** involves thinking about what you hear and your reaction to it. It is the route to understanding what is being said or shared.

A person's point of view and behaviour is influenced by listening to what is going on. The trouble is that individuals are often so busy talking and so eager to be heard that they cannot be bothered to listen to others. Even when conducting assessments and reviews little thought may be given to what someone else is saying. The candidates will be quick to spot when the assessor is not listening to them. Once this happens mutual understanding becomes impossible, effective communication ceases and little is accomplished.

> The assessor will need to maintain with the candidate a conversation link by promoting creative listening.

> Good listeners are able to understand and reflect back what is being fed to them. An assessor should be a competent listener.

Need for clarity

Information shared should be clear-cut and detailed. Vague and generalised comments are not helpful when giving feedback. Comments, whether descriptive or evaluative, should be narrowly focused. Arguments should be avoided and defensive attitudes discouraged. Candidates will expect to be told or otherwise helped to discover just what it is that they need to do to put things right when things go wrong. They will not appreciate assessors's attempts to evade the truth or to introduce vagueness and ambiguity.

It has been suggested that candidates prefer the assessor to use descriptive rather than evaluative statements when commenting on performance. Descriptive accounts of what the assessor saw or heard during the observation give tangible examples of good and bad practice that candidates can grasp in their minds. These accounts are of more use to them than bland statements that are open to many interpretations like: 'That was OK' or 'You did that well' or 'I think you're capable of doing it better'.

Open-ended questions have a place in the review process, throughout learning and when assessing underpinning knowledge and skills but feedback must be specific.

> The assessor will need to be explicit when discussing aspects of a candidate's performance. Reference should be made to particular incidents observed during the demonstration or to features of process or product. Actual examples should be quoted.

> Feedback given should enable the candidate to identify exactly where further action is needed to meet the standard demanded or to confirm competent performance.

Avoid delay

Feedback must be immediate. Delay allows thought and recollection to blur with the passage of time. Candidates will have a desire to show that they can meet performance criteria, to overcome obstacles and to do something quickly and well. But they will also need early recognition of their 'achievement' or of 'failure'. Feedback and 'knowledge of results' reinforces and produces faster learning and permits correction of errors provided that it is received soon after the event.

> Assessors should strike while the iron is hot.

Behaviour change

All learning and experience involves behaviour change. **Behaviour** concerning memorising, understanding and doing things may be readily evaluated and fed back to candidates. In this instance, while feedback about performance may not greatly affect the candidate, it can result in their making rapid changes in opinion and attitude.

Personality may be defined as: 'the characteristic ways of behaving that determine how individuals will adjust to their surroundings'. However, ignoring the effect of situational circumstances, a person's personality may in the short term be regarded as being shaped by inborn potential. It could be represented by an individual '**trait profile**' which is: 'as characteristic of a person as his or her fingerprints'.

> Trainers and assessors will need to be aware of the tendency for themselves to operate outside their briefs. They may attempt to promote change in a candidate's approach to life or work which is beyond their capability. The temptation to take such actions that may be considered to be unethical should be avoided.

The act of unfairly or unreasonably attempting to secure changes in matters that are beyond the control of the candidate or asking them to do things that are incapable of being done should be rigorously avoided.

> Feedback intended to promote change should be restricted to approved action that is feasible and likely to help candidates achieve attainable objectives. Feedback should be restricted to knowledge, skills and attitudes that can be changed.

When reviewing assessment outcomes candidates should be encouraged to take decisions about whether or not to make use of any feedback provided. Choosing the course of action to be taken must be theirs. Any attempt to push them into remedial activity or imposed retraining will probably be met with considerable resistance.

A negotiated approach which allows all concerned to examine the 'pros' and 'cons' of taking a certain decision is recommended.

> Telling or directing people to do it 'your' way will probably not result in the desired outcome.

Reinforcement

Reinforcement is often thought of as being some form of strengthening or support and this may be true when applied to the learning process. But in the training sector **rewards** are known as **positive reinforcers** and **punishments** as **negative reinforcers**. In other words, rewards can help matters while punishments tend to hinder.

Some psychologists believe that rewarding a person is much more effective than punishing when attempting to promote learning or when seeking co-operation. Punishing someone for a wrong may help to inhibit that behaviour pattern but it will not necessarily wipe it out once and for all. Rewarding someone for doing what is required will, however, often reinforce good behaviour.

When assessing or being assessed we must be careful to avoid arousing feelings of resentment, dislike or fear. A few careless words may destroy rapport and arouse strong unhelpful emotional responses in others involved. It is better to be positive and to highlight the good than to concentrate mainly on the not-so-good.

The assessor when reviewing others will need to be able to:
- Establish contact and communication link.
- Reward candidates with compliments for doing good work.
- Welcome suggestions from candidates for improving their performance.
- Thank candidates when appropriate for efforts made in carefully preparing for and presenting their demonstration of competence.
- Give positive reassurance to candidates that their contributions to improving quality of work in the occupational area is important.
- Turn aspects of 'failure' into opportunities for candidates to accept the challenge to master whatever is holding up progress.
- Use their 'power' properly and sensitively.
- Be aware that any indication of pleasure derived from 'putting down' the candidate should be avoided.
- Arrange debriefings so that the presence of others does not cause candidates any loss of status or image.
- Avoid abusing candidates by misjudging the severity and intensity of the effect of comments made to them or criticism offered.
- Ensure that adverse constructive criticism is not repeated to others nor used for the purpose of providing a lesson for the whole group unless the candidate concerned is in agreement.
- Realise that quiet 'soft' private remarks made during reviews are more effective and will be better remembered by candidates than 'loud' public pronouncements to all and sundry.
- Avoid feelings that loss of image will occur if observers note that no fault can be found in the candidate's performance.

Giving feedback
- Encourage. Start with the good news. Give some positive aspects of candidate's performance.
- Be explicit. Be definite and relate to particular instances, evidence and tangible things. Make specific points and avoid generalities.
- Turn negative constructive criticism into positive intent.
- Tell candidates how criteria have or have not been achieved. Give praise where due. When criteria are not met suggest achievable alternatives or ways forward.
- Be descriptive. Say what you saw or heard. Be objective and avoid making value judgements.
- Stand by your feedback. Admit ownership of what you say. Let what you say be worth listening to.
- Offer factual feedback. Allow candidates to make decisions and select courses of future action. Leave them with facts to chew over and allow them to choose their way forward. Never attempt to impose a decision.
- End on a high.

Figure 9.4 Giving feedback – summary of aspects

Keeping records

Records

Records are an account in permanent form of achievement or performance. Information gathered during identification of prior achievements and assessments may be used to support learner's claims for the accreditation of competence. Some typical sources of information together with a note of those who may be involved in its selection and processing are given in Figure 9.5.

In some government-sponsored training schemes Training Agents and Training Managers are responsible for recording the achievement of competence for their own staff and also for trainees. During training, assessment records may be stored in Part One of the candidate's NROVA together with the action plan.

Source	Administration	Agent
Accreditation of prior learning	School College Employer	Trainee Assessor
Initial assessment	Training provider	Trainee Trainer
Training programme	Scheme co-ordinator Employer	Trainee Trainer
BTEC registration examination entries and certification	BTEC Assessor	Exams officer Moderator Trainee
CGLI examination entries and certification	CGLI Scheme co-ordinator Assessor	Trainee Trainer
Industrial Training Board documentation	Countersigning Officer Key person	Trainee Trainer Assessor
NROVA registration updating and transfer	Scheme co-ordinator Government agency	Trainee Trainer
Skills tests	Industrial Training boards Training manager	Trainee Trainer Assessor
Monitoring of work experience	Employer Scheme co-ordinator Liaison officer	Trainee Trainer Workplace Assessor
Reviews	Training provider Liaison officer	Trainee Trainer Counsellor Assessor Employer
Logbooks	WP training/assessor Training provider	Trainee Trainer

Figure 9.5 Learner documentation

NROVA
The **National Record of Vocational Achievement (NROVA)** is a cumulative lifelong record of credits and qualifications. Its use enables credits accumulated to be collated and recorded. Any certificates awarded or other forms of accreditation will be held by individuals in their NROVA. It is also used to hold action plans and personal training plans.

The NROVA is published by NCVQ and the contents are made up of two parts:
- Part One comprises an 'action plan' and 'assessment record'.
- Part Two holds 'Record of Achievement Certificates'. This part is separated into three sections: Section 1 for 'NVQ Units'; Section 2 for 'Other Qualification Units' and Section 3 for 'Programme Units'.

Action plan and assessment record
The **action plan** stated in the form of units of competence gives details of the qualification being pursued or training programme to be followed. It lists what needs to be done and what will be assessed in order to attain the award sought.

Action planning may take place during initial assessment or induction or as the need demands. The object being for trainee and training provider to agree a plan of activity that will provide opportunities for competences to be achieved.

The **assessment record** comprises award body designed and approved assessment report forms and other records of assessments relating to elements of competence and performance criteria relating to each unit of competence that the trainee is working towards.

> The assessor or project supervisor is normally responsible for maintaining relationships with vocational qualification awarding bodies and for arranging for certification and issuing of certificates or units of competence to the candidate.

Record of achievement certificates
The **record of units of competence achieved in NVQ** is located in Section 1. It holds certificates for full NVQ awards and also records and certificates showing units achieved which are credits towards NVQs. A specimen Joint Certificate relating to the Part One Certificate in Cooking for the Catering Industry is given in Figure 9.21.

Units of competence and credits achieved in vocational qualifications other than NVQ are recorded in Section 2. A list available from NCVQ details bodies whose qualifications are approved for inclusion.

Section 3 holds records and certificates issued by approved education and training agencies. These relate to units of competence achieved in nationally or locally devised programmes not included in Sections 1 and 2.

NROVA in Government Sponsored Training
The NROVA was adopted by managing agents and made available to all Youth Training trainees from April 1990. All new recruits are issued with a NROVA.

Individual **action plans** indicating intentions and methods to be pursued in order to meet objectives to be achieved, and assessment records for those elements of competence realised during the process are filed in Part One.

In Youth Training, as with other sponsored training, NVQ awards and traditional vocational qualifications are held in the first two sections of Part Two, as previously described.

In the interim period between full coverage for occupations by NVQs it was agreed that non-NVQ certificates for units of competence achieved in national programmes such as Employment Training and Youth Training should be filed in Part Two, Section 3 of the NROVA.

The introduction of NROVA into Youth Training greatly reduced the burden of record keeping previously undertaken by managing agents. For the trainee, the main advantage of maintaining a NROVA is that in the eyes of prospective employers their standing and esteem is raised. The value of NVQs awarded can quickly be established in terms that may be readily understood by those concerned.

Learner documentation

'Filling in' training records

A **form** is a printed document normally with spaces in which to insert facts and answers. Application forms are used when applying or asking for something such as a training place or job. In training circles forms are used to record in a systematic way information about progress, achievement and competences. Some **Records of Progress** are printed in a specified format and needed for the trainee's portfolio of evidence that will be used to support claims of achievement.

Form filling can be very time consuming. In some cases forms are completed as a matter of course by people who have little or no idea of the use to which data supplied will be put – nor how their time and effort will be rewarded. Few seem to bother about checking about why the form needs to be completed in the first place.

Some people experience difficulty in accurately filling in forms and handwriting **log-book entries**. For many, putting things in writing can be painfully slow, requiring great effort and a lot of hard work. Others will say, 'What's behind all this?'.[2] They may not feel well-disposed to handling the paperwork needed as evidence to support claims for NVQ or other accreditation and certification.

Well-designed forms that are easy to read, understand and fill in, with enough space to record information asked for in logical sequence, should be provided.

> Trainees will happily fill in holiday request forms, football pools entries, etc. but record-keeping needs to be carefully explained and justified. This is when the staff trainer will need to lend a hand and guide the trainees at least until they are able to cope reasonably well with the task.

Achievement records

An **achievement** is something that has been accomplished often by hard work and considerable effort. It implies successful completion measured against some kind of criteria. An **achievement record** is used to express concisely the evidence collected against elements and performance criteria. The summary in the form of a written statement is used as an aid to assessment. The record usually contains details of:

- Skills demonstrated while carrying out an activity or performing work. These skills are called 'process skills' and relate to what the Candidate does in order to control the conduct that enables tasks to be performed. These skills involve planning work and problem solving and may be characterised by thinking and controlling.
- Skills demonstrated while producing a product such as a sheet of typed paper or a brick wall. These skills are called 'product skills' and relate to what the Candidate does in order to produce a desired clearly defined outcome such as typing a letter or building a brick wall.
- The content and circumstances that are relevant to the demonstration of competence.
- The categories and amount of evidence produced in support of a claim for accreditation.

Training cards

A **training card** is a summary of training programme outcomes. The example given in Figure 9.6 relates to the job of Sales Assistant in a large store. The card contains essential information relating to job responsibilities and training factors.

Three main job responsibilities are defined (see: Codes A1–A3) and key training factors have been listed against each code. The training programme will be planned and trainee performance will be assessed against each set of factors listed.

Training is carried out and performance assessments made using checklists similar to that given in Figure 9.7. The assessments are made on a 'can do' basis and in this instance the checklist covers the A3 training factors. When the trainee and trainer agree that competence has been achieved and demonstrated the trainee dates and initials the card.

When training is completed the trainee, trainer and departmental manager discuss performance and review outcomes. Comments are written on the card and initialled. Certification is completed when the store manager as countersigning officer is satisfied that training content and performance meets company standards.

Assessing record-keeping

Training Department staff and candidates seeking workplace trainer's and assessor's awards will need to maintain high standards of record-keeping as it pertains to their role.

Records that would normally be kept by workplace trainers engaged in Government sponsored training are listed in Figure 9.8. Each of the records reflects aspects of the trainer function such as: planning, preparing, delivering or assessing. Many of the records would be used without exception by the trainers engaged in other forms of training and staff development.

The 'ticks' shown in Figure 9.8 indicate those pieces of supporting evidence that would be needed when performance criteria making up given elements of competence are being assessed.

> **Examples of checklists, programmes and other records listed should be filed in the trainer's portfolio of supporting evidence for presentation to the assessor when achievement is being assessed.**

Trainer documentation

Trainers will be expected to keep records of trainees and to maintain assessment records. Trainee records are a requirement of some government-sponsored training schemes and essential to their operation. Elsewhere, employers normally keep records of staff skills, qualifications, training and achievements for use when carrying out **skills audits**. In each case care should be taken to operate within the provisions of the Data Protection Act, 1984. Records kept include:

- Lists of people in training.
- Date of birth and sex.
- National Insurance number.
- Address and phone number.
- Qualifications on entry.
- Start date.
- Statement of any long-term health problems or disability that may affect the kind of work done.
- Standard Occupational Classification (SOC) relating to trainees' types of job and skill level within their employment or occupation.
- Location or workplace.

Trainers could usefully develop a framework for monitoring, evaluating and recording training programme implementation and outcomes. Records kept vary according to providers' needs but may often include:

- Action plan and training programme details.
- Training start and finish dates.
- Details of Special Training Need category.
- Anticipated NVQ level of achievement.
- Achievements during training.
- Destination post training.

The use of assessment matrices and schedules when planning and making assessments and collecting evidence helps to promote an organised approach to the record keeping task. Notes may be made during the candidate's actual demonstration of achievement rather than relying entirely on memory. Documentation will normally be completed at the time of assessment or during review sessions immediately afterwards.

Instruments that could be used when assessing and recording performance would include:

- Elements of competence and performance criteria.
- Assessment questionnaires and checklists.

CHARLTON SUPERSTORES PLC

Job responsibilities and training summary card	**Trainee's name:** *Simon Alastair*
Job title: *Sales Assistant*	**Employee's clock no:** *7*
Store no: *1*	**Responsible to:** *J. Ankwill* Manager
	Starting date: *18 August*

This training card is a summary of the Sales Assistant's training programme and should be used to record in-store training. In the interests of both the Trainee and the Company it is essential that the training programme is followed and that training is completed within two weeks of the employee's starting date.

Code	Main responsibilities	Training factors	Trainee	Date
A$_1$	To ensure that all Company policies and procedures relating to the store are complied with	*Company Policies* Staff dress and appearance Hygiene Health and safety, including usage of equipment Security	*SA*	*20/8*
A$_2$	To foster and maintain the highest level of customer care and service through salesmanship and customer contact	*Customer care* Customer courtesy and service in the store. Commodity knowledge – especially Produce	*SA*	*27/8*
A$_3$	To operate a cash register and weighing scales efficiently and according to Company policy	*Customer service point* Spoilage Bag packing procedures Buying change Void sheets Luncheon vouchers and coupons Cheque handling Float checking Credit cards Customer refunds Cleaning programme Overheads Use of intercom	*SA*	*1/9*

	Dept trainer	Dept manager	Trainee	Date
Training completed – comments				
Credit Card Voucher Completion – of 70 vouchers handled one voucher value £18.43 had not been signed by the customer. XA SW				
Company rules and procedures clarified. Need to implement correct procedures agreed. SW XA				
Void sheets – voids in excess of 50 pence to be countersigned by supervisor. SW XA	SW	PH	XA	1/9

Full name: | Employee clock no.

Training content:	Start date	Completion date	Signatures			
				Dept trainer	Dept manager	Trainee Date
Sales Assistant Programme						
Job Training Elements A.1-3	16/8			SW	PH	XA 3/9

Comments

Need for employee to comply with Company Policy and Procedures in every instance stressed and agreed.
SW PH XA

On-the-Job Training Completed 1/9
(2 weeks)
Ref (A1, A2, A3)

Store manager J. Ankwill 3/9

Figure 9.6 Training summary card

Charlton Superstores PLC

Performance assessment A3

Candidate's name: *Simon Alastair*   Date of assessment: 24/8

Assessor's name: *Martine Griffiths*

Criteria	Can do		Observations
	Yes	**No**	
Till operation			
Dexterity:			
Use of hand on keyboard	✓		
Entering Amount Tendered	✓		
Change Selection	✓		
Change Giving	✓		
Accuracy	✓		
Speed (Items per minute)	✓		
Security:			One credit card
Use of 'no-sale' button	✓		voucher unsigned
Use of Void button	✓		by customer.
Error-free scanning	✓		
Use of 'Sign On/Off' Key	✓		Supervisor to
Maintenance:			countersign voids in
Change till roll	✓		excess of 50 pence.
Keyboard Area Tidy	✓		
Scale operation			
To Company Policy	✓		
Department identification			
Grocery	✓		
Meat	✓		
Produce	✓		
Delicatessen	✓		
Liquor	✓		
Bakery	✓		
Bagging			
Service Performed	✓		
Correct Bag	✓		
Customer service			
Smile/Greet	✓		
Friendly/Courteous	✓		
Thank You	✓		
Offer Carry Out Service	✓		
Other Help	✓		
Housekeeping			
Cleanliness/Tidy	✓		
Terminal Drawer/Notes Tidy	✓		
Check Out Area Tidy	✓		
Goods Left Behind	✓		
Appearance			Demonstrated correct
Company Policy	✓		procedures to adopt.
Attitude			
Good/Interested	✓		
Service calls			
Correct Use of Codes	✓		

Figure 9.7 Assessment checklist – sales assistant

Assessment matrix - records

RECORDS	ELEMENT					
	20.1	20.2	20.3	20.4	23.1	23.2
Induction Checklist	✓					
Workplace Admin	✓					
Training Programme	✓	✓		✓		✓
Training Action Plan		✓		✓		✓
Trainee Review		✓		✓	✓	
Lesson Plan	✓	✓		✓		
H & S Checklist			✓			
H & S on YT			✓			
Assessing Workplace Safety						
Performance Criteria	✓	✓	✓	✓	✓	✓
Trainee Log Book	✓	✓	✓	✓	✓	✓
Training Agreement Employed Status Trainee Status	✓	✓		✓		✓

Figure 9.8 Assessment matrix - records

- Hazards checklists.
- Session plans.
- Induction checklists.
- Forms for recording achievement (see Figure 9.9).
- Candidate's assessment and achievement handbooks and records (CGLI, RSA, Caterbase, RTITB, etc.).
- Work experience logs and employer reports and evaluations by other trainers and job supervisors.

Certification

Awarding certificates

Certificates are official documents that may be issued by an awarding body to a person who has completed one or more units of competence or an entire award. **Certification** is the act of certifying or confirming in written or printed form that the person named has been assessed, his or her achievement recorded and a certificate issued.

Forms of certification

Besides the formal certification carried out by awarding bodies there are several other possibilities. These range from informal self-assessments communicated orally, to strictly objective, impersonal computer-marked and certificated outcomes.

A certificate may serve as evidence that the holder meets the standards of performance needed for progressing to other studies or for employment at a level compatible with achievement. But due to the diversity of certification in use and the varied needs of employment selection interviewers and study guidance counsellors, there will be demand for each type of recording and certification.

Very often employers will need to know rather more about a person's achievements than is written on some forms of certificate. This is where continuous assessment records; initial, formative and summative assessments; profiles, diaries, records of achievement and units listing performance criteria may be helpful. There is also the NROVA that will contain vocational qualifications, NVQs, evidence of occupational competences demonstrated, credits for units of competence and other evidence of experience and achievements. Some instruments are discussed below.

Summative statement of achievement

A form of certification known as a '**summative statement of achievement**' is sometimes used to validate achievement. Competence is established using evidence collected against specified elements and performance criteria and recorded during a process of continuous assessment. Certification of units or elements of competence may result from the combination of formative assessments carried out over an unspecified period and a summative or final assessment.

Personal profiles

A statement in the form of a **personal profile** may be used to summarise assessed achievement. It also gives an estimate of development potential at the end of a course of training. The statement derives from learner self-evaluation of all the

Candidate's Assessment Record

Name _____   Registration date _____

Unit D32
Assess candidate performance	Date achieved	Assessor signature
D321		
D322		
D323		
D324		

Unit D33
Assess candidate using diverse evidence	Date achieved	Assessor signature
D331		
D332		
D333		

Date of APL _____   Date assessment plan agreed _____   Date candidate pack sent to NVQ Services _____

Assessed by _____

Figure 9.9 Candidate assessment record

experiences and outcomes obtained while learning backed by a final review with the trainer/assessor. The profile builds on earlier in-course developmental reviews and takes into account the process of continuously monitoring, evaluating and recording learning achievements.

In some circumstances summary statements may be used to support bids for final awards. Features indicated on the relevant personal profile include:

- Details of learner.
- Prior learning and achievement.
- Details of action plan.
- Essential details of training programme completed.
- Experience gained during training.
- Work-based learning provider's comments.
- Attendance record.
- Performance criteria and competences attained.
- Vocational qualifications achieved.
- Comments on reviews.

Profiling

Profiling is a means of recording achievement and competence and it plays an important role in workplace accreditation and in vocational training programmes that are now offered. The profile or record of achievement produced contains details of the **formative assessments** made during training and a **summative statement of achievement** recorded on completion of the programme.

According to Garforth and Macintosh[3] the contents of profiles should contain the following three basic elements:

- A list of items forming the basis of the assessment. These may be called 'criteria' and may be in the form of a list of skills and qualities or may be embodied within a course description.
- A means of indicating the level and/or nature of performance reached for each item in this list. Almost any means can be used including marks, grades, percentages, histograms, bar graphs, statements and descriptive assessments.
- An indication of the evidence used to arrive at the description provided. This element is unfortunately often ignored but it is vital to indicate the context in which a particular skill is assessed if the nature of its performance is to be fully understood.

These three elements can be seen in the progress profile report of the City and Guilds of London (CGLI) shown in Figure 9.10. The level of performance for each item is identified by indicating the most appropriate statement in the five boxes on the right hand side of the report. The tutor then uses the blank section on the left to describe in what context the skill was displayed and to indicate the kind of evidence on which the assessment is based.

With the CPVE Profile given in Figure 9.11 students are assessed against **competence statements** but there are a number of different style profiles in use and it may be necessary for readers to familiarise themselves with some of these or to design their own to suit needs of clients.

When designing profiles Garforth and Macintosh[4] suggest key criteria to be considered include:

- What are the main purposes of the profile?
- Who is to be profiled?
- What is to be assessed?
- How is assessment to be undertaken?
- Who is to be involved in the assessment process?
- How are the results of the assessment to be recorded?

National Vocational Qualifications

The National Council for Vocational Qualifications (NCVQ) does not itself award certificates, but decides which organisations are approved to offer qualifications within the framework.

A National Vocational Qualification (NVQ) is a statement of competence clearly relevant to work and intended to facilitate entry into or progression in employment, further education and training. It is issued by a recognised body to an individual. If the qualification meets the national standards required for employment it is given the **NCVQ seal of approval**. The statement of competence should incorporate standards in:

- The ability to perform in a range of work-related activities.
- The skills, knowledge and understanding which underpin such performance in employment.

Awards within the NVQ framework consisted initially of four **levels** each indicating different attainments of competence with each accredited qualification assigned to a level within the framework. An example of how NVQ level is linked with occupational role is given in Figure 9.12.[5] NCVQ identify the following list of factors concerning role, performance level and work activities. The combination of these will vary from award to award according to the area of competence and the level of the award.

- Breadth and range of competence attained.[6]
- Complexity and difficulty.
- Degree of skill.
- Ability to undertake specialist activities.
- Ability to organise and plan work.
- Ability to transfer competence to an increasing and wider variety of situations.
- Ability to innovate and cope with non-routine activities.
- Ability to supervise and train others.

Accreditation of prior learning and achievement (APLA)

In the Further Education Unit (FEU) project report 'The Assessment of Prior Learning and Achievement – the role of expert systems'[7] Geoff Stanton writes:

> The accreditation of prior learning and achievement is becoming an increasingly important area of development for all those involved in the education and training of adults. NCVQ, with assistance from the Training Agency, is developing systems for the accreditation of prior learning and achievement in relation to vocational qualifications, and CNAA, FEU and the Learning from Experience Trust have undertaken a considerable amount of work aimed at improving access for unqualified adults to higher education.

City and Guilds of London Institute   Progress

Main Activities:

		ABILITIES	EXAMPLES OF ABILITIES
COMMUNICATION		TALKING AND LISTENING	
		READING	
		WRITING	
PRACTICAL & NUMERICAL		USING EQUIPMENT	
		NUMERACY (I)	
SOCIAL		WORKING IN A GROUP	
		ACCEPTING RESPONSIBILITY	
DECISION-MAKING		PLANNING	
		COPING	
		OBTAINING INFORMATION	
ADDITIONAL		WORKING WITH CLIENTS	
		USING SIGNS AND DIAGRAMS	
		NUMERACY (II)	
		SAFETY	
		COMPUTER APPRECIATION	

Profile

Profile No ....

Name of Centre and Course ....
Period covered by this Review   From ....   To ....
Signed ....   Signed ....
(Trainee/Student)   (Supervisor/Tutor)

PROGRESS IN ABILITIES

Can make sensible replies when spoken to	Can hold conversations and can take messages	Can follow and give simple descriptions and explanations	Can communicate effectively with a range of people in a variety of situations	Can present a logical and effective argument. Can analyse others arguments
Can read words and short phrases	Can read straightforward messages	Can follow straightforward written instructions and explanations	Can understand a variety of forms of written materials	Can select and judge written materials to support an argument
Can write words and short phrases	Can write straightforward messages	Can write straightforward instructions and explanations	Can write reports describing work done	Can write a critical analysis using a variety of sources
Can use equipment safely to perform simple tasks under guidance	Can use equipment safely to perform a sequence of tasks after demonstration	Can select and use suitable equipment and materials for the job, without help	Can set up and use equipment to produce work to standards	Can identify and remedy common faults in equipment
Can count and match objects, can recognise numbers	Can add and subtract whole numbers to solve problems	Can use × and ÷ to solve whole number problems	Can add, subtract and convert decimals and simple fractions	Can multiply and divide decimals and simple fractions
Can cooperate with others when asked	Can work with other members of the group to achieve common aims	Can understand own position and results of own actions within a group	Can be an active and decisive member of a group	Can adopt a variety of roles in a group
Can follow instructions for simple tasks and carry them out under guidance	Can follow instructions for simple tasks and carry them out independently	Can follow a series of instructions and carry them out independently	Can perform a variety of tasks effectively given minimal guidance	Can assume responsibility for delegated tasks and take initiative
Can identify the sequence of steps in everyday tasks, with prompting	Can describe the sequence of steps in a routine task, after demonstration	Can choose from given alternatives the best way of tackling a task	Can modify/extend given plans/routines to meet changed circumstances	Can create new plans/ routines from scratch
Can cope with everyday activities	Can cope with everyday problems. Seeks help if needed	Can cope with changes in familiar routines	Can cope with unexpected or unusual situations	Can help others to solve problems
Can ask for needed information	Can find needed information with guidance	Can use standard sources of information	Can extract and assemble information from several given sources	Can show initiative seeking and gathering information from a wide variety of sources

Can help someone to carry out clients' requests	Can carry out clients' requests under supervision	Can carry out clients' requests without supervision	Can anticipate and fulfil clients' needs from existing resources	Can suggest realistic improvements to services for clients
Can recognise everyday signs and symbols	Can make use of simple drawings, maps, timetables	Can make use of basic graphs, charts, codes technical drawings, with help	Can interpret and use basic graphs, charts and technical drawings unaided	Can construct graphs and extract information to support conclusions
Can estimate answers to tasks involving whole numbers decimals and simple fractions	Can calculate percentages and averages	Can solve problems involving simple ratios and proportions	Can express a problem in terms of a simple formula and solve it	
Can remember safety instructions	Can explain the need for safety rules	Can spot safety hazards	Can apply safe working practices independently	
Can recognise everyday uses of computers	Can use keyboard to gain access to data	Can enter data into the system using existing programs	Can identify potential applications for computers	

Figure 9.10 Progress Profile Report

CPVE PREPARATORY MODULE PROFILE					CENTRE _GEORGE PALMER SCHOOL_
MODULE P00034					
MODULE TITLE VISUAL ARTS PRESENTATION					_Don Courtnage_
STUDENT NAME					

No	Competence Statement	Assessment Record				Where and how Demonstrated
		I	II	III	IV	
1	Adopt the required standard of dress and conduct		SW Dc	SW Dc		Preparing CPVE ① display 6/2
2	Establish and maintain relationships with clients	SW Dc	SW Dc			①
3	Respond to clients' questions from own knowledge or by reference to others		SW Dc			Display for ② incoming first years 10/10
4	Identify a range of printing, drawing and painting techniques and materials		SW Dc			②
5	Identify a range of materials and techniques used for 3-dimensional items		SW Dc			②
6	Provide the conditions required for given items during display and storage	SW Dc	SW Dc			②
7	Handle and store items and associated materials	SW Dc	SW Dc			①
8	Carry out minor repairs and maintain tools and equipment in good order	SW Dc	SW Dc	SW Dc		① and ③
9	Work co-operatively in a team	SW Dc	SW Dc	SW Dc		②
10	Use the terminology relating to the visual arts	SW Dc	SW Dc			②
11	Plan the layout of an indoor exhibition	SW Dc	SW Dc			① and ②
12	Plan the layout of an outdoor exhibition	SW Dc	SW Dc			Arts Centre s/s ③
13	Select and use a range of fixtures and fittings	SW Dc	SW Dc			Work experience ③
14	Select and use lighting effects in display	SW Dc	SW Dc			②
15	Assemble audio-visual equipment for use in display	SW Dc	SW Dc			①
16	Design an exhibition guide	SW Dc	SW Dc			②
17	Apply the appropriate safety measures and regulations	SW Dc	SW Dc	SW Dc		①
18	Maintain the security of items and the environment	SW Dc	SW Dc	SW Dc		①

Key to Performance – self assessment   Dc 23/6

Enter initials and date

 – tutor assessment   SW 23/6

I – has started but needs further experience

II – competent with help or under supervision

III – competent unaided under supervision

IV – competent unaided – able to help others

Figure 9.11 CPVE Preparatory Module Profile

Source: The CPVE Handbook and Issues of Practice (13)
Sample documentation provided by Joint Unit for CPVE & Foundation Programmes. Reproduced with permission

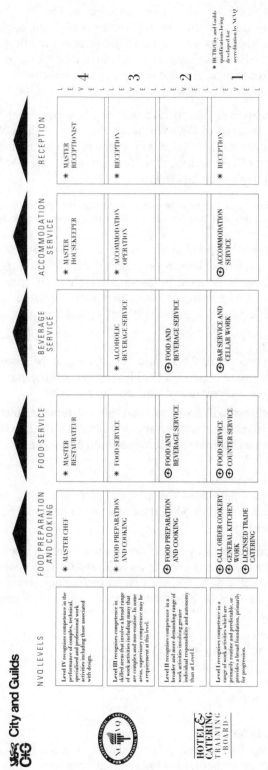

Figure 9.12 NVQ levels

Source: 'National Vocational Qualifications – giving credit where credit is due'[5]

According to the report, one option suggested by NCVQ is that: 'The simplest and most convenient method of APLA is to submit the applicant to the formal tests, assignments, etc. associated with the course or qualification under consideration'.[8] But the FEU report indicates concern that there may be a possibility that performance tests of specific occupational competence may not take into account the possession or otherwise of a wider range of basic skills.[9]

The report analyses the APLA and shows how computer-based expert systems may profitably be used to assist tutors in the process. Jack Mansell, the author of the report, suggests that a basic expert system can be used as a tool by tutors who are involved in APLA but that some tutors and managers will need new skills to carry out APLA. He concludes that:

> . . . the project does little more than confirm the potential of using expert systems in this area, and even at this stage the limitations of the technology are already apparent.[10]

When accrediting prior achievement, account must be taken of the difficulty in **verifying** and **authenticating** evidence of competence and evaluating the **currency** of achievements claimed by candidates. This can arise from differences in work practices and techniques, together with updated or revised underpinning knowledge essential to effectively performing the work for which a credit is sought after.

> **Assessors must be able to distinguish between 'learning' and 'achievement' since NVQ philosophy dictates that accreditation must be based on achievement and not learning.**
>
> **Accreditors will need to establish as genuine and of undisputed origin all evidence produced to support claims for accreditation of competence. Signatures validating claims should be authentic.**

Credit accumulation
Credit accumulation is the process of certificating and aggregating units of competence over a period of time as a means of achieving the competence needed for an award.[11]

NCVQ is promoting a system of credit accumulation that enables candidates to gain **unit credits** that count towards an **NVQ award**. This system enables people to build up their qualification at a pace that suits their needs and individual circumstances. Competence may be achieved using a variety of formal and informal methods including:

- experience
- on-the-job training
- college courses or other off-the-job training
- distance learning
- private study.

Credit transfer
Credits may be awarded to candidates for units of competence achieved or for sections of an examination syllabus satisfactorily completed. **Credit transfer** may

occur when leaving a school or college to enrol at another or when changing over from one qualification to another. In certain industries **phase testing** is used to assess competence and modules awarded may be compatible with other occupational areas. Core skills may likewise be transferred.

Today, with modular teacher training and degree courses, credit may be given for prior learning and awards gained earlier may be accepted as credits towards the new qualification.

Frameworks for awards

Many colleges, employers and other training providers now operate a combination of continuous assessment, phase testing and final tests or examinations. Instruments and methods used for assessment include:

- Work experience performance.
- Simulated work experience carried out in a realistic environment with the training provider.
- Projects and assignments.
- Phase tests and other practical tests.
- Oral examinations and guided discussions.
- Written papers.
- Objective tests and short-answer tests.
- Computerised assessments.

Many current qualifications reflect the requirements and standards of occupational competence now demanded by employers. An NVQ is a statement of competence clearly related to work and intended to facilitate entry into or progression in employment. The ability to perform a range of work-related activities and to demonstrate the knowledge, skills and understanding that underpin performance at work is an essential feature of the accreditation of achievement. It has been said that qualifications based on a restricted range of tests are unlikely to guarantee role-competence. It is therefore reasonable to expect that properly designed schemes of assessment will draw on and clearly reflect learning developed when performing work. Assessments must test the attainment and application of underpinning knowledge as well as the product.

Moderation

Locally assessed elements or units will often be subjected to moderation by an accreditor or representative of the awarding body before certificates are issued. In some cases **verifiers** are used to check and confirm the validity of assessments and to seek evidence that candidates are getting a fair deal and that the right standard and quality is maintained.

Accreditation

'**Accreditation** is the formal act by which the NCVQ simultaneously recognises statements of competence and awarding bodies, and approves qualifications for inclusion within the NVQ framework.'[12] For some other vocational and non-vocational qualifications different systems of assessment and validation operate. There is no one right way of assessing competence or for recording and certificating achievement. The examples that follow are intended to illustrate good practice although there are many others that would serve the purpose equally well.

The Certificate of Pre-Vocational Education (CPVE)

CPVE Framework

CPVE is for anyone over the age of 16 who has completed full-time secondary education and who seeks a balanced and relevant programme of pre-vocational study. There are no formal entry qualifications.

The CPVE framework is based upon the **Core, Vocational Studies** and **Work Experience** supported by **Additional Studies**. The five **core areas** that provide the foundation for a broad range of learning opportunities are designed to build upon requirements of the National Curriculum. Each core area has a series of objectives that provide for a process of continuous development through ongoing critical self-review and performance assessment. Personal and career development and the achievement of practical and creative skills are essential aims of CPVE. The Core objectives are not competence statements to be ticked off when completed. Students are assessed by recording their achievements in the most demanding context.

Vocational studies are **modular** in form and provide a means for integrating the development of core skills. Students explore a range of vocational activities according to individual need and interests and, where appropriate, may acquire specific entry-level skills for a variety of occupations.

All students must complete at least 15 days' planned work experience during which time relevant core and vocational studies objectives may be achieved.

Additional studies in CPVE allows for and encourages achievement in leisure activities or additional academic and vocational studies.

Opportunities exist throughout CPVE to integrate learning opportunities with those of GCSE, AS, A level, BTEC, RSA and CGLI vocational courses by studying modules with common outcomes.

The Joint Unit for CPVE and Foundation programmes published a paper outlining how the National Curriculum Council (NCC) core themes may be delivered in CPVE. Figure 9.13 shows the link.

The education and training process is seen as being part of a lifelong continuum of learning opportunity and the **entitlement curriculum** places the student at the centre of the learning process. It is designed to facilitate post-16 education and training for students wishing to acquire appropriate national qualifications, allowing progression into work and into further and higher education. CPVE would provide a useful framework within which the 16–19 entitlement curriculum, NVQs and TVEX may be delivered.

The Award

Students will be entitled to receive The Certificate of Pre-Vocational Education provided they complete:

- 500 hours of pre-vocational study
- At least three vocational modules including one each at Introductory and Exploratory stages.
- 15 days' planned work experience.

NCC Core Themes	Delivered in CPVE through . . .
Economic and industrial understanding	– Economic awareness (CA) – Exploratory modules
Environmental education	– Cultural and environmental awareness (CA)
Education for citizenship	– Social, industrial and economic awareness (CA)
Careers education and guidance	– Exploratory modules – Work experience preparation and review – Tutorials – integral to CPVE
Health education	– Social, industrial and economic awareness (CA) – Preparatory module: Health studies
Scientific and technological understanding	– Science, technology and IT (CA) – Range of preparatory modules
Aesthetic and creative understanding	– Cultural and environmental awareness (CA) – Preparatory module: Product design

NCC has also highlighted the need for a project which is work or community based. This links particularly closely with the project requirement for all students found in the Exploratory modules.

(Note: CA = CPVE Core Area)

Figure 9.13 Linking NCC core themes with CPVE delivery

Source: CPVE and the NCC Post 16 Core (October 1990) Joint Unit for CPVE & Foundation Programmes. Reproduced with permission

In addition, all students will be entitled to receive:

– a Summary of Experience
– a Work Experience Report
– individual Module Summaries.

The Award documentation has been designed to reflect and compliment Records of Achievement.

Award documentation
The programme leading to the award provides for initial assessment, effective guidance and counselling including an ongoing review procedure and final assessment of achievements.

Details of award documentation are given in Figure 9.14 and examples of completed documents are given in Figures 9.15, 9.16, 9.17, 9.18 and 9.19.[13]

CaterBase
'CaterBase is a national qualification scheme for operational staff in accommodation and catering jobs in the hotel, restaurant, licensed trade, leisure and other service industry sectors including public service operations.'[14]

CaterBase is modular in format and awards are made through continuous assessment of performance in the workplace. Each CaterBase module specifies for

---

Introduction
The CPVE award documentation, illustrated below, has been designed to complement award documentation issued elsewhere, e.g. LEA produced records of achievement.

Certificate
The Certificate is awarded to all students who have successfully met the criteria for its award. (See Section E)

Summary of Experience
A Summary of Experience is available to all students and is normally completed at the end of the CPVE programme. It is reflection of achievements throughout the programme, not simply a repetition of details given in Module Summaries. It is normally as a result of discussion between tutor and student and may be written in the first or third person. Where a local authority provides a comparable summary in its own record of achievement there is no need to complete a second summary of experience for CPVE.

Work Experience Report
A Work Experience Report is written after the period of work experience has been completed. It should be written as a result of discussion between student, tutor and employer, and may be written in first or third person. Where a local authority provides a comparable work experience report in its own record of achievement there is no need to complete a second report for CPVE.

Module Summary
A Module Summary is normally written as an integral part of a vocational module (Introductory, Exploratory or Preparatory). It describes the student's achievements in context. A centre must produce a minimum of three Module Summaries for each student. It is strongly recommended that these are written during the programme.

Full details of assessment procedures in CPVE, with illustrations, may be found in *Issues of Practice – Assessment, Profiling and Certification.*

Portfolio
In addition to the award documentation, CPVE students maintain a Portfolio of their work which serves as an illustration of their achievements.

Figure 9.14 Award documentation

Source: The CPVE Handbook and Issues of Practice (13)
Sample documentation provided by Joint Unit for CPVE & Foundation Programmes. Reproduced with permission

the task it covers, clear and concise performance criteria (see Figure 1.4 for Module WMO5) all of which must be met consistently to gain the award for a module.

> **Assessments are carried out in the workplace by the staff who have day-to-day responsibility for supervising candidates' work and who are technically proficient in the skills being assessed. Each assessor is trained in the skills needed to operate CaterBase and awards they make are checked and countersigned by a qualified senior member of staff. A central contact takes overall responsibility for implementing, administering and maintaining the quality of CaterBase within an organisation.**

Module sheets are jointly signed by the assessor and candidate when competent in module content and work methods. The modules are then entered in the candidate's personalised **CaterBase Passbook** and jointly signed by the assessor and **countersigning officer** and sent to CaterBase for authorisation.

The passbook is the focal point for recording achievement in CaterBase. Modules properly entered in the passbook and overstamped by the CaterBase office to

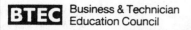 Business & Technician
Education Council

 **City and Guilds**
of London Institute

The Certificate of Pre-Vocational Education

is awarded to

JOHN SMITH

WHO SUCCESSFULLY COMPLETED A COURSE OF STUDY AT

TOOTING HIGH SCHOOL

Listing FIVE CORE AREAS

Stating completed a minimum of 15 days
WORK EXPERIENCE
in one or more VOCATIONAL AREA

Listing INDIVIDUALLY ACHIEVED MODULES

AWARDED JULY 1988

Chairman
Joint Board for Pre-Vocational Education

On behalf of
The Secretary of State for Education and Science
and
The Department of Education for Northern Ireland

Figure 9.15 The Certificate of Pre-vocational Education

Source: The CPVE Handbook and Issues of Practice[13]
Sample documentation provided by Joint Unit for CPVE & Foundation Programmes. Reproduced with permission

Summary of Experience

NAME   JAMES FORD ....

CENTRE   LINTON UPPER SCHOOL ....

After doing GCSEs, I decided to do A levels in Geography and French. My teachers and I thought the CPVE programme would be interesting and would help me to decide on a career.

Over the last two years, I have studied modules in Business and Administrative Services, and did Preparatory Modules in "Geography of Tourism" and "Travel Agency Services". These fitted in very well with my A levels. At Easter of the first year, we had a residential week in Wales. I helped to plan the travel and accommodation, and found out about the region before we went. The weather was dreadful, so we had to plan things to do as well as get on with each other. At first, it was not very easy, but by the end of the week, we had all learned a lot about communicating and solving problems together!

During my work experience, my school managed to arrange for some of us to work in France for a week. I worked in a bakery, with another boy from school. It was very interesting to see the different ways things are done in France and my French improved enormously. We were staying with French families, which felt very strange at first, but the people were very kind.

My next two weeks of work experience were in a travel agency. I learnt how to arrange holidays and make travel plans. It was hard work to get up at 6.30 each morning, but I had a long way to go and I did not want to be late for work. Although it was tiring, I was given some interesting jobs to do, as well as making tea.

I am much more confident now than I was at the beginning of the course. I did not know what would be involved, but it has been very interesting to find out about jobs, especially in the travel industry. I want to go on to qualify in Travel and Tourism at college and have plans to work in a different travel agency during the summer holiday.

Signed (Student) .... Date ....

Signed (Tutor) .... Date ....

Figure 9:16 Summary of Experience
Source: The CPVE Handbook and Issues of Practice[13]

BTEC Business & Technician Education Council

City and Guilds of London Institute

Work Experience Report

NAME   SARAH TAYLOR ....

CENTRE   ST WILFRID'S HIGH SCHOOL ....

In March, I spent two weeks working in a playgroup. I worked with small groups of children, mainly 3 and 4-year olds, helping with different crafts for them, reading stories and singing songs with them. Some of the children were really fun and loved doing things. The sandpit was a great favourite with them and there was a play house where they played at keeping home. One or two of the children were very quiet and it was hard work to make them join in. Some of them wanted to be looked after all the time. I had to toilet them and help to feed them. The staff were very patient and I learnt a lot about dealing with small children. It was very important to be on time every day and to be cheerful and friendly all the time. I enjoyed working there, but I would not want to work with small children all the time.

The second work placement I did was in a residential home for mentally handicapped adults. I helped at meal times, as some of them had difficulty feeding themselves properly. Sometimes we played games like Bingo and Snakes and Ladders. Some of them were very good at cards and they taught me some games I did not know. On Wednesday, they go shopping in the town and I went with them and helped them to buy the things they needed. We all met for tea before catching the bus back. I really enjoyed working with handicapped people. I now want to study for City and Guilds in Caring. In the holidays and at weekends I hope to go and help in this home again, as they were very keen for me to go back.

Signed (Student) .... Date ....

Signed (Tutor) .... Date ....

Figure 9.17 Work experience report

Source: The CPVE Handbook and Issues of Practice[13]

Exploratory Module Summary with Core Areas Headings

NAME   Sabina Parkinson ....

CENTRE   Hometown High School ....

MODULE TITLE Media Industries and Services ... TYPE: EXPLORATORY

Description of Work and Achievements Demonstrated:

Communication and Social Skills
Sabina displayed a variety of skills through interviewing local employers, producing a leaflet on leisure activities in the school holidays and writing and producing two short films. She co-operated well with a variety of people and demonstrated considerable tact and maturity.

Applied Numeracy
Sabina had to calculate running times for her films and to edit the sections appropriately. She had to produce her films and leaflets to a budget and keep accurate accounts.

Problem - Solving
Sabina had to identify subject matter for a leaflet and two films and then decide what filming and material were required to make interesting and balanced content. She displayed innovation in her approach to a film on sex stereotyping.

Science, Technology and Information Technology
Sabina used her time in film studios to find out how film is developed and processed and how this can affect the finished product. She also found out how information technology is being used in newspaper production and used a word processor to produce a leaflet.

Social, Industrial and Economic Awareness
Sabina considered the role of the media nationally and locally and made a film on the use of stereotyped images.

Vocation Skills Developed
Writing, word processing and editing material. Filming using a video camera. Film editing. Making taped interviews.

Signed (Student) .... Date ....

Signed (Tutor) .... Date ....

Figure 9.18 Module summary

Source: The CPVE Handbook and Issues of Practice[13]
Sample documentation provided by Joint Unit for CPVE & Foundation Programmes. Reproduced with permission

BTEC Business & Technician Education Council

City and Guilds of London Institute

CPVE

PORTFOLIO

COURSE DATES: FROM _____ TO _____

NAME _____

CENTRE _____

The Portfolio will contain a selection of student work demonstrating the breadth and quality of experience. The material should be useful and relevant, both for the student and for a potential employer. It should serve to illustrate achievements.

Those who will examine the portfolio and read its content are likely to be busy people so to be more effective, material for inclusion should be carefully selected and evaluated.

Figure 9.19 Portfolio

Source: The CPVE Handbook and Issues of Practice[13]
Sample documentation provided by Joint Unit for CPVE & Foundation Programmes. Reproduced with permission

validate them are fully accredited to the individual concerned within the national system of vocational qualification for the industry. The passbook with validated module entries is **certification** in its own right. The Hotel and Catering Training Company monitors and reviews assessor and countersigning officer training methods of assessment thereby ensuring the maintenance of quality, validity and reliability.

Joint certification

The award of a Joint Certificate denotes the achievement of knowledge and skill and the ability to apply these in a working situation. The Joint Certificate is awarded at the successful conclusion of an integrated programme of education and training based on the combined strengths of the City and Guilds of London Institute's 706 Part 1 and the Hotel and Catering Training Company's CaterBase system of work-based assessment.

The Joint Certificate in Food Preparation and Cooking awarded by CGLI and the HCTC illustrated in Figure 9.21 was the first qualification to be approved for the Hotel and Catering Industry by NCVQ.[15]

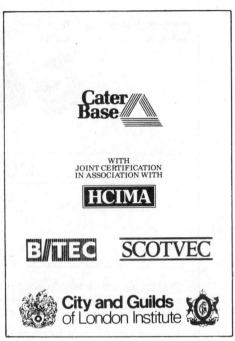

Summary of
Modules Achieved

Module No: Module No:

_____   _____
_____   _____
_____   _____
_____   _____
_____   _____
_____   _____
_____   _____
_____   _____
_____   _____
_____   _____
_____   _____

12

	Nα
ASSESSOR	COUNTERSIGNING OFFICER

Signed _____   Signed _____

Date _____   Date _____

Position _____

Organisation _____

	Nα
ASSESSOR	COUNTERSIGNING OFFICER

Signed _____   Signed _____

Date _____   Date _____

Position _____

Organisation _____

13

Figure 9.20 CaterBase Pass Book – summary of modules achieved

 **City and Guilds**
of London Institute

National Vocational Qualification

FOR FOOD PREPARATION AND COOKING – LEVEL OF AWARD 2

**This Joint Certificate
is awarded to**

MICHAEL OWEN

THIS AWARD IS ACCREDITED BY THE NATIONAL COUNCIL FOR
VOCATIONAL QUALIFICATIONS AT THE LEVEL INDICATED ABOVE

**The holder has one or more formal Records of Achievements
by which this Certificate was earned**

Awarded   JUNE 1990   012345/7061/00009/1/00/00/00

*Director-General
City and Guilds of London Institute*

*Chief Executive
Hotel and Catering Training Board*

The City and Guilds of London Institute is incorporated by Royal Charter and was founded in 1878

N66

Figure 9.21 Joint Certificate

Joint certificates of the City and Guilds and the Engineering Industry Training Board

Candidates who achieve both City and Guilds certification and successes in the appropriate Engineering Industry Training Board's training programme at the same level will be entitled to claim a joint certificate of the City and Guilds and the Board.

In courses such as: 'CGLI Fabrication and Welding Competences', all candidates successful in any assessment will receive a record of achievements towards the certificate for which they aim. For written papers, there will be three grades of success: distinction, credit and pass.

Each practical qualifying task will test core competences. Success in practical tasks requires the satisfaction of all performance criteria for a pass and differing grades of success will not be given.

> Grading of performance for the practical qualifying tasks as a whole should be recorded simply as 'Pass' and 'Fail' to indicate whether a competence has been obtained. For a 'Pass', all the performance criteria listed in the assessment schedule must be met.

The records of achievements will make no mention of assessments for which the candidates did not enter, which they failed or from which they were absent. Candidates will receive a certificate when they complete successfully all the required assessments.[16]

> The assessor when assessing practical qualifying tasks will require a knowledge of the candidate over a period of time and have access to a system of continually updated assessments, culminating in the assessment of the tasks at the end of the candidate's course.

Road Transport Industry Training Board

Skills assessment and certification

The RTITB **modular training scheme** provides a flexible approach to training. Two types of self-contained modules are available: **foundation modules** containing basic skills and **post-foundation modules** detailing specific jobs, operations or procedures.

Trainees undertaking modular training register with the Board and a **computerised record** of each trainee's progress through the scheme is kept. The register is used to provide evidence of achievement in skills assessment.

Prior learning and achievement in respect of selected modules may be ascertained by referring to existing training records and test results or by using other procedures for APLA (see Chapter 7).

Trainees undergoing assessment will receive a certificate providing a personal **record of achievement**. A detailed record of their performance in the tests will also be available. Any areas of weakness where additional training may be needed will be indicated.

TRAINING STANDARDS

<table>
<tr><td></td><td>MODULE
REFERENCE</td></tr>
<tr><td></td><td>LV
107B</td></tr>
</table>

MODULE   CARBURETTOR AND AIR SUPPLY SYSTEMS –
REMOVAL, REPLACEMENT AND ADJUSTMENT
OF COMPONENTS

Complex   Light Vehicle

ENTRY
REQUIREMENTS

Preferred   Foundation Module MV 014F and
Module LV 001A

Minimum   Foundation Module MV 014F and items 12 to 18 incl. of
Module LV 001A

STANDARDS   The standards for this module have been achieved when the trainee:

i)   can demonstrate the skills and perform the operations detailed in the training specification to the prescribed standards and tolerances specified by the vehicle or system manufacturer AND those required by the company

ii)   works safely

iii)   has passed the skills test for this module

KNOWLEDGE   Complementary knowledge is an important part of this module.

The trainee should be aware of:

the working principles of the components and systems specified; the procedures for their removal and replacement; the methods of adjustment and their effects.

NOTES   i)   On completion of this module, the trainee may progress to module(s):
LV 108C

ii)   Associated module(s) are:
LV 109B; LV 003C; LV 004C; LV 006C; LV 007C

© RTITB July 1986

CONTINUED OVERLEAF

Figure 9.22

TRAINING SPECIFICATION & RECORD

| MODULE |
| REFERENCE |
| LV |
| 107B |

†**To be completed by the trainee when each task, operation or procedure is completed**

TASK, OPERATION OR PROCEDURE	† RECORD (√)
Air Supply	
Remove and replace:	
1 – air cleaner	
2 – inlet manifold	
3 – automatic air control valves	
4 – hoses and ducts	
5 – manifold heater (liquid or electric)	
Carburettor	
Remove and replace:	
6 – carburettor	
7 – fuel tank and filler	
8 – fuel pump	
9 – control linkages and cables	
10 – fuel lines	
11 – anti run-on valve	
12 – cables and connectors	
13 – choke units	
14 – diaphragms	
15 – valves and seats	
16 – jets and needles	
Dismantle and reassemble:	
17 – carburettor	
18 – fuel pump	
Set or adjust:	
19 – engine idle speed	
20 – fuel/air mixtures	
21 – carburettor controls	
22 – jets	
23 – choke units – manual	
24 – choke units – automatic	
Measure:	
25 – exhaust emissions	
26 – engine speeds	

© RTITB July 1986

Figure 9.22 (cont.)

TRAINING SPECIFICATION & RECORD

MODULE REFERENCE
LV 107B

† To be completed by the trainee when each task, operation or procedure is completed

TASK, OPERATION OR PROCEDURE	† RECORD (√)

Training Supervisor to sign and date when satisfied with the trainee's performance in this module	SIGNATURE:	DATE:

© RTITB July 1986

Figure 9.22 Training specification and recording system

Source: Module reference LV 107B 'Carburettor and air supply systems – removal, replacement and adjustment of components' © Road Transport Industry Training Board, Wembley, Middlesex July 1986[18]

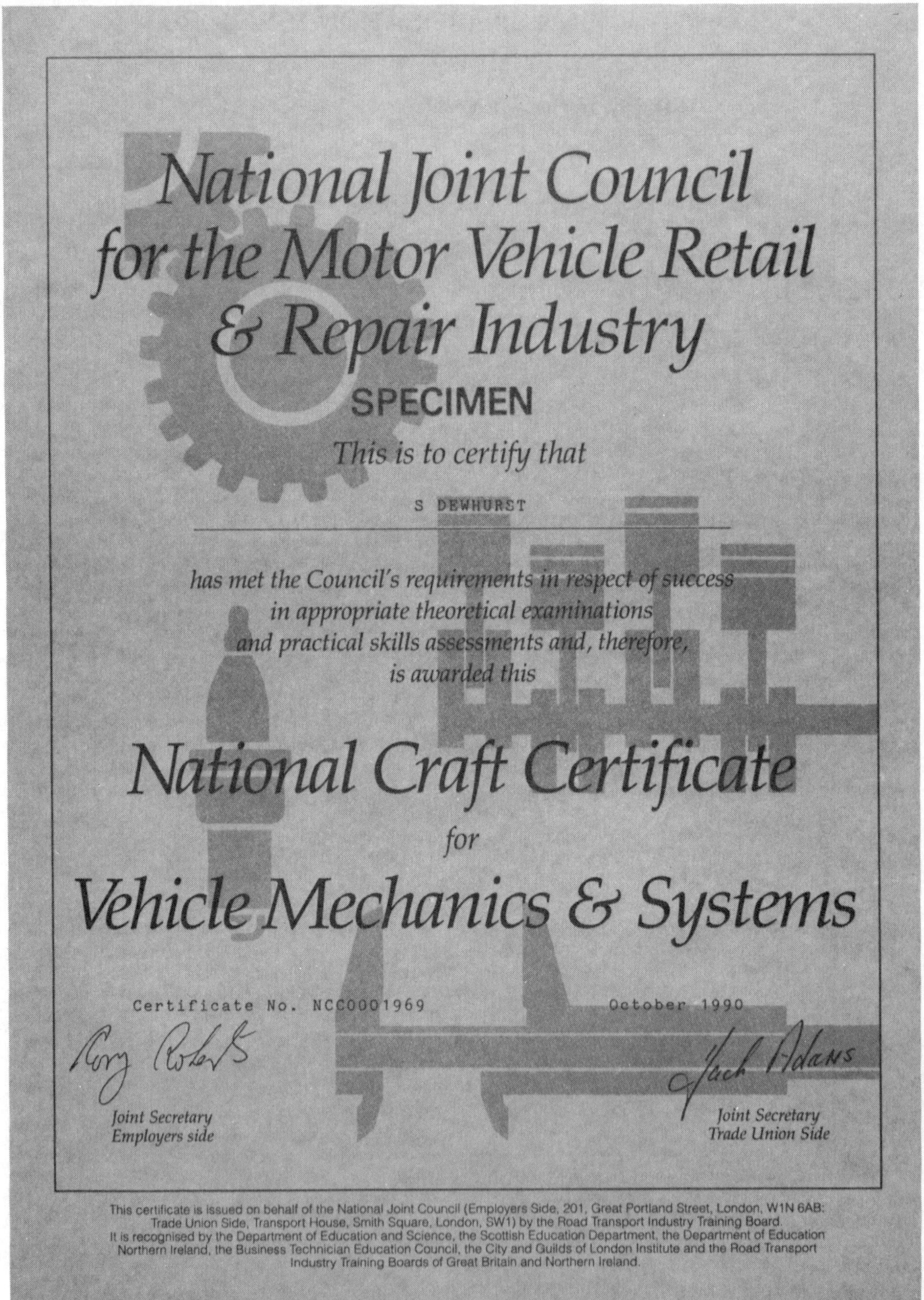

National Joint Council
for the Motor Vehicle Retail
& Repair Industry

SPECIMEN

This is to certify that

S DEWHURST

has met the Council's requirements in respect of success
in appropriate theoretical examinations
and practical skills assessments and, therefore,
is awarded this

National Craft Certificate
for
Vehicle Mechanics & Systems

Certificate No. NCC0001969 October 1990

Joint Secretary
Employers side

Joint Secretary
Trade Union Side

This certificate is issued on behalf of the National Joint Council (Employers Side, 201, Great Portland Street, London, W1N 6AB: Trade Union Side, Transport House, Smith Square, London, SW1) by the Road Transport Industry Training Board. It is recognised by the Department of Education and Science, the Scottish Education Department, the Department of Education Northern Ireland, the Business Technician Education Council, the City and Guilds of London Institute and the Road Transport Industry Training Boards of Great Britain and Northern Ireland.

Figure 9.23 National Craft Certificate for Vehicle Mechanics & Systems

Source: RTITB © Road Transport Industry Training Board, Wembley, Middlesex

Recording the training

Each module includes provision for recording training. Progress is monitored by comparing record entries and module completions against the individual's training plan. The method of recording is as follows:

The **trainee** ticks the column headed '**Record**' against an item when first shown how to complete a task, operation or procedure and again on subsequent attempts and practice, ideally until all the columns are complete.

The **supervisor** who is responsible for the training and assessment signs and dates the back page of the module when satisfied that the trainee can do the work completely, correctly and safely.[17]

The training specification and recording system for RTITB post-foundation module entitled: '**Carburettor and air supply systems**' is reproduced in Figure 9.22.[18]

The National Craft Certificate (NCC)

The National Craft Certificate (see Figure 9.23) is awarded by the National Joint Council for the motor vehicle retail and repair industry (NJC). In order to qualify for the award, candidates must pass the motor vehicle studies examinations and skills tests listed in Figure 9.24.

A **Record of Progress and Achievement** is maintained for each trainee and a form similar to that shown in Figure 9.25 is given to the trainee on completion of training.

Certificates may be awarded for success in assessments of practical skills and related knowledge. Passes in modules available within the Modular Training Scheme are recorded. A specimen certificate is shown in Figure 9.26.

NCC	*STAGE 1	STAGE 2	STAGE 3	NCC NCVO LEVEL 3
Further Education	CGLI 381 Part 1 BTEC First	CGLI 381 Part 2 (Year 1) BTEC 4N Units	CGLI 381 Part 2 (Year 2) BTEC $2\frac{1}{2}$N Units	CGLI 381 Part 2 BTEC $6\frac{1}{2}$N Units
RTITB Module Skills Tests	Foundation and Scheduled Servicing	8 Post Foundation Modules at Level B	7 Post Foundation Modules at Level C	Foundation Scheduled Servicing 8 at Level B 7 at Level C

*Accredited at NCVQ Level 1

Figure 9.24 NCC – Schedule of further education and skills tests

Source: RTITB National Craft Certificate Guide: *Light Vehicle Mechanic.* © Road Transport Industry Training Board, Wembley, Middlesex

RECORD OF PROGRESS AND ACHIEVEMENT	TRAINEE:
	N.I. NO.

	STAGE 1						
	MODULE REFERENCE	SKILLS TEST RESULT & DATE				FURTHER EDUCATION	EXAMINATION RESULT & DATE
		A	B	C	D		
	MV 014F					CGLI PART 1	
	LV 001A					BTEC FIRST	

WORK AREA	STAGE 2					STAGE 3				
	MODULE REFERENCE	SKILLS TEST RESULT & DATE				MODULE REFERENCE	SKILLS TEST RESULT & DATE			
		A	B	C	D		A	B	C	D
ENGINE	LV 101B					LV 102C				
COOLING	LV 118B					LV 119C				
FUEL SYSTEMS	LV 107B					LV 108C				
STEERING	LV 207B					LV 208C				
EXHAUST						LV 105C				
BRAKES	LV 213B					LV 214C				
ELECTRICS OR ELECTRONICS	LV 301B									
	LV 304B									
SUSPENSION	LV 201B					LV 202C				
TRANSMISSION						LV 221C				
BODY	LV 401B									
IGNITION	LV 114B					LV 005C				
	LV 116B									

FURTHER EDUCATION	EXAMINATION RESULT & DATE			
	CGLI PART 2 YEAR 1		CGLI PART 2 YEAR 2	
	BTEC 4 N UNITS		BTEC 6 ½ N UNITS	

NOTE
- At least one skills test success is required in each of the work areas colour shaded above.
- Ignition is not a compulsory work area for the NCC but success in the skills tests for ignition modules will count towards the 8 'B' and 7 'C' module skills tests needed for the award.
- Skills test results are graded A, B, C, or D. Only an A or B result is a pass.

Figure 9.25 Record of progress and achievement – NCC

Source: RTITB National Craft Certificate Guide: *Light Vehicle Mechanic.* © Road Transport Industry Training Board, Wembley, Middlesex

SPECIMEN
ROAD TRANSPORT INDUSTRY
TRAINING BOARD

This

Certificate

is awarded to

A BURNS

For success in an assessment of practical
skills and related knowledge in the following :

MODULAR TRAINING SCHEME

LIGHT VEHICLE MODULE GROUPING NO.1

PASSES IN THE FOLLOWING MODULES:
LV301B GRADE A   LV304B GRADE B   LV114B GRADE A
LV118B GRADE A   LV213B GRADE A   LV101B GRADE A

Certificate No. M/135686   Candidate No. GL011/0017/03

Date: 25 OCT 89

C. C. Hodgson.

C.C. HODGSON,
Director of Training Research and Development

Figure 9.26 Specimen certificate – Road Transport Industry Training Board

The London Chamber of Commerce and Industry Examinations Board

The London Chamber of Commerce and Industry (LCCI) in association with Centra, The Further Education Centre for the Regional Association and The East Midland Further Education Council, offers awards accredited by the National Council for Vocational Qualifications.

The NVQ Business Administration Level 1 is one example of the awards on offer. Designed to certify foundation competences in practical business skills, it is ideally suited for people who are embarking on a career in office work or who wish to enter office work at a junior level.

Their system of approving local centres and procedures that enable candidates to register for awards, to be assessed, to record achievement and to seek certification provides a model that may be transferred to other situations.

Training may be offered by providers and once approved as a local centre a member of staff is appointed as course co-ordinator and the LCCI appoints an independent consultant.

Role of LCCI Course Co-ordinator

The course co-ordinator will have responsibility for:
- Overall administration of the scheme.
- Submitting all forms and organising the course, ensuring that candidates are adequately supervised.
- Ensuring that when results listings are submitted to the London Chamber of Commerce and Industry Examination Board (LCCIEB) his or her signature guarantees that all results are bona fide.

Role of LCCI Consultant

The main functions of the consultant are to monitor:
- The integrity of the centre.
- Centre standards, and to ensure that national standards are being maintained.
- The competence of accreditors or proposed accreditors.
- The validity and reliability of the assessment process.

When candidates are enrolled a requisition form is sent to the LCCI requesting files and packs for the appropriate level.

Each candidate is then issued with a course file. The file will have a number printed on a label which is stuck on the inside front cover. This is the candidate's exclusive course file number – it must not be passed on to other candidates unless for some reason the candidate does absolutely no work concerning the award at all. The file will contain:
- A Competence Transcript. This is a document in which the candidate will record evidence of achievement against specified performance criteria and details of units achieved (see Figure 9.30, page 204).
- A set of LCCIEB assignments.
- Other evidence to support achievement claimed.

NVQ Process

Process for candidate:

The candidate:

- Receives advice and guidance on NVQ levels and courses.
- Produces a portfolio of evidence needed to support requests for accrediting prior achievement (APA).
- Negotiates an individual 'action learning programme' which is reviewed and revised as the candidate progresses (see Figures 9.27 and 9.28).
- Receives formal input or training.

Student: Paniang Tamprateep
Trainer: Tara Henley
Award: Business Administration
          LCCI NVQ Level 1

Autumn Term 1998
　　　　Units : 1, 4, 6 and 9

Spring Term 1999 *Units : 2, 5, 7 and 8*

Summer Term 1999 *Unit : 3*
　　　　Progress to Level II NVQ

Final Examinations to be taken
　　　　Pitman Word Processing Elementary
　　　　Pitman Typing Elementary

Note: Although this form relates to a standard college academic year, once a candidate is registered programmes should be flexible since there is no time limit involved in gaining the award.

Many training programmes reflect local demand and operate a 'roll-on/roll-off' system. Registration and certification may therefore take place at any time.

Figure 9.27 Individual learning programme

1.1 Element: File documents and open new files within an established filing system

1.2 Element: Identify and retrieve documents from within an established filing system

Competence elements	In college		In workplace	
	Input/knowledge	Practical	Input/knowledge	Practical
1.1 & 1.2	Investigate systems and methods of filing	Complete assignments	Induction into filing system and methods	Carrying out filing (under supervision)
			Supervisor to check work	When competent do the filing unaided
	Induction into Assessment Centre filing system	Help run the filing section 2/3 days	Produce a report on work done	
	Question and answer session to confirm knowledge		Supervisor or lecturer to certify work	

Figure 9.28 Programme for Unit 1 (Level I)

- Completes assignments and practical work in college, in other training provider's premises and in the workplace.
- Before seeking accreditation ensures that all competence criteria are achieved.
- Is assessed. Note: Colleges and training providers are responsible for designing and maintaining their own course records (see specimen given in Figure 9.29).
- If the required competence is not achieved then further training, help and guidance should be given and the candidate assessed at a later date.
- In order to gain accreditation candidates must prove that they have successfully achieved a particular competence on several occasions, over a period of time and, if possible, in a variety of situations.*
- When the candidate has achieved the required competence and the evidence is accepted a statement is agreed between themselves and the accreditor. This is entered into the 'Evidence of Achievement' statement by the candidate and is signed by the accreditor and dated (see Figure 9.30).
- When candidates have completed the required units of competence a Results Form is completed by the training provider, signed by the Co-ordinator and sent to the Consultant who will sign it and pass it on to the LCCIEB. The Consultant will visit the college or provider at least twice during the year to ensure that standards are being maintained.
- LCCIEB will then issue the LCCI Unit or full NVQ Certificate as appropriate (see Figures 9.31 and 9.32).

*See guidance issued by Board in Units in Assessment Guidelines Range of Application.

Student: Paniang Tamprateep
Trainer: Tara Henley
Award: Business Administration
           LCCI NVQ Level 1

LCCI NVQ LEVEL I   Progress Record

BUSINESS ADMINISTRATION

	Unit Started	Progress Indicator	Unit completed
Unit 1 Filing			
Unit 2 Communicating Information			
Unit 3 Data Processing			
Unit 4 Processing Petty Cash and Invoices			
Unit 5 Stock Handling			
Unit 6 Mail Handling			
Unit 7 Reprographics			
Unit 8 Liaising with Callers and Colleagues			
Unit 9 Health and Safety			

Progress Indicators

Insert:
  I   Assignment issued
  X   Criteria achieved
  R   Assignment referred
  N   Assignment not submitted

Note:
Formative rather than summative assessment should characterise Centre Records. Start and finish dates would be purely arbitrary and meaningless without an indication of progress towards competence. Mastery of criteria and demonstration of competence could be achieved within one day for someone already competent. However it may take much longer to train people with learning difficulties, or with literacy or numeracy problems or with other special needs.

Figure 9.29 Student record

LONDON CHAMBER OF COMMERCE AND INDUSTRY EXAMINATIONS BOARD

BUSINESS ADMINISTRATION LEVEL I

COMPETENCE TRANSCRIPT

Candidate Name *Paniang Tamprateep*   Candidate No *0045 1948*

Centre *Charlton Marshall College*   Centre No *D.01743962*

UNIT 1 – FILING

ELEMENT OF COMPETENCE 1.1 – File documents and open new files within an established filing system

PERFORMANCE CRITERIA	EVIDENCE OF ACHIEVEMENT
1.1 (a) All documents are filed, without undue delay, in correct location and sequence	On several occasions filed documents using College numerical system. Filed correspondence daily at workplace using alphabetical system.
1.1 (b) All materials are stored without damage in a safe and secure manner	Papers were handled carefully and placed neatly and securely in files. No document missing nor damaged.
1.1 (c) All documents are classified correctly	Identified filing unit. Pre-sort documents into correct sequence prior to filing. Checked correct classification of file & document before filing. Random checks by supervisor confirmed correctness.
1.1 (d) Classification uncertainties are referred to an appropriate authority	Referred problems to office supervisor. Clarified classification of document where non-conformance was detected.

Assessor's signature *T. Henley*   Date *23 June 1999*

Position *Course Tutor – NVQ Assessor*

Figure 9.30 Competence transcript

London Chamber of Commerce and Industry Examinations Board

in association with
The East Midland Further Education Council
Centra–Further Education Centre
for the Regional Association

NCVQ

Unit Certificate
Business Administration
A N OTHER

5013377

having satisfied the requirements of the awarding bodies is hereby certified competent in the following unit(s):

```
1  Filing
2  Communicating information
3  Data processing
4  Processing petty cash and invoices
5  Stock handling
6  Mail handling
7  Reprographics
8  Liaising with callers and colleagues
9  Health and safety
```
Total of Nine NVQ units

MAR 1991   PZZZTEST/1234567

The unit(s) listed above count as credit(s) towards a National Vocational Qualification.

R. Ainscough,
The East Midland Further
Education Council

Clive Bateson, (Prof.)
Director of the London Chamber of Commerce
and Industry Examinations Board

R. S. Welsh,
Centra Further Education Centre
for the Regional Association

Figure 9.31 Sample LCCI Unit Certificate

Reproduced with kind permission of the London Chamber of Commerce and Industry Examinations Board.

6004137

The London Chamber of Commerce and Industry Examinations Board

in association with
The East Midland Further Education Council
Centra – Further Education Centre
for the Regional Association

National Vocational Qualification

Business Administration Level I

A N OTHER

having satisfied the requirements of the awarding body is hereby certified competent in the following units:

```
1  Filing
2  Communicating information
3  Data processing
4  Processing petty cash and invoices
5  Stock handling
6  Mail handling
7  Reprographics
8  Liaising with callers and colleagues
9  Health and safety
```

MAR 1991   PZZZTEST/1234567

Clive Bateson (Prof)
Director of the London Chamber of Commerce
and Industry Examinations Board

Figure 9.32 LCCI NVQ Certificate

Reproduced with kind permission of the London Chamber of Commerce and Industry Examinations Board.

Note: The design of this certificate may be reviewed and updated.

Notes

1 *Standard Occupational Classification* Volumes 1 & 2 ISBN 0 11 691284 7 and ISBN 0 11 691285 5
   HMSO 1990
   Note: Volume 1 outlines principles and concepts of the classification, approaches certain technical
   problems and shows the structure with designations of unit groups.
   Volume 2 consists of a detailed alphabetical order index of job titles preceded by a description of the
   index and notes on coding occupations.
   Volume 3 covers topics related to occupational coding including derivation of socio-economic
   classifications from occupation and employment status information.

2 The Data Protection Act, 1984 is designed to protect people from misuse of computerised information.
   Non-computerised information is not covered by the Act. The Act entitles individuals to have access
   to their personal details held as computerised records (including computerised personnel records)
   and to seek compensation in the courts for damage due to inaccuracy or their unauthorised
   disclosure. The Act also requires all users of computerised information to register with the Data
   Protection Registrar.

3 D Garforth and H Macintosh, *'Profiling: a user's manual'*, Stanley Thornes (Publishers) Ltd,
   Cheltenham 1986, pp. 2–4
   This is a valuable source of reference for those wishing to familiarise themselves with a variety of
   performance profiles.

4 Ibid, pp. 21–30.

5 Leaflet: *National Vocational Qualifications – giving credit where credit is due*, City and Guilds of
   London Institute, London (Undated).

6 Range relates to the limits to which the person concerned can function effectively and the extent of
   activities. Range statements describe the products and processes relating to a particular element of
   competence and the conditions and circumstances applying to the related performance criteria.

7 Jack Mansell, *The Assessment of Prior Learning and Achievement – The Role of Expert Systems*, FEU
   1990 p. vii Note: Geoff Stanton is Chief Officer, Further Education Unit.

8 Ibid p. 11 See also: 'Assessing and Crediting Prior Achievements in Relation to National Vocational
   Qualifications', NCVQ Information Note 5.

9 Ibid p. 13. See also: 'Basic Skills', FEU 1982.

10 Ibid p. 30.

11 Source: 'Accreditation procedures' NCVQ London. January, 1988 p. 21.

12 Ibid p. 21.

13 Much of the text under the heading: 'The Certificate of Pre-Vocational Education (CPVE)' and
    Figures 9.11 to 9.16 inclusive is reproduced from *The CPVE Handbook*, DES/Joint Board
    Publication. January 1990.

14 Leaflet: *Assessing vocational skills at work – The CaterBase System*, Hotel and Catering Training
    Company, Ealing, London (undated).

15 Text based upon information provided in Hotel and Catering Training Company literature.

16 Source: Pamphlet *229 Fabrication and Welding Competences Part 2*, SP-90–0229 City and Guilds
    of London Institute. London 1988–90 pp. 4/5 and 10.

17 Source: *Guidelines for the use of modular training*, Road Transport Industry Training Board,
    Wembley, Middlesex (Undated).

18 Source: Module reference LV 107B 'Carburettor and air supply systems – removal, replacement and
    adjustment of components', Road Transport Industry Training Board, Wembley, Middlesex July
    1986.

Note: Relating principles of assessment effectively to the aims and objectives of
training is discussed in: L Walklin, *Teaching and Learning in Further and Adult
Education*, Stanley Thornes (Publishers) Ltd, Cheltenham 1990, pp. 134–163.

ASSESSING PRIOR LEARNING AND ACHIEVEMENT

Chapter coverage

Assessor role – APLA
Accreditation of prior achievement
Claiming credit for competence
Experiential learning
Assessment centre staff
Evidence from prior achievement
Recording achievement

Assessor role – APLA

The accreditation of prior learning and achievement is fast becoming a key function of teachers and trainers who are involved in the education and training of adults. Its importance lies in the need to recognise and give credit for the knowledge, skills and attitudes that together make up the many competences already owned by people who are seeking acknowledgement in the form of NVQs and other qualifications.

Basic techniques used involve tutors or helpers working with candidates to assemble a portfolio of evidence of previous learning and achievement which can then be presented to a qualified APL assessor for evaluation and accreditation either manually or with the help of computer-based 'expert' systems.[1]

How the process of assessment is planned and conducted and how it links to the wider learning programme has already been described in the main text. What follows is intended to provide greater insight into the concept of APLA and perhaps to promote further interest in current developments in this important topic.

The impact of change

There is now a powerful force challenging the *status quo* and compelling almost all educators and trainers to re-address their way of assessing. As traditional barriers between education and training break down, more and more teachers, trainers and workplace supervisors will find themselves in new style 'assessor' roles. Experienced practitioners are being asked to learn new tricks and consequently the need to breathe fresh life into teaching styles is fast becoming an essential requirement rather than an optional extra. The need to keep up with developments in learner assessment and assessment in a real work environment must now be nagging away in the back of teachers' minds. If it isn't, then it should be.

Full implementation of **National Vocational Qualifications (NVQs)** and **Scottish Vocational Qualifications (SVQs)** will call for considerable change in training philosophy and the assessment of work-related competences in every occupational area as well as in the National Curriculum, GNVQs and other recent innovations. The arrival of competence-based qualifications impacts on the standards required to achieve vocational qualifications. It also affects the way students and trainees are assessed, the way assessment relates to learning and also, therefore, the learning process itself. The impact of the change described will stretch right back to the moment learners begin their courses or negotiate their assessment plans.

The use and understanding of a wide range of assessment techniques is now an essential ingredient in the teacher's pack of skills. Acquiring these and becoming certificated for doing so is essential not just for full-time teachers in the education and training system but also vital for the growing army of assessors in industry who may be in supervisory or other positions which bring them into contact with the NVQ process.

Initial assessment

People seeking access to education and training opportunities are entitled to an **initial assessment** designed to help them plan their future education and training programme. Initial assessment helps both provider and learner sort out what it is they wish to achieve. **Action plans** can be negotiated, credit for prior achievement can be given and relevant training arranged to meet identified needs and the ability of individuals. Matching needs and expectations within the education and training provision is the key to success in the attainment of vocational competence or achievement in academic subjects.

Motivational aspects

Showing approval and giving credit for good work can motivate people to strive even harder to meet self-imposed goals. Formally acknowledging skilled status and recognising a candidate's claim of being competent to carry out certain tasks at work or in a simulated work environment can also serve as effective motivators. This is why it is so important to give recognition for prior achievements when a client is seeking access to a new learning opportunity. Knowing that they will not have to 'jump through the hoops' again before moving on to fresh ground gets learners off to a good start and acts as a spur and motivator. Time is precious and adult learners will not relish the idea of wasting several attendances going over old ground just because it happens to suit the teacher's scheme of work.

Accreditation of prior learning and achievement

Prior learning and achievement

Prior learning is learning that has occurred in the past. Prior learning leads to **prior achievement** and it is the 'achievement' aspect that is particularly relevant when a client is seeking admittance to a particular course or formal learning opportunity, and not the formal or informal learning process that led to the achievement. Evidence of prior achievement is used by assessors to give credits toward NVQ units.

Unintentional learning deriving from everyday life experiences, independent self-study out of college such as by correspondence courses and watching TV programmes, and experiential learning in the workplace, home or on DIY projects are prime examples of the means by which prior learning and achievement may occur.

The client is now seen by many providers as the central figure in the educational process. This was not always the case and even today there is still much evidence of teachers adopting the role of authoritative central figures who direct and control every aspect of what is offered to learners. These 'pillars' or 'guardians' of institutional standards often held the key to the door of learning and could easily exclude anxious learners on the grounds that they 'did not meet the formal entry qualifications for the learning opportunity sought'.

Nowadays the introduction and growth of formal **accreditation of prior learning and achievement (APLA)** is changing matters for the better. Candidates are now better able to claim their entitlement to a place on a given course and exemptions or credits toward a particular qualification.

Route to progression

Initial assessments and APLA sessions provide opportunities to collect and judge oral and written evidence brought forward from existing experience. Present levels of achievement can be established by asking a series of carefully framed assessor-devised questions or administering pre-set tests covering the performance criteria of the unit or element being assessed.

Being able to objectively specify just where the candidate stands enables the APLA assessor to outline what is on offer and to negotiate the learner's way forward up a 'ladder of opportunity'.

Claiming credit for competence

Assessment in NVQs

NCVQ says of the use of evidence from prior achievement:

'Evidence of past achievements, if properly authenticated, may be equally or more valid than evidence from a test or examination. . . . Prior achievements are simply those which have occurred in the past. . . . If a candidate has practised the required competencies, in work or outside, and can produce evidence of his or her competence from past performance, this could provide an alternative source of evidence that could be taken into account for the award of a qualification.'[2]

Experiential learning

The term **experiential** may be applied to learning deriving from experience. In vocational training the term **prior experiential learning** describes learning and associated achievement demonstrated as a result of learning by 'doing' things in everyday life rather than from contrived learning situations in classrooms, workshops or simulations. Informal learning evidenced by correctly performing tasks in **real work environments** (natural performance) therefore provides a valuable source of evidence of prior achievement.

Experiential learning is defined as:

> The knowledge and skills acquired through life and work experience and study which are not formally attested through any educational or professional certification.

> It can include instruction-based learning provided by any institution, which has not been examined in any of the Public examination systems.

> It can include those undervalued elements of formally provided education which are not encompassed by current examinations.

Source: *Curriculum Opportunity* FEU, 1983, para. 1.

Assessment centre staff

Trained assessors

Trained and qualified assessors must be aware of the regulations, assessment processes and requirements of the awarding bodies and they must be able to consistently meet quality assurance procedures administered by internal and external verifiers.

Assessors will be required to make decisions about the **amount** of evidence needed to support candidates' claims for the accreditation of competence. They will need to be able to judge the **validity** of evidence presented and ensure that the content adequately underpins the competence claimed. They must ensure that **sufficient** evidence is presented so that all performance criteria comprising the element being assessed are covered. Evidence gathered from more than one source must be **consistent** and must support the notion that the competence has been correctly demonstrated on a number of previous occasions in different contexts and can still be demonstrated at the required standard – it must be **current**. They must be satisfied that the evidence presented is **authentic** – it must be genuine and must relate only to the candidate.

APL Advisers

An **APL adviser** is someone who is qualified to give guidance, on-going support and direct help to candidates who are seeking recognition of previously acquired learning and achievement. Advisers will suggest how to gather and put forward evidence drawn from past achievements and past demonstrations of competence when seeking accreditation of current competency.

APL advisers will indicate how information stored in **NROVAs** or **National Records of Achievement (NRA)**, and evidence such as certificates, training records, employers' letters, skills tests, projects, assignments and reports stored in personal portfolios can be used to validate claims of prior achievements. Products may also be presented to assessors but supplementary evidence in the form of oral questioning, multiple choice tests or short written answers to pre-set tests may be needed to allow valid assessments to be made.

Advisers may offer suggestions regarding how to set about making initial self-assessments and writing lists of evidence to be gathered before an assessment plan is devised. They will arrange access to trainers and tutors who are able to help the candidate top-up their achievement so as to match outstanding elements or performance criteria. Or they will refer the candidate to assessors with whom they can negotiate formal assessments against award criteria.

Vocational Assessors

Vocational assessors will be responsible for judging evidence of prior learning presented, and negotiating and agreeing with the candidate a suitable assessment plan covering remaining elements. Candidates will be briefed on the assessment process and how a valid assessment specification will be used when making assessment decisions.

Occupational area assessors must be familiar with all types of evidence that may be provided in a real work environment and must adopt the agreed assessment process. Immediately after the work or assessment task has been completed the assessor must give the candidate accurate, objective and constructive feedback.

Where all performance criteria are met assessors will make known their decision and complete all relevant assessment records and other documentation needed. Where criteria are not met the assessor and candidate will together agree the way forward and update the candidate's **assessment plan** accordingly.

Internal Verifiers

Internal verifiers are quality assurance agents and as such they must be able to confirm whether or not standards are being maintained within their assessment centre and among assessors. This is necessary to ensure that a reliable assessment service may be provided. Verifiers will need to check the process and determine the correctness of vocational assessors' use of valid assessment specifications. They will audit assessors' interpretations of qualification standards or performance criteria, the consistency and accuracy of judgements made, usefulness and completeness of feedback shared with candidates, and completeness and correctness of records kept.

Think QUALITY!

When we do it right no one remembers.

When we do it wrong no one forgets.

If in doubt check the assessment specification.

External Verifiers

External verifiers are the guardians of awarding body standards. Their role is to ensure that internal verifiers are doing their job properly, to clarify procedures, to answer questions raised and to offer advice whenever needed. External verifiers will check that assessment centre systems and documentation, candidate achievement records, and internal verifiers' and vocational assessors' performance consistently meet agreed specifications. They will assess whether or not requirements of the award body concerned are being met. In this way, national standards can be assured.

Evidence from prior achievements

Gathering evidence

Candidates will be responsible for gathering and assembling evidence that they intend to present during an APL session. In principle this is fine, but in practice it is time-consuming and is often the cause of people withdrawing from the process or simply failing to turn up on the day. The burden of responsibility for organising themselves and their material proves too much for some candidates and they walk away from the task. Others after initial discussion will declare their intention to start from scratch and will subsequently confirm that they find it easier to provide new evidence than face the ordeal of trying to meet all elemental requirements with what they originally had in mind to offer.

The prospect of going over once again what they have already achieved as a 'revision' or 'confirmation' appeals to some candidates. They seem happy to do so provided that they are not made to 'jump through hoops' just to please assessors. But there will always be occasions when there will be a need for candidates to convince assessors that evidence presented is: accurate and soundly based, covers all specified performance criteria, is representative of competence deomonstrated over an acceptable period, is genuine and confirms that knowledge and skills claimed are still current.

For those wishing to go ahead with APLA sessions, methods of assessment will include:

– Asking the candidate questions relating to essential underpinning knowledge. (This will entail assessor competence in asking open-ended, closed and confirmation type questions.)

- Reviewing portfolios.
- Examining reports, documents and products, design work, computer programs, projects and assignments, peer group reports, testimonials and letters of validation from employers. (This will entail assessor competence in establishing and matching evidence with relevant performance criteria, and checking authenticity, validity, currency and sufficiency of evidence presented.)

Supplementary evidence

Supplementary evidence may be called for where assessors are not satisfied that evidence of prior achievement alone is entirely satisfactory. Or when they are unable to assess, by observation of performance, a candidate's competence over the full range outlined in the assessment specification for the element concerned. Assessors must be convinced that the candidate can or will be able to perform competently in the full range of contexts in which they can reasonably be expected to work. Various methods can be employed when assessing the knowledge and understanding that underpins competent performance. Typical sources of evidence that could provide the confirmation sought include:
- oral questioning
- guided discussion
- open-ended written answers given in short or long essay form
- multiple-choice tests
- skills tests
- demonstrations
- interview notes
- computer interrogation and printouts
- live or video-taped demonstrations
- simulations
- role plays
- projects and assignments
- products.

Credit transfer

Credits for prior achievement can be awarded against one or more element of a qualification offered by a school, college or training provider. For example, a candidate holding a C&G 9292 Staff Assessor Award would be entitled to credit for six of the seven elements comprising the updated C&G 7281/12 Vocational Assessor Award, provided that satisfactory evidence of prior achievement was presented to the APL assessor. Recent C&G 7305/7 FAETC Awards would probably be acceptable as credits for Parts I and II of the Certificate in Education (FE) leaving only Part III to be obtained. Credits for prior achievement are usually offered before a detailed learning programme is negotiated.

Credit accumulation and transfer schemes operate for NVQs and a wide range of other qualifications offered in further and higher education.

Client portfolios

As suggested above, gathering and collating evidence is not an easy task for some candidates. They really struggle to sort out valid and acceptable supporting evidence from archives, ring binders and material from sources that may well be widely dispersed. The task can be so off-putting that it deters candidates from going any further. They tend to give up unless there is someone on hand that they can turn to who is experienced in reviewing with them what is required. Help will be needed when cross-referencing evidence selected with award performance criteria, indexing portfolio content, writing up self-analyses and specifying what further evidence needs to be gathered before going to the APLA session.

Recording achievement

Statement of achievement

A **statement of achievement** is recorded during or immediately after the assessment of evidence gathered and presented by candidates who are seeking accreditation of prior learning achievements. Its content confirms competence deriving from earlier experiential learning or contrived learning situations. Evidence of current competence is inferred from an assessment of the candidate's claim of prior experience when judged against relevant assessment specifications.

It is the actual achievement that is recognised and not simply participation in learning experiences that led to attainment of the competence achieved. A learner can take part in a learning opportunity but may not meet all specified performance criteria that indicate competent performance and hence achievement of a particular NVQ element.

Statement of competence

A **statement of competence** lists the performance criteria, range statements and sources from which evidence has been collected and evaluated during the assessment of a candidate against, for example, a NVQ unit or element. Achievement is judged against specified criteria and then records of assessment are completed and processed. Successful candidates will have their training log, diary, National Record of Achievement or NROVA endorsed or a statement of achievement will be printed out.

Accreditation

Accreditation of an awarding body's NVQ qualification means that NCVQ has accepted and validated its submission. Candidates for the NVQ award may then be assessed and certificated. The candidate's performance will have been 'certificated', 'credited with NVQ Units' or 'accredited', and they will then receive a certificate relating to their individual NVQ award.

Notes
1   See: 'The Assessment of Prior Learning and Achievement – The Role of Expert Systems', RP448, FEU London 1990.
2   'Assessment in National Vocational Qualifications – the use of evidence from prior achievement' NCVQ. See: Foreword by Geoffrey Melling, Director, Further Education Staff College in Richard Gorringe, Coombe Lodge Report Volume 21 Number 5 'Accreditation of Prior Learning Achievements: Developments in Britain and Lessons from the USA.' The Further Education Staff College 1989 p. 320

INDEX